GAY MEN AT THE MILLENNIUM

This *New Consciousness Reader* is part of a new series of original and classic writing by renowned experts on leading-edge concepts in personal development, psychology, spiritual growth, and healing. Other books in this series include:

The Awakened Warrior
edited by Rick Fields

Creators on Creating
edited by Frank Barron, Alfonso Montuori, Anthea Barron

Dreamtime and Dreamwork
edited by Stanley Krippner, Ph.D.

The Erotic Impulse
edited by David Steinberg

Fathers, Sons, and Daughters
edited by Charles Scull, Ph.D.

Healers on Healing
edited by Richard Carlson, Ph.D., and Benjamin Shield

In the Company of Others
edited by Claude Whitmyer

Meeting the Shadow
edited by Connie Zweig and Jeremiah Abrams

Mirrors of the Self
edited by Christine Downing

The New Paradigm in Business
*edited by Michael Ray and Alan Rinzler
for the World Business Academy*

Paths Beyond Ego
edited by Roger Walsh, M.D., Ph.D., and Frances Vaughan, Ph.D.

Reclaiming the Inner Child
edited by Jeremiah Abrams

Sacred Sorrows
edited by John E. Nelson, M.D., and Andrea Nelson, Psy.D.

The Soul Unearthed
edited by Cass Adams

Spiritual Emergency
edited by Stanislav Grof, M.D., and Christina Grof

The Truth about the Truth
edited by Walter Truett Anderson

To Be a Man
edited by Keith Thompson

To Be a Woman
edited by Connie Zweig

What Survives?
edited by Gary Doore

Who Am I?
edited by Robert Frager, Ph.D.

Founding Series Editor: Connie Zweig, Ph.D.

Gay Men at the Millennium

SEX, SPIRIT, COMMUNITY

edited by

Michael Lowenthal

JEREMY P. TARCHER/PUTNAM

a member of Penguin Putnam Inc.

New York

Most Tarcher/Putnam books are available at special quantity discounts for bulk purchases for sales promotions, premiums, fund-raising, and educational needs. Special books or book excerpts also can be created to fit specific needs. For details, write or telephone Putnam Special Markets, 200 Madison Avenue, New York, NY 10016; (212) 951-8891.

Jeremy P. Tarcher/Putnam
a member of
Penguin Putnam Inc.
200 Madison Avenue
New York, NY 10016
http://www.putnam.com

Library of Congress Cataloging-in-Publication Data

Gay men at the millennium : sex, spirit, community / edited
    by Michael Lowenthal.
        p.   cm.—(New consciousness reader)
    Includes bibliographical references.
    ISBN 0-87477-892-1
    1. Gay men—United States—Social conditions.
    2. Gay men—United States—Sexual behavior   3. Gay
    men—Religious life—United States. 4. Spiritual life—
    United States.   5. Gay communities—United States.
    I. Lowenthal, Michael.   II. Series.
    HQ76.2.U5G387   1997   97-21683   CIP
    305.38'9664—dc21

Book design by Ralph Fowler
Cover design by Susan Shankin

Printed in the United States of America
10 9 8 7 6 5 4 3 2 1

This book is printed on acid-free paper. ∞

Acknowledgments

I'd like to thank Kevin Bentley, who introduced me to the wonderful Joel Fotinos, who made this book possible. I'm also grateful to the other staff members at Jeremy P. Tarcher, especially Irene Prokop, David Groff, and Ken Siman; and to Tom de Kay, Robert Drake, and Janet Lowenthal, who offered helpful advice.

Contents

PART THREE: Community

GAY MEN AT THE MILLENNIUM

Introduction

MIL•LEN•NI•UM

1. A span of one thousand years.
2. A hoped-for period of joy, serenity, prosperity, and justice.

FOR CHRISTIAN FUNDAMENTALISTS—WHO BELIEVE CHRIST'S
Second Coming will be preceded by an apocalyptic battle between the forces
of good and evil—it may come as no surprise that as we reach the end of
this millennium, the gay rights movement seems closer than ever to success.
To many of them, I imagine, the recent rise of homosexuality is, in fact, reassuring. It is in their worldview a sign of the moral decline and decrepi-
tude prophesied in the Book of Revelation—the last gasp of the Antichrist.
Just when it seems the forces of evil are poised to triumph, Jesus will appear
and initiate his thousand-year reign of holiness. Thus, Ellen DeGeneres's
coming out on TV is not just media hype, it's a coded sign: The End Is
Near.

But as a gay man, I have a different view. For one thing, I don't hold
to a millennial ideology. Even if I did, though, I'm not sure I'd read the signs
the same way. To my mind, the recent progression of the gay movement
seems not so much apocalyptic as Sisyphean.

On the one hand, gay people are undoubtedly thriving openly as never
before, making marked strides in politics, culture, and family life. And yet,
each step forward is almost inevitably accompanied by a discouraging set-
back. Scanning any given day's newspaper, I'm as likely to find an account
of fag-bashing in the heartland or the halls of Congress as the report of a
legal victory for gay rights.

It is unclear to me, as we close in on the year 2000, whether we are
speeding toward the hoped-for period in which justice will triumph, or if
the backlash will be stronger and steal our ground.

Probably both.

Consider some recent history in the following areas:

Marriage

In one of the most stunning achievements of the gay rights movement, gay marriage is on the verge of becoming legal in the state of Hawaii. In late 1996, the First Circuit Court ruled that the denial of marriage licenses to same-gender couples is unconstitutional. The implementation of the decision has been delayed pending final appeal, but observers widely expect that by sometime in 1998, the state Supreme Court will reaffirm the judgment and order the issuing of marriage licenses. Gay marriage will be fully sanctioned in the Aloha State.

But the progress of the gay-marriage cause in Hawaii has already provoked one of the most rapidly organized political counterattacks in history. In 1996, Congress passed (and President Clinton signed) the Defense of Marriage Act, which allows the other forty-nine states to deny recognition to potential "Hawaiian marriages." As of this writing, seventeen states have specifically banned same-gender marriage (something which none of them, prior to 1995, had thought to do). And in the first months of 1997, similar measures have been introduced in the legislatures of eighteen additional states.

The dark prospect of constitutional amendments banning gay marriage looms at both state and federal levels. Of course, if attempts to ratify such amendments were to fail, it could be the greatest victory yet for the gay rights movement. It's anybody's guess in which direction things will go.

Nondiscrimination

1996 saw another major milestone in the battle for gay civil rights when the United States Supreme Court, in *Romer vs. Evans,* ruled Colorado's Amendment 2 unconstitutional. Amendment 2, which had been approved by a majority of Colorado voters, prohibited the state or any localities within it from passing nondiscrimination laws protecting gay men and lesbians. By voiding the amendment, the Supreme Court—for the first time—included homosexuals within the concept of equal protection under the law.

Romer vs. Evans marked the effective end of antigay ballot initiatives like Amendment 2, which had a been a staple of the right wing's antigay strategy for more than five years. Beyond that, however, it is not clear what effect the ruling will have. *Romer vs. Evans* seems implicitly to contradict the Court's previous finding, in *Bowers vs. Hardwick*, that the constitution grants no inherent protection to gay people. But it remains to be seen if this implicit overturning of precedent will in fact be played out in future cases. William Rubenstein, former director of the American Civil Liberties Union's Lesbian and Gay Rights Project, has asked: "Will *Evans* knock out the five state sodomy laws that ban only same-sex sodomy (not to mention the other fourteen that ban all sodomy)? Will *Evans* reverse custody rulings that discriminate against queer parents?"

Furthermore, while *Romer vs. Evans* rendered unconstitutional the *prohibition* of gay nondiscrimination laws, it did nothing to promote the passage of such laws. At present, discrimination on the basis of sexual orientation is outlawed in only eleven of the fifty states. The majority of gay Americans can still lose their jobs or housing because of their sexuality, and have no legal recourse.

Schools

Society's increasing openness about homosexuality has begun to trickle down to our schools, where the American youth who will lead us into the next millennium are being educated. The Gay, Lesbian, and Straight Teachers Network is active on a national level, offering support and training to educators about sexual orientation. Gay/straight alliances have been formed in hundreds of schools, promising an antidote to the isolation endured by generations of gay teenagers. The first national alliance of such groups, Pride USA, was founded in 1996 by a seventeen-year-old.

Perhaps the most encouraging sign of progress came in late 1996, when twenty-one-year-old Jamie Nabozny was awarded nearly a million dollars in damages from his former high school in Wisconsin. Nabozny had sued school administrators, claiming they failed to protect him from antigay abuse by other students. The federal jury's finding marked the first time school officials have been held accountable for allowing antigay harassment.

But Nabozny's success is hardly an indication of universal advancement. Nineteen ninety-six was also the year in which the Utah state legislature passed a measure explicitly intended to ban gay clubs in public schools, and another threatening to punish teachers who engage in illegal behavior (i.e., sodomy). Even in progressive Massachusetts, the only state with a government-funded "safe schools" program for gay youth, nearly 25 percent of all reported antigay hate crimes in 1996 took place in schools.

Having faced defeat on the national level with *Romer vs. Evans,* the religious right is concentrating on smaller gains at the state and local level—particularly regarding school curricula and library purchases. Public schools in targeted areas could become more dangerous than ever for gay youth.

The Military

Bill Clinton, the most gay-friendly president in history, famously reneged on his 1992 campaign pledge to lift the military ban on gay and lesbian servicemembers. But even if gay people were bitterly disappointed by Clinton's failure to end the ban, most acknowledged his "don't ask, don't tell, don't pursue" compromise as a step forward. Yes, gay military personnel were still officially barred from serving, but the witch-hunts were over.

After almost half a decade under the new regime, however, the evidence indicates that the plan has backfired. According to the Servicemembers Legal Defense Network, 850 gay military personnel were discharged in 1996—the highest number in five years, and the highest rate of discharge since 1987 (in other words, a higher rate than at any point during Bush's presidency). Perhaps in an angry response to having had its authority to discriminate challenged in the civilian realm, the Defense Department routinely violates its own policy. Many gay servicemembers contend that their position is worse now than it was before Clinton's "enlightened" intervention.

Aids

Sixteen years into the AIDS epidemic, everything has changed. Or has it?

At the 1996 International Conference on AIDS researchers presented breathtakingly encouraging reports. Protease inhibitors and other new drug therapies have reduced the viral load of HIV-positive patients to undetectable levels. Individuals who had been near death are now back on their feet, returning to work, planning for the future.

Dr. David Ho, one of the leading scientists working on the new antiviral regimes, was named Man of the Year by *Time* magazine.

The New York Times Magazine ran a long cover story by Andrew Sullivan titled "When Plagues End." "A diagnosis of HIV infection," Sullivan wrote, "is not just different in degree today than, say, five years ago. It is different in kind. It no longer signifies death. It merely signifies illness."

In early 1997, the government reported that the number of yearly AIDS deaths has declined significantly for the first time since the epidemic began. And yet:

- Protease inhibitors do not work on all patients. Nor do they seem to eradicate HIV entirely, but only to reduce its presence or force it to hide in hard-to-observe locations. Once started, the drugs must be taken every day for the rest of a patient's life.

- As activist Larry Kramer pointed out in a *New York Times Magazine* article titled "A Good News/Bad News AIDS Joke," the new drugs are exorbitantly expensive. The vast majority of HIV-positive individuals throughout the world will not have access to them for years—if ever.

- Although rates of new HIV infection have plateaued among gay men, the rates among other groups—particularly blacks, Latinos, and women—are skyrocketing.

- Rates of infection among gay men in their twenties are climbing as well.

There is also the possibility that the recent relatively good news about AIDS will in fact have counterproductive effects. Young gay men, hearing that AIDS is no longer a death sentence but merely a "chronic manageable illness," may feel permission to engage in risky sexual behavior. A new cycle of infections could begin.

Will the next century see the end of the plague? A cure? Will AIDS have been a phenomenon unique to the twentieth century? As much as we hope and pray that the answer will be yes, it seems entirely premature to predict with any conviction.

And so, when we toast the turn of the millennium, will the glass of champagne gay men lift be half-full or half-empty? A case can be made for either interpretation. The political and cultural war in which gay men are engaged is one of daily skirmishes and incremental victories; a definitive battle of flying horsemen seems unlikely.

But the future of gay men in America is unpredictable not only because of our advance-and-retreat relationship with the mainstream. A good deal of the uncertainty stems from the fact that *within* the gay community, this fin de siècle is also a crucial—and confusing—time of flux.

In 1969, when the contemporary gay rights movement was born in the wake of the Stonewall riots, it was a common cry of the counterculture not to trust anyone over thirty. But the millennium's approach means that the gay movement itself is about to turn thirty. And like Jerry Rubin, the sixties radical who eventually landed on Wall Street, the gay movement is in some ways becoming part of the very establishment it initially sought to overthrow.

The transition is not an easy one, nor is it by any means a fait accompli. While some gay men settle into conventional stability, others resist, clinging to youth and rebellion. Thus, the often schizophrenic tension: The gay movement is in midlife crisis.

The rifts within the gay community are perhaps best exemplified by the nearly simultaneous publication in 1996 of two books: *Beyond Queer,* edited by Bruce Bawer, and *Anti-Gay,* edited by Mark Simpson. The first collection, subtitled *Challenging Gay Left Orthodoxy,* represents a full-scale critique of radical gay activism, which it posits as outmoded and childish. (The jacket copy uses the word *mature* or *maturity* three times to distinguish its contributors, who it says are dismayed by the "puerile and counterproductive 'queer' image that represents neither the lives nor the goals of most gay people.")

Anti-Gay is equally critical of the gay movement, but this attack comes from the other direction. The gay community is not too radical, the volume's contributors suggest, but not radical enough. Gay culture has become bland and mediocre and commodified; the cutting edge has been dulled. This book's jacket copy calls it "the shameful antidote to prideful feel-good politics."

Here are two books that move so far in opposite directions on the globe of ideology that they almost (but don't quite) meet on the other side. And if both gay conservatives and gay radicals are now rejecting the identity of "gay" as the term is commonly understood, perhaps it's time to ask what—if anything—such an identity constitutes.

In fact, assumptions that have held fast for years within the gay male community are being challenged from all sides. In the realms of sexuality, politics, religion, and family, what it means to be "gay" is an increasingly open question. Some say gayness is too broad, others say it's too narrow. Some argue that the notion of "gayness" as a distinct, all-important identity has lost its relevance. Isn't it just as important to examine and celebrate one's identity as a Buddhist, a Texan, a storekeeper? In particular, many gay men who are members of other disenfranchised groups—African-Americans, Latinos, Asian-Americans—are speaking about the impossibility of identifying themselves on the basis of their sexuality alone, to the exclusion of race and ethnicity.

There are also generational and demographic trends at issue in what Tony Kushner has called the "understandable perplexity . . . of our transitional moment." A younger contingent of gay men—who have come of age taking for granted the relative freedom gained by their forebears—often see things differently from their elders. They are by turns impatient with the mentality of the closet (whose oppressive grip defined the previous generation) and dismissive of the need to be "out and proud" at every possible moment. (The promotional copy for *Anti-Gay* asks, with tongue only partly in cheek, "Have you ever wondered . . . whether the closet is perhaps not quite as awful a place as you've been led to believe?")

Recent years have witnessed both a post-AIDS resurgence of urban gay ghettos with their concomitant "fast-lane" scenes, and an unprecedented move of gay men to suburban and rural locations. As Michelangelo Signorile writes in the introduction to his book *Life Outside,* "The fast lane is getting faster, but the slow lane is getting wider." In the late 1990s, depending on where you look, it seems that gay men are simultaneously becoming more and more like our stereotype in the popular imagination (we are narcissistically obsessed with gym-pumped bodies, addicted to hedonistic sexual licentiousness), and less and less like that stereotype (we are getting married, raising kids, joining churches and synagogues).

My use of "we" in the previous paragraph is problematic, and intentionally so. At a time of such change, and given the multitude of directions in which gay life is headed, is it possible (or even desirable) to speak of gay men as a group?

Gay Men at the Millennium addresses this large question by addressing many smaller questions—about sexuality, relationships, AIDS, spirituality, activism, race relations, aging, identity. The book assesses the state of the gay community as we near the year 2000 with full acknowledgment of the fact that there may be no such thing as *the* "gay community."

The writers included in this volume span a wide spectrum of political and personal points of view. Some of them agree with one another, but many disagree (and I disagree with some of them, too). Despite their diverging views, however, they share a general perception that gay culture is at a turning point, and a sincere commitment to guiding the direction in which it will turn. Gay men have always been masters of self-invention; the contributors to this volume all wrestle with the boundless possibilities of who we are and how we might create ourselves anew in the years to come.

In choosing selections from the vast array of recent writings on gay-related topics, I attempted to be evenhanded and inclusive. (For example, I have reprinted one essay each from *Beyond Queer* and *Anti-Gay.*) However, the book is not definitive. There are countless voices worthy of inclusion that are not represented in *Gay Men at the Millennium,* because in an infinitely diverse community, full representation is not possible. (It should also be noted that while many of the issues addressed in the book are of relevance to lesbians, the focus is explicitly on gay men. I have encouraged the publisher to consider a companion volume, *Lesbians at the Millennium.*)

I think of this collection not as a manifesto or guidebook but rather as something of a salon—a gathering of twenty-nine articulate, provocative gay men engaged in heartfelt discussion about the most pressing issues of our day. It is my hope that the book fosters further conversation as the gay movement grows into midlife and beyond.

I have always believed firmly in the power of words, but that they must also coincide with and be backed by actions. I offer *Gay Men at the Millennium* with full confidence that an era of joy, serenity, prosperity, and justice awaits. But we cannot count on divine intervention; we must initiate a new millennium with our own hard work and humanity.

Michael Lowenthal
Boston, March 1997

PART ONE

Sex

INTRODUCTION

It is by now the tiredest of clichés to joke that "the love that dare not speak its name" has become "the love that just won't shut up." From its cloak of secrecy just thirty years ago, homosexuality has emerged as fit subject matter for Ask Beth and "All My Children," for *USA Today* and the United States Senate.

And yet, for all the barriers that have come crashing down, the emphasis of the newfound openness has been almost entirely on "homo" to the exclusion of "sexuality." As journalist Wayne Hoffman has observed,

> Since the 1970s, gay men have become increasingly visible in mainstream popular culture. Ironically, however, as gayness becomes more visible as a lifestyle or identity . . . , publicly visible *homosexuality*—that is, sexual behavior—seems to shrink in stature. The abundance of asexual, gay-identified characters circulating in public discourse does nothing to counteract the devolution of public sexual culture for gay men.[1]

In America in 1997, it is still largely taboo to talk about what gay men actually do with their bodies—in other words, those very acts which are arguably the core of our difference, for which we have been willing to risk our lives, our careers, our families. Gay men can be depicted on television as lovers, but not making love. We can bare our souls on "Oprah," but not our chests.

With the turn of the millennium, however, things may be changing.

At this writing, the scandal of the moment centers around *Esquire*'s reversal of its decision to publish David Leavitt's novella "The Term Paper Artist." The novella's plot is simple, if salacious: a gay novelist (named David Leavitt) breaks a long bout of writer's block by ghostwriting term papers for male college students in return for the chance to give them blow jobs. *Esquire* accepted the story (and paid Leavitt $13,000), but at the last possible moment, editor-in-chief Edward Kosner pulled it. Some—including the magazine's literary editor Will Blythe, who resigned in protest—charge that Kosner was pressured (or acted in anticipation of pressure) by corporate advertisers who objected to the story's explicit gay sexual content. Kosner claims that he made the decision on his own, as a matter of taste.

The Leavitt controversy prompted major coverage in *The New York Times* and countless other publications. A gay bookstore in Boston placed a copy of Leavitt's new book (which includes "The Term Paper Artist") in its display window with a sign that read: "Banned by *Esquire*."

Now, I agree that the cancellation is outrageous. It seems a classic case of economic censorship—which in our age is more pervasive and perhaps more insidious than legal censorship. Leavitt argues that if his story were about heterosexual characters, it would have run in the magazine—and he is probably right.

But what no one seems to be registering, and what to me is the truly shocking aspect of the saga, is that *Esquire* accepted the novella in the first place! *Esquire*—that most mainstream of men's magazines, available in every Wal-Mart and corner newsstand—had planned to run a story that has one male character telling another, "Your balls are pretty hairy. I could shave them for you, if you wanted."

The level of outrage at Leavitt's treatment is a measure of the extent to which gay men have come to expect society's acceptance of our sexuality. We now feel *entitled* to what only a few years ago would have been *unthinkable*. And the fact that Will Blythe, a straight editor, quit over the flap, proves that we are not without allies in our demands for equal treatment.

This is not to say that mainstream America is ready to turn its family rooms into back rooms. (Remember: *Esquire* did kill the story.) The specter of two men getting it on is still so haunting to the popular imagination that all Senator Nunn had to do during the gays-in-the-military debate was to visit a submarine, stoop into the sleeping quarters, and mention how "tight" they were.

It's still a major event—prompting letter-writing campaigns from both armies of the culture war—when two gay men share a single kiss on television.

Furthermore, it bears pointing out that "sodomy"—which is how squeamishly unimaginative lawmakers still refer to gay sex—remains illegal in nineteen states. (In other words, a fair share of you reading this sentence are likely criminals.)

And yet, unquestionably, things are becoming more open:

- AIDS has made phrases like "receptive anal intercourse" part of the public lexicon. Schoolkids learn about condoms before they learn chemistry.
- The Internet has brought gay cruising literally within the push of a button for millions of Americans.
- Volumes of gay sexual writing (such as the *Flesh and the Word* series, and the *Best Gay Erotica* books) are available in nearly every Barnes & Noble superstore in the land.

This is how culture stumbles along: one step ahead, a half-step back, another forward. The leather bullwhip protruding from Robert Mapplethorpe's anus in one of his famously censored photographs lashes at society, and society lashes back, but no matter—the silence has been shattered.

And now that gay men don't need to expend quite so much energy defending the simple *fact* of gay sex, we are increasingly free to engage in discussion about more nuanced aspects of our sexuality.

The debates within the gay community are at least as heated as those between gays and straights. There are plenty of gay men, for example, who would have joined Edward Kosner in squelching the David Leavitt story, or who would have rejected it to begin with. How will we win acceptance, they ask, if we continue to confirm mainstream society's view that gay men are sex-compulsives who flagrantly flout propriety? But others ask how gay men will ever win true acceptance *without* being honest and public about our sexual natures.

The writers in the following section address these and other questions about gay sex and relationships.

In "Making Sex Public," Michael Lassell concedes that sex has become almost shockingly prevalent in American life. Paradoxically, though, he argues that we are much *less* comfortable with sexuality than previous societies; the kind of sex that has become public is in his view false, commodified, distracting from the gritty truths of the human condition. Far from quieting down about sex, as the social conservatives would have us do, Lassell believes gay men must now be more vocal than ever. In his powerful call for art that deals openly with sexual themes, Lassell suggests that in this precarious cultural moment, it should be the special role of gay men to push society further into honest and accurate explorations of sex.

Gay men, however, are by no means immune from the effects of inauthentic, commercialized sexuality. "Why Gay Men Can't Really Talk About Sex" is Michael Bronski's lucid critique of the gay community's own inability to discuss the emotional realities underlying our seemingly liberated physicality. Decrying the commodification of gay pornography, Bronski worries that gay men increasingly speak in a vapid default lingo of "tits and ass" that avoids how we *feel* about sex. The growing legal and social acceptance of gay pornography may in fact, he contends, have hindered the possibilities of honest sexuality. If we are truly going to liberate ourselves, Bronski writes, gay men must learn to talk about our most intimate fears and fantasies.

In the era of AIDS, when each sexual encounter requires a negotiation about safety, the kind of honest talk Bronski longs for has become a matter of life-and-death importance. But the difficulty of candid discussion—in the mainstream as well as within gay circles—has posed significant problems for sex education. There has been sharp debate about what messages are most appropriate, and most effective.

The notion of "safe sex" was invented virtually overnight by early AIDS activists, and the gay community's response is legendary. In San Francisco, New York, and other cities, the rate of new HIV infections dropped dramatically among gay men, proving the possibility of widespread behavioral change through public-health campaigns. Recently, however, the evidence points to a disturbing trend of "slippage" among gay men. The safe-sex message is reaching them, but they are not heeding it. Jesse Green's "Flirting with Suicide" takes a hard look at safe-sex education and at the psychology of HIV-negative men living through the epidemic. Green tries to assess why some men, despite their knowledge of the risks, continue to engage in dangerous behavior. His frightening chronicle addresses issues that will be essential to confronting AIDS as the current and future generations of gay men come of age: self-esteem, self-hatred, guilt.

If it has been difficult to talk candidly about sexual decision-making among HIV-negative men, it has been virtually impossible to discuss the sexual choices and responsibility of those already infected. For fear of offending the sick and dying, gay men have resisted any criticism of the HIV-positive. In "To Protect and Serve," Gabriel Rotello dares to include HIV-positive men in the public-health equation. Pointing out that each new HIV infection results from the failure of both a negative partner and a positive partner, he calls for renewed commitment to safety on both sides of the HIV divide. Rotello's point is not to assign blame but rather to inspire a truly communal response to the crisis as it enters its next phase.

Scott O'Hara rejects such a notion outright, arguing in "Talking with My Mouth Full" that being HIV-positive has liberated him from responsibility. Sex can never be safe, he declares; each person can only act according to his own desires and boundaries. O'Hara's libertarian position is pointedly inflammatory, but beneath the bravado there is real bravery: He refuses to let being a person with AIDS mean that he's a person without sexuality. And far from curtailing his sexual adventurousness, O'Hara's AIDS diagnosis has spurred him to be even more fervid in his defense of promiscuity. "Monogamy," he insists, "is unnatural behavior."

Monogamy is also the subject of D. Travers Scott's "Flexibile Fidelity," but he takes a more open-ended position. As a young gay man who came of age after both the free-sex seventies and the dawn of the AIDS epidemic, Scott speaks for a new generation investigating creative ways to navigate relationships. He rejects pronouncements about the relative morality of monogamy and nonmonogamy, arguing instead that any number of possible configurations can succeed, as long as the partners communicate. Utterly pragmatic, and offering the positive example of his own long-term relationship, Scott argues that nonmonogamy does not necessarily equal lack of commitment. In fact, he says, the kind of serious, loving negotiation it takes to make a flexible partnership work often exceeds the degree of commitment in a traditional marriage.

Michelangelo Signorile also writes about the nuances of being what he calls "Not-So-Single." In a gay culture so dependent on flirtation, pick-up bars, and (at least the pose of) perpetual availability, he asks, How does one act if one is part of a couple? Signorile is honest about his own ambivalence; he confesses to meeting men and delaying the revelation that he has a boyfriend, attempting to have his sexual cake and eat it too. Yet he is critical of a gay world that places such a premium on singledom and renders invisible those in relationships.

The final selection is an excerpt from Bernard Cooper's deeply moving essay "If and When," about his lover Brian's HIV-positive diagnosis. The couple have devoted themselves to each other for more than a decade, Cooper tells us, only to discover that their very desire poses a life-threatening risk. He describes the guilt and worry that suddenly accompany physical intimacy, but how he and Brian—on the strength of their longtime commitment—forge a path into a creative and satisfying sexual future. His affirmation of desire offers inspiration for gay men as we move into the next decade and beyond.

Notes

1. Hoffman, Wayne, "Skipping the Life Fantastic," in *Policing Public Sex,* Dangerous Bedfellows, eds. (Boston: South End Press, 1996), 340.

I. MICHAEL LASSELL

Poet and editor Michael Lassell combines his wicked wit with an incisive critique of censorship to speak out in favor of openly sexual art. He presented an early version of this in-your-face argument at a conference honoring the late gay writer (and pornographer) John Preston.

Making Sex Public

AS A WRITER OF POEMS AND STORIES THAT ARE OFTEN FRANKLY sexual (sometimes, I am told by editors, *too* sexual to print), I spend more time than others may consider healthy thinking about sex—not the act, per se, necessarily, but sex in relation to the notion (and legal principle) of privacy. The two, of course, are inextricably connected in the current repressive political climate. I am prompted in my musings on the privacy and publicity of sex (to coin an electronic-age antithesis) by my almost daily contact with Times Square, in whose tacky embrace I actually work.

Once known as "The Crossroads of the World," the Broadway theater district (particularly along Forty-second Street) later slid into a far-from-unique urban decline into drugs, prostitution, and pornography. This, we all know, is Sin Central, both to those whose erotic fantasies are corseted in limited imaginations and to the dictators of public "morality." The neighborhood to which I travel each day on the subway is not a geographic destination in the minds of the martinets of the mundane; it's the symbol for all that is vile and unholy, the long-predictable end of the ethical world given the too-permissive liberal agenda.

The truth is, it's difficult, even for me, to walk past one porn shop after another and not actually agree in some sense with the poseurs of rectitude: Nowadays, sex is unavoidable. These streets of our cities are ablaze with fluorescent crimson announcing the availability of amateur videos, glossy magazines, and "marital aids" for the acutely or occasionally single. Call me a closet conservative, but this hard-sell sexuality *does,* I believe, misrepresent sexuality and *does* damage innocence. Nor is this pushing of the act down our throats, so to speak, limited to arcades of arcane eroticism. Sexuality oozes from the pages of many a consumer magazine, not only rubbing our noses in our reproductive urges but smacking us on the snout with its most mundane aspects. (A good deal of mystery is lost when K-Mart advertises cheek-by-jowl with condoms and K-Y Jelly.)

I am nonetheless seriously put off by the current "clean-up" of Times Square (not only a local New York City fact, but a metaphor for the rightward rush of the country). I can barely look at the southwest corner of Broadway and Forty-second. Once the turf of Damon Runyon's prebowdlerized guys and dolls, it is now dominated (*not* in the B&D sense) by a gigantic toy store. Indeed, the corporate descendants of Unca Walt Disney own not just this store and an adjacent theater, they have been given a municipal green light to "develop" the northwest corner of Forty-second and Eighth, where the Mouse that Whored will someday erect (pun noted) a family-style tourist hotel hung like a transvestite gypsy with garish neon ("to preserve the integrity of the environment").

Staring through the plate-glass show windows at all those semiclad Disney characters, I am confronted every day with the absolute failure of our society to accommodate the fundamental, existential, animal reality of sex. Instead, we prefer the illusory, the sanitized, the anthropomorphized, and the animated. In America, cute little fawns drop no spoor. Hinds do not carry Lyme disease or decimate vegetable gardens; harts never go into rut. Here in the land of the not-really-free, Bambi has no balls.

Keeping sex—that primal need of every species—at the center of public social dialogue seems so reasonable and necessary, it seems lunatic that we continue to give the notion any energy at all in 1997, which is more than a few calendar years since the invention of sex, even of public sex, much less the artistic representation of sex—which were once not forbidden at all. In virtually every society the world has known, sex has been considered a public matter as well as a private one, as naturally addressed as midday dining or life after death. It took the three great conundrums (some might say evils) of the Middle East—Judaism, Christianity, and Islam—to institute an official dichotomy between body and spirit, between society and the basic biological realities of human existence, between—therefore—the individual and God (except via a priestly class whose privileged status has been so routinely ripe for corruption that the wormy fruit is invariably plucked).

So let us look at the public sex that sticks in the craw of censorious fundamentalists of every ilk and stripe (usually a shade of yellow—and shouldn't they be forced to drop the "fun" from their name?). There is too much sex available to the public, they sneeze, and this sex will corrupt children and undermine Western Civilization (making the assumption, of course, that such a thing exists or that it is, for some unspecified reason, worthy of preservation if it does). These biophobics are, in fact, quite accurate: There has never been, I suspect, a society as obsessed with sex and as ignorant as ours. As sexually saturated as our lives are, sex itself is in as much trouble in this American fin de siècle as it was in the previous three.

Sex, we of profligate erotic expression concede, is already public. But only in a *quantitative* sense. Qualitatively, it is not, at least from the point of view that diversity (a word I now use with trepidation in its nonironic sense) is a good thing. Sex is everywhere: films, television, videos, the Internet. However, it is highly and grotesquely significant that what is being decried by the phrase-makers of righteousness in their mad scramble for attention is *not* the use of sex to hawk wares in the marketplace of products. ("Yes," we say as a culture, "sex sells; please feel free to attach a wallop of unexamined sexuality to every product from diet cola and toilet cleaners to phone cards and vacation trailers.") No, the objection among the moralists is not to the commercialization of a highly prescribed and limited kind of sexuality but to the introduction of sex, sexuality, sexual orientation, sexual practice, sexual representation, gender deviance (and other such "minority" issues) to the marketplace of *ideas.*

I am generalizing, of course, but only partly for effect. Among the most interesting turns of fairly recent events was the public outcry over a Calvin Klein ad campaign that featured extremely young (or apparently young), barely clad or seminude kids (depending on your point of view) in poutingly provocative come-hither poses. I, too, despised the ads, but not because I found the pictures disgusting. I found them genuinely and legitimately erotic. (Teenagers *are* sexual creatures, the self-hypnotic blindness of their parents notwithstanding.) What rankled was geriatric Calvin's use of teenage sexuality to sell jeans. I couldn't care less if the Dorian Gray-like designer is a pederast, or whether or not he comes clean about it, so to speak. What is loathsome is his exploitation of what should be the precynical sexuality of his young models for personal gain. Klein was pushing the envelope not of public sexuality but of the outer limits to which he will go to generate profit. (I must, however, admit to a certain glee that the once-again-single ambisexual-scentmeister has given new meaning to "Calvinism.")

It is the conceit of power Mafia—from Old Testament stonecasters, through the censorious clergy of the Middle Ages, to the witch-burning Puritans of Salem and the Jessie Helmsian *jihad* of the U.S. Senate—that certain forms of sexual expression are good, others bad. They oppose the more humane construct that some sex works for some people and some sex works for others, as the evidence from time immemorial clearly attests.

Faced with diversity, the (predominantly male and overwhelmingly heterosexual) powers-that-be write laws that define as obscene everything different from their own sexual practices, which to read the news, seem frequently to involve the nonconsensual participation of female employees, including minors. (Given the sexual practices in the U.S. military, for example, wouldn't morale, as well as the defense of the nation, be better served if the Pentagon banned heterosexuality from the armed services rather than queer sex?—a suggestion, by the way, with actual historic precedents according to Plato. And are these not legitimate public questions?)

It is useful to note that the issue of public obscenity is as old as recorded Western cultural history. The word itself—*obscene*—refers to the stage house of the Greek amphitheaters that reached their architectural apogee in the fifth century B.C.E. The *skene* was the stage building itself, in front of which the actions of gods and heroes unfolded. *Obskene* (literally, off-stage; behind the scene house) was where things took place that were too difficult, too horrific, too potentially harmful for the audience to witness. In Athens, seat of Hellenism in its flower, what was considered obscene was not sex, but violence. When Oedipus puts out his eyes to punish himself for his crimes, he goes behind the stage house, because self-mutilation in Greek society was considered overtly *obscene*. We have begun to censor violence in the media in this country, but generally speaking, we would rather be entertained by dismemberment than tumescence. "They gave me a medal for killing a man," says the gravestone of Sergeant Leonard Matlovich, "and a court-martial for loving one."

We must also realize as we come to the end of this millennium that sex has always been a central component of art. Oedipus is the story of a man who kills his father and sleeps with his mother, who fathers children with his mother (and rather prodigious children they turn out to be). Most of the extant Greek tragedies involve some sort of transgressive sexuality (the multigenerational incest/adultery dramas of Agamemnon, Jocasta, and Electra, for example)—as do all the comedies of Aristophanes, which are not only overtly and comically sexual but political as well, taking contemporary domos to task in characteristically scabrous language.

Less known is that these most noble Greek tragedies were performed in trilogies that were followed by so-called Satyr plays. These broadly sexual farces were burlesques of the tragic events that had directly preceded them. Enormously popular, these on-stage lampoons included choruses of highly sexualized satyrs (half-men, half-goats), who wore little except extremely large leather phalluses. The Greeks, who were repressive enough in their own way, did not seem to think it wise to repress sexuality.

So we do not need to ask ourselves the question whether or not sex and/or politics is and/or are appropriate to art (as the "finest" of all public venues): Sex and politics are not only inextricable one from the other, as the women's movement taught us, they are equally inextricable from art and public discourse. It is worth noting, further, that these raucous Satyr plays, like the more familiar comedy and tragedy, were performed as part of an annual *religious* festival, a community-wide homage to the god Dionysus, god not of repression but of orgiastic abandon. So sex and politics are, in a traditional Western sense, inextricable also from religion. Does anyone miss the erotic content of the Sistine Chapel ceiling, or the Pietà? Or doubt that all this papal art is deeply involved in internecine struggles for the Throne of Peter?

The twin problems we then face are how to introduce the full palette of sexuality into public dialogue through the medium of contemporary art, and how to rescue from the politicians the right to make art about whatever we want to make it about: sex, politics, and religion, or any combination we choose. In other (perhaps impertinent words): How do we stop people who know so little about sex from silencing those of us who know more? After all, many a homosexual is a former heterosexual; but the vice is infrequently versa.

Another question—and it's their question, of course, not ours—is, "Why do queer people insist on confronting sexuality so directly in their work?" This is a version, of course, of "Don't frighten the horses." There would be no NEA conflict at all, we are misled, if only the queers weren't so *explicit*. Apparently, we not only kiss and *tell*, we do it in a style too compelling to ignore!

The answers to all these questions of theirs *seem* more or less obvious. Performance artists, like the four who had their National Endowment for the Arts grants rescinded because of the subversive and/or queer content of their work, make art about being queer because they themselves are queer (although not necessarily homosexual). Similarly, Andres Serrano makes art about religion, religious iconography, and the abasement of religion in a capitalist world, because he is religious—in a sense that clearly transcends the unexamined church-on-Sunday religion practiced by most Americans. He photographs plastic crucifixes submerged in urine and blood because sex is as inextricable from religion as it is from art.

It is a general principle in psychotherapy that the more the patient resists, the more need there is to press forward. The same is true in culture. The more the power elite wants us to shut up and go away, the louder we need to remain in keeping our agenda afloat. It is not art about sex that is causing a sexual identity crisis in this country but commerce about sex.

As Julia Cameron writes in her very persuasive *The Artist's Way: A Spiritual Path to Higher Creativity,* the artist part of creative individuals is a child—the inner child, if you will forgive the contemporary self-help jargon. It's an arguable position, I concede, but it does seem true that the artist-self behaves in many ways as a child (given traditional notions about childhood), which is precisely why it is invaluable as well as dangerous: It has not bent to the socialization that kills creativity in favor of the status quo, in favor of those things that make the most people feel the most comfortable. Artists are not animated characters out of Disney: In the real world, artists (like children and religious visionaries) turn the world upside down.

Defying authority is not *only* or even predominantly an adolescent or immature gesture. That's what they kept saying in the sixties, those who were in control of the money and the rules they could buy with it: that the peace movement, the youth movement, the women's movement, the black movement, the sexual revolution, the gay/lesbian movement were adolescent. What they meant was, *they* had the money, and it irritated them to the point of apoplexy that *we* managed to acquire power without it, in our numbers (as in a paradigmatic democracy).

Additionally, we queers-who-write write about sex because it is a normal thing for us. We write about our kind of sex because it is the normal thing for us to write about. We write about sex because our perspective on sexuality as outsiders, as outlaws in many cases, is precisely the piquant ingredient we have most legitimately to offer the conformist sociocultural stew, social conformity being the perfect bell-jar environment for the ignition of fascism. It is in large measure *because* gay men and women (and our other queer cohorts) have lately forced our sexual expression on the rest of the culture that the rest of the culture has in many ways liberated itself from strictures of missionary positions and once-a-week nuptial trysts for the primary purpose of propagation.

But there is a fundamentally more important reason for writers to write about sex, for writers of minority sexuality to write about minority sexuality, and the reasons are so fundamental they go back, again, to Greece, to a period that predates the writings of fifth-century B.C.E. Periclean Greece, to the very origins of the god Eros. Now, Eros, of course, is the root of the word *erotic*. Like many words, it has come to have a specific cultural meaning that entirely eclipses the breadth and depths of its origins in the culture from which ours derives.

In fact, there were two different gods called Eros in mythology. One is familiar to us, having descended through the history of Latin culture to the chubby little boy of Valentine's Day cards (the arrow being a hieroglyph of the penis, as the heart is of the vagina). But this toddling *putto* is an emasculation of the original god, who belongs to the Greek creation myth. In this older, more important view, Eros is the force of cohesion, creativity and, in essence, society itself (and in this sense relates to Freud's theory of repressed libido as the animus of art). Sadly, we have lost this far more complex and authentic notion of Eros as the force in nature of all creation, associated with sexuality, certainly, but far greater than sexuality. Eros is the life force in nature and embraces everything that opposes Thanatos, or the force of death.

As many of us have learned far too early in this age of AIDS, life consists of coming to terms with the shifting balance of these forces of life and death. It becomes increasingly necessary to preserve this original all-nurturing notion of Eros not only because it is under attack but because it underlies all human interaction. It is a mistake to separate body and spirit (the force of religion and of art), and we have suffered from that schism. If we suppress sexuality, we suppress creativity. If we suppress creativity, society dies. If society excludes those of us who have by virtue of our outsider status a more complete understanding of sexuality, then society will be stuck with more network sitcoms and fewer works of literature.

Among the additional reasons to keep sex a matter of public dialogue (and of public education) is to put it on public record, to rescue future generations from the ignorance of those who have gone before. One of our great responsibilities here, of course, is to make sex public *accurately,* which is to say, in its wide variety, and in its real-life role, which includes sexuality inside committed relationships. I understand the tendency to revel in pure sexual expression, both in life and on the page, to bring into the light the full weight of our imagination and experience with unmitigated sexuality—in other words, erotic writing, or pornography, if you will, since it has a long and noble history. It is *normal* for us to want to get it into the canon that pure sexuality exists and that it is or can be a good thing; it is an *abnormal* though perniciously persistent impulse to exclude it.

One of the most liberating moments of my own sexual education came at a West Hollywood bathhouse called the 8709. Back in its heyday in the late seventies, the 8709 had a barely lit maze, and its denizens frequently doused even the dim lights to create a labyrinth of pitch-darkness. Freed from prejudices about visual attraction, I came to understand that chemistry does in fact exist. In that totally dark corridor, it was possible to come into contact with hundreds of naked men in a single night, and eventually to happen upon a single arm, or leg, nipple, earlobe, or erect penis that created an absolutely uncensored and uncensorable chemical or electronic or, for all I know, spiritual erotic charge. Had I not "transgressed"—this was, after all, *illegal* behavior—I would still be ignorant about my own body.

But sex can become addictive. As an oppressed minority—the only single minority in this country whose oppression is still a matter of law—our community has come to include a disproportionate number of alcoholics and drug addicts, addiction being a function of, among other things, eroded self-esteem. We endanger ourselves with other self-destructive behaviors, too, including sexual compulsion, obsession, and addiction. The pursuit of sex has led many to premature and ugly deaths.

When we talk about making sex public, the temptation is to assume that we are making *our* sexuality public for *their* consumption, as if among the queer confraternity sexuality is already known, that we cannot each inside the community profit from information about sexuality other than our own—about leather sex, for example, if we do not walk in that part of the forest, or transgenderism, or any other kind of sexual expression, including sex inside relationships both traditional and nontraditional. As we know, sex is *part* of a life, not a life, or a life *style,* per se. Our community's obsession with sex, with youth (our own *elusion* of death, we might call it), is a direct result of buying into the heterosexual lie that we dykes and fags *are* our sexuality and nothing more.

But all art, all writing, public utterances of any kind, whether or not they are about sex, ought to aspire to great expression, because it is the expression that makes the experience live. "Pornographic," "indecent," "noble," or "liberating" are impermanent labels that are reaffixed over time. Shelley, that now-tame exemplar of Romantic poetry and one distilled liqueur of English literature, was hounded out of London not only for his free-love take on sex and marriage but for a scandalous little poem called "Sonnet: England in 1819," an overtly political poem that was an attack on the king and his irresponsible minions—the Jesse Helmses of his day.

Rather than bow to pressure that we tailor the suits of our own writing to the fashions of the current lamentable day, we must rather invoke that renegade of the night who won widespread public approval, Tennessee Williams: "I do not write to shock," said our impish sage of Key West when thus accused. "I write the truth, and the truth shocks."

It is authenticity in this world of mendacity that speaks louder than Senate resolutions about the Defense of Marriage (an institution sorely in need of defense, given those who practice it), and we must continue to be authentic even after we become legitimate, which is inevitable.

Author of the groundbreaking *Culture Clash: The Making of Gay Sensibility,* Michael Bronski has long been an astute observer of gay culture. Here he analyzes the paradoxical limitations of the recent proliferation of gay sexual writing and videos.

2. MICHAEL BRONSKI

Why Gay Men Can't Really Talk About Sex

GAY MEN ARE ACCUSED OF A LOT OF FAILINGS IN OUR CULTURE, but the inability to talk about sex is never one of them. I mean, after all, gay men *talk* about sex. It's something we do. We do it well. We do it a lot. At least that's what I've thought over the past twenty-five years. But recently I'm coming to the conclusion that most of our sexual talk is simply an attempt to avoid really talking about sex. The discussions of what, or who, we do in bed, of how big someone's dick is, of who we want to fuck, or what went on in the bushes last night are fine as far as they go, but they are more posturing than professional, more obfuscating than observing, more pruriently licentious than profoundly liberating.

It is rare, in my experience, for gay men to discuss honestly their sexual feelings, their sexual needs, or their sexual fantasies. This isn't about gay men being unable to open themselves up emotionally—problems in expressing intimacy are endemic to being human, although their manifestations are certainly influenced by a wide array of gender, race, ethnicity, and class factors—but about how sex, sexuality, and sexual activity have shaped and been shaped in gay male life. The irony is that while talk about sex has always been a salient, vital part of gay male culture, honest discussion about sex is as scarce as good acting in a porno movie.

I first started to think seriously about gay men's inability to discuss sex after I started presenting a piece I had written entitled "Death, AIDS and the Transfiguration of Grief: Thoughts on the Sexualization of Mourning" at conferences. In the piece (which originally appeared in *Gay Community News* in 1988), I talked about the physical connections between sex and grief, about my sexual fantasies about my ex-lover Jim who had recently died of AIDS, and how I discovered, for me, the reality that sexual fantasy and activity had become inextricably intertwined with dealing with the miasma of death and grief with which I found myself surrounded. The piece began with a description of my jerking off on Jim's brass bed a few hours after he had died—an image which, though shocking, conveyed both the visceral and emotional sense of my ideas.

When I wrote the piece I was aware that some of the images and ideas might be challenging. I had no idea that they would disturb listeners so much. The first time I read "Death, AIDS and the Transfiguration of Grief" in public was at a panel on AIDS writing at the 1990 Gay Games in Vancouver. Each of the panelists did their presentations and received appropriate applause. When I finished my piece, there was a sort of stunned, embarrassed silence. I thought maybe it was because they felt I was not taking AIDS seriously, or perhaps because my solution to the grief that immediately followed a hospital visit was to go and cruise Boston's outdoor, reedy Fenway area. But it became clear to me later on that much of the distress was caused simply by my elaborating on sexual fantasies concerning Jim's doctors and other sick PWAs on his hospital floor.

This I thought was most curious since most gay men I know will be more than willing to tell you how big last night's trick's dick was, how many people they blew in the bushes, and exactly what they would like to do if they ever got porn star Jeff Stryker in bed, or over a kitchen table. Why should my sexual fantasies—and rather mild sexual fantasies at that—be so threatening? Of course it was possible that I had broken some gay cultural taboo by talking about AIDS and positive sexuality in the same breath, but it seemed that the problem was deeper, that by simply recounting actual masturbatory fantasies I had crossed some unspoken line of sexual and social demarcation: Sure, everyone agrees, sex fantasies are great—we just don't want to get too personal about it.

Keeping this in mind the next time I presented "Death, AIDS and the Transfiguration of Grief," I built my presentation around the idea that men needed to talk more openly and honestly about their sexuality. The venue was perfect—a panel called "Gay Men and Sex" at the 1991 Creating Change conference. I began with a short rap about how hard it is to talk about sex, and read portions of the article (once again to great discomfort in the room). Then I spoke about how gay men, myself included, found it hard to talk about the more intimate aspects of our sexual lives: not how many times we got porked the other night, but what it meant to us, how we felt about it. I talked about how we never really talk about jerking off—perhaps the most common private sexual act we all perform with astonishing regularity—and asked how many men jerked off last night? (some hands were raised), how many men jerked off this morning? (a few more hands went up), and then I asked how many men were willing to tell us, as a group, what they had thought about while they were jerking off. Most of the hands disappeared. This was, obviously, moving into the more dangerous territory. A few hands lingered, and when their owners spoke, the results were amazing: Almost all of their private, intimate, personal masturbatory fantasies sounded like tired scenarios from a porn film or a dog-eared copy of *Honcho*. The audience seemed pleased; sex was being spoken about in the most explicit terms and everyone (but me) seemed to think that gay men had no problem being open and honest about their sexual fantasies, desires, and needs.

What puzzled me most about that episode was that I could never figure out if the men who presented their fantasies were avoiding the truth or were, in fact, simply recounting it. Did they mask their real thoughts with shopworn, store-bought erotic fantasies or—a more frightening thought—were these mundane, commercialized, processed images and actions really their fantasy life? If either one is correct, what does this tell us about gay men, about our ability to fantasize and explore our erotic needs and desires? What does it tell us about gay male culture, and what does it tell us about our lives?

The ease with which gay men can talk sex—probably better than any other cultural group—emanates from a desire for self-expression, a need for public space, and an urge to be socially rebellious. In a culture that tells us that our sexual lives and feelings are bad, or nonexistent, gay male talk about sex is a form of survival. The articulation of sexual desires—"I want to suck your cock," one man says to another in a bar—is the first step to action and satisfaction. The articulation and gesticulation of gay male sex in public—queers talking loudly on the street, softcore gay porn on newsstands, blatant cruising, sex in restrooms or in the bushes, openly sexual modes of dress like the leather queen, the clone, the drag queen—are all a reclamation of a public space that we would be denied. All of these actions are—in the broader scheme of things—a form of social and sexual protest, an attempt to break down those social boundaries of "private" and "public" that have enforced silence and shame for so many for so long.

Gay men have learned how to use our sexuality as a social marker, as a disrupter of the social and sexual status quo, and as a way to make our presence felt in the world. The problem is that we have begun to see these actions and effects as ends in themselves. The blatant public sexual persona has obscured the need, the desire, and the ability to talk about a more private sexuality. Gay men have learned to talk sex by emulating the bravado of straight male locker-room talk and mixing that with the rhetoric, conventions, language, and images of commercialized pornography. By adopting this ready-made set of attitudes, words, phrases, postures, and desires—a one-size-fits-all notion of gay sexuality—gay men can talk sex all we want without ever revealing anything about ourselves.

Over the past forty years porn has played an important part in gay male culture. It has given us a visibility, it has given clear imagining to gay male desire, and it has made it perfectly clear to both gay men, and heterosexuals the answer to, "What *is* it that they do in bed?" For many gay men, softcore and hardcore porn was one of the ways that they validated their sexual desires. Be it paintings by George Quantice in the *Physique Pictorial* of the 1950s, the famed *Song of the Loon* by Richard Amory in the 1960s, or the newest Falcon video of last week, porn not only gets us hard but shows us new possibilities; it is incitive as well as instructional.

But porn has also had a deeply destructive effect on gay male sexuality. The increasing commercialization of porn over the decades—*Physique Pictorial* gave way to *Mandate* and *Honcho,* 8mm porn loops have given way to the assembly-line productions of Falcon and Bijou Studios—has left us with a porn world of homogenized, mass-produced images that have little emotional or sexual resonance. Sure, porn stars are well built with big dicks and fashionable haircuts, but they have little connection with real life. They are commodities like new cars, expensive shoes, or Gap fashions. It is no surprise that the men who appear in Bruce Weber's early photographs for

Calvin Klein advertisements have become one of the basic molds for porn stars: Calvin Klein is selling clothes, pornography is selling sex. The same is true of other male porn-star types: the boy next door, the Marky Mark clone, the gym body. And it is no surprise that they all have made-up, generic names: Corey, Scott, Lane, Rod, Casey, Erik, Rob, Mitch, Ty, Alex.

The commercialization, and codification, of gay male sexual fantasy is a powerful social force. As with all merchandising, "the market" has rules and parameters; it stipulates what is "hot" and what is not, it sets standards, and it promotes what sells. The problem is that our general culture is so homophobic that none of us are encouraged to cultivate, stimulate, or act upon our own incredible wealth of sexual fantasies. In such a context, the fantasy factory of porn rushes in to fill a need created by fear, ignorance, and lack of encouragement. I don't mean to imply that pornography has completely stolen our inner erotic resources—everyone's libidinous mind is always working, spurred by some man on line in the supermarket, a photograph of a Missouri flood worker in *Time* magazine, or the fleeting remembrance of a trick from twelve years ago—but it has made it far easier to rely on prepackaged, physically approved, and commercially available images.

This is not only true of sexual images but of sexual language as well. Everyone has a story of going home with someone who—once sex began—fell into porno-talk: "Yeah, take that big dick," "Bite those tits," "Yeah, that's right, suck it, yeah." The frightening thing is that this happens far more often than people will admit. An intimate, personal language of passion and desire and physical heat has been supplanted by the dialogue of porno films and novels. When our culture tells us that it is not all right to talk about sex, it makes sense that we would not be very good at it. The language of passion must be as practiced, experimented with, and honed as any other type of communication. I have a friend who recently was being picked up in a bar. When he asked what the other man, who was slightly younger, was interested in, he replied, "You know, like having a hot time." And what would that entail? my friend asked. "You know, like two hot dudes doing it. Like, you know, getting together and like making it . . ." What struck my friend the most was that the other man's language was nothing more than a series of porno-phrases combined with advertising slogans. It was communication for the nineties—all pitch and no substance, provocative without ever being evocative.

None of this is a recent problem. John Preston remembers that in the late 1970s when he was working on magazines like *Mandate* and *Honcho* it was not uncommon to hear of men in urban centers simulating specific looks that the magazines published each month: the cowboy, the mechanic, the biker. John speaks of this to illustrate how few models men have in their lives to teach them how to be sexual. The lesson for me is a little more frightening. Did these images—really, just a series of half-put-together costume accessories—really resonate with these men's inner lives or were they simply responding to what they had been told by the media they read was "in" or "hot"? This is not uniquely a gay male problem—did all those straight men *really* want to look like John Travolta in 1978, did all those women *really* want to look like Marilyn Monroe in the 1960s? The lure, and the trap, of the media image has always been with us. A consumer culture tells us we are not good enough (in any number of ways) and that we have to buy something—anything—to make us different.

Some might argue that "fantasies"—and porn is, like all imaginative creations, a fantasy—*don't* have any relationship with real life, but this misses the essential point: Our fantasy life is as integral to our emotional, psychological, and material life as eating and sleeping and fucking. The problem with almost all gay male porn (and most other porn for that matter) is that it has little connection with our real fantasy lives. The gay artist Blade talks about how, in the 1940s and early 1950s, his erotic drawings were so rare and so legally dangerous, they would be left in bus-station lockers or in sealed, plain envelopes behind bars to be passed from one man to the next. Such early porn had far more personal energy and honesty to it than anything mass produced later in the century. Look at the early drawings of Tom of Finland and then at his later work—it is the difference between an artist and an industry.

The power of pornography is that it can arouse us (and thus, generally make us forget how boring it is) and that it offers us social visibility. But like other mass-produced genres of commercial writing—the mystery, the romance—it also allows us to forget that we have an inner life that is more varied, more exciting, and dirtier than most of what we might read and see. We are told by porn (and TV, movies, advertising), as well as by heterosexual culture, that this inner erotic life—different for every man, completely idiosyncratic to his desires and needs, fantasies and longings—is inferior to the approved (and sanitized) sexual images that are made for popular consumption.

I think one of the reasons why my piece "Death, AIDS and the Transfiguration of Grief" was so disconcerting to gay male listeners was that for a few minutes it broke through the silence of gay men's fantasy lives: It actually said what was on someone's mind in images and terms that were not represented in porn films or *Drummer* magazine. It connected sex with the real world—in this case the world of friendship and AIDS—and it did so explicitly but without the usual language and rhetoric that make other writings about sexual fantasy acceptable and emotionally safe.

The prevalence of casual, nonimportant sexual talk in gay men's lives has been, in many ways, a positive presence. It has helped us form visible communities, it has helped us formulate safe-sex education skills and techniques, it has—in the long run—challenged the all-encompassing antisex attitudes that have so long been the bulwark of Western culture. But it has also prevented us from exploring the many ways in which our sexual desires and ideas, longings and needs do manifest themselves in our lives. How many of us are willing to talk freely about the whole *range* of sexual fantasies we choose to have—not to mention those that occur to us in sleeping or waking dreams, or while we are in the midst of masturbating, or having sex or coming?

What about those dreams of sex with a best friend whom we have never before thought of as sexual, or about sex with a family member, or with women, or a daydream about an S/M activity we would never (well, probably never) really do, or fantasies about underage boys, or with animals, or with lovers who have died of AIDS, or men who are very ill, or sex that is not, or might not be, consensual, or sex that occurs in connection with extreme violence . . . ? The list goes on and on and on. There are whole areas of sexual fantasy and imagination which are never discussed because we are embarrassed by them, either because they are "taboo," or too personal, or too frightening. If we are to grow as people and as a community, we have to find ways to discuss our actual sexual lives and thoughts, our real sexual fears and longings. And not in the language or the posturing of porno novels or the images of porn videos but in honest, open discussions with ourselves and with others until we have broken through the inhibitions and the embarrassments, the anxieties and the terrors of really knowing—without fear and without shame—the complexity and the glory of who we are and who we might become as fully sexual beings.

3. JESSE GREEN

When this provocative article about the failures of safe-sex campaigns appeared as the cover story of the *New York Times Magazine,* readers responded viscerally to the account of a man struggling to stay HIV-negative. Jesse Green's award-winning journalism has also been featured in *GQ, Mirabella, Out,* and many other publications.

Flirting with Suicide

MARK EBENHOCH HAS ON HIS "COMMAND" VOICE: THE VOICE OF fearless authority he learned during twelve years in the Marines. A fearless voice hardly seems appropriate now, in my hotel room, talking about sex; he wants to get rid of it, but it keeps re-emerging. If he had the money, he'd also like to get rid of the tattoos: the one on his left arm that reads "U.S.M.C. and damn proud" and the one under his left nipple, the so-called meat patch, with his Social Security number and blood type—B-positive. Which could be his catch phrase. Be positive.

So he talks about what has brought him to this state—he is HIV-negative but wonders how long he can hold on—as if he were announcing a baseball game. "Heck, I'd been such a good boy, followed my church upbringing, wouldn't cuss, even in the Corps. I was celibate for thirteen years instead of being gay! So then, last year, when I finally came out, I came out flying like a bat out of hell. Wednesday, Friday, Saturday I'd go to this bar called Friends, which was outside a military base that was notorious for gay-bashings. I'd walk in and it was a really friendly atmosphere, so I'd sit down and order a beer. I felt really good, like I didn't have to look for somebody, because I was fresh meat and they would come to me. Like once, this guy, not even my type really, sat down next to me. He was military, which I could tell from his haircut, and it didn't take that long, a drink or two and a couple cigarettes, before he said, 'Do you want to go do something?' And it was like, okay, let's go.

"He followed me home in the car and there was this incredible anticipation, with his headlights in the rearview mirror. *I wonder what he's like . . . I wonder what we're going to do.* And I'd show him the house and offer him something to drink, but then the first time somebody swings that first kiss, you can just forget it. From there, it's: Here's the Christmas wrapping, and I'm going to unwrap the present. And by now it's midnight, I've had four or five beers. I don't have any rubbers and stuff. In California, the bars give you the condoms free; not in North Carolina, where I was living then. And no one brings it up. It's not thought about. Well, for a split second, but I say to myself: I know this is a Marine, I know he gets checked every six months and he's probably the safest bet in the world. And *this* one was married.

"It was like I was finally inside the candy store I'd been looking at forever. I wasn't about to deny myself now. So during that time, those two or three months, I guess I had over twenty partners. A lot of the time I was drunk, though, so I can't say for sure. Sometimes you'd go home with somebody you might not really want because of loneliness or something, and in that position I sure wouldn't mention safe sex. I'd always wait for them to say something about it." He nods his head sharply, as if dismissing an underling. "But no one did."

That no one mentioned safe sex to Mark Ebenhoch does not mean no one knew what it was. Gay men have had more than a decade to get the message—and for the most part, have. In the years after AIDS was first reported, in 1981, the gay community, largely on its own, masterminded what may be the most intensive public-health intervention ever. Armed with explicit fliers and scary ads urging the use of condoms for every sexual contact—and, later, with subtler messages trying to promote this new behavior as fun—educators undertook the complete reorganization of gay mating habits. By some measures, the effort was amazingly successful: a 1994 New York City study showed that gay men's average number of unsafe-sex contacts dropped from more than 11 per year in 1980 to 1 per year in 1991. But by other measures, as Mark Ebenhoch's story and a thousand others like it demonstrate, the effort failed. Which leads to a question of perspective: Are the cemeteries half-full or half-empty?

Getting people to change their private behavior for the public good, or even for their own well-being, has been a chronic national problem. Recent reports—much politicized this election season—show that drug use by teenagers, after a period of steady decline, more than doubled between 1992 and 1995. Highly visible efforts to combat the problem of "children having children" haven't worked either: 4 out of 10 American women become pregnant by the time they reach age twenty—almost a million teenagers a year. Indeed, despite decades of effort, there is no clear consensus on what kinds of interventions even make a difference. Prescriptive, authoritarian campaigns like Just Say No may be effective in certain already-motivated populations, but they virtually repel those who most needed addressing. And even if successful interventions are found, they tend to stop working long before anyone is willing to give them up.

An examination of AIDS-prevention efforts in the gay community shows why. For a while, the safe-sex posters and fliers worked well, at least while it was still believed that the disease might disappear momentarily. The optimism engendered by the early statistics led some AIDS organizations to conclude that their educational mission was complete; San Francisco's Stop AIDS Project disbanded in 1987. But when it became clear that no cure was imminent, and that the changes adopted for a finite emergency would have to be sustained over a lifetime instead, the gay community was caught short. By 1991, it was common knowledge that men who had been safe for at least six years were slipping more and more often, and that many men who had never been safe saw no point in starting now.

The Stop AIDS Project reconstituted itself in 1990, but the renewal of prevention efforts there and elsewhere took place in a much grimmer context. It was by then evident that black and Latino men (whose seroconversion rates were much higher than those of white men) had never been adequately reached, and that young homosexuals especially were on the brink of a disaster. According to a 1991 study, more than half of the nation's twenty-year-old gay men will contract HIV during their lifetime, if current trends continue. But even among the population of older, white gay men who most successfully absorbed the original prevention message, things began to look less golden in the light of the new decade. Though the annual rate of new infections in San Francisco had decreased from well over 10 percent in the early eighties to 1.4 percent in 1990, that rate has nearly doubled in just the last six years. Perversely, even the good news about a new class of drugs called protease inhibitors—which have reduced blood levels of HIV in some patients to undetectable levels—has backfired: Many gay men are now talking about AIDS as a manageable disease, and using this premature hope as an excuse for returning to the unsafe practices of the past.

Despite these reversals—and despite studies suggesting that between 20 percent and 40 percent of gay men still report at least occasional anal intercourse without condoms—the one-note educational strategy of the prevention organizations has barely changed since 1985. That strategy basically boils down to normative, hand-slapping variations on Just Say No, which are almost interchangeable with similar preachments about driving drunk, smoking cigarettes, and motorcycling without a helmet. "These things can become jokes very quickly," says Lloyd Johnston, who as program director at the University of Michigan's Institute for Social Research has studied adolescent drug use for twenty-five years. "Remember the fried egg campaign? *This is your brain. This is your brain on drugs.* It was only a slogan, and the best you can say for a slogan is that it may work for a little while. This one did. It definitely spoke to kids, at least for a time; then it lost its persuasive power and maybe even became negative. In a way, the more successful these things are, the shorter their shelf life."

Aside from the paternalism of such campaigns, Johnston blames their eventual failure on a phenomenon he calls "generational forgetting." Improvement in one decade means that young people in the next see fewer examples, either first hand or in the media, of the consequences of risky behavior. At the same time, that improvement allows public-health officials to let down their guard, and government agencies to cut back financing. With less negative *and* positive reinforcement, the cycle starts again. "Which is a strong parallel to AIDS," says Johnston. "At the beginning of the epidemic many young gay men knew about or cared for people who were dying; they felt that tragedy and pain personally. Now we have a new generation replacing them who haven't gone through it. The most convincing prevention message in any field is direct experience—but it's also the most costly."

How cost is measured is the crux of the problem. Our current notions of public health are based on old, even ancient, models. Developed to contain everything from the plague to polio, classical interventions addressed more cohesive and tractable societies, and made less intrusive demands: *Cover your mouth and nose when sneezing.* But how do you "do public health" (as public health people like to say) in a democracy? How do you weigh individual liberty against statistical risk? And what happens when the behavior in question isn't a sneeze but part of a person's deepest core of identity? What if it's something he profoundly enjoys and does not *want* to give up?

When a natural drive like sex gets tangled in unintended and even tragic results, public health is at its worst. "Moralistic slogans and intervention programs based unrealistically on no-sex vows do *not* reduce teen pregnancy or sexual activity," says Gloria Feldt, president of the Planned Parenthood Federation of America. "In fact, there have been studies that show they may actually *increase* the desire of teenagers to experiment: to find out what it is they've been told to say no *to*. And then because they haven't been given the tools with which to experiment safely—and because they've been told that they are bad people if they prepare—the likelihood of pregnancy only goes up. Basically such programs don't work," she concludes, "because ignorance is *not* bliss."

This is a phrase I've also heard from a Berkeley psychologist named Walt Odets, but Odets goes even further. Suggesting that coercive messages like "a condom every time" are unjustifiably broad, he has condemned AIDS-prevention efforts as at best counterproductive and at worst dishonest—"not only withholding information from gay men but lying to them." In response to the huge stir such proclamations have caused in the AIDS community, Odets has dug in his heels; the question of whether prevention efforts have succeeded or failed is to him almost obscene. Indeed, though you can look at studies of gay men and make a credible case for either proposition, looking at gay men themselves, you cannot. Many of those who show up in the data as HIV-negative are struggling in ways statistical analysis won't pick up until it's too late; some consider themselves *statistics to be.* Such men exist in an illogical limbo: They are not sick but don't feel safe and, despite years of posters and pamphlets, can barely tell the difference.

A living rebuke to the status quo in AIDS education, these men were largely ignored until Odets started asking a series of contrarian questions: *Have some prevention campaigns actually increased the likelihood of transmis-*

sion? Are risk-elimination strategies for gay men actually homophobic? For the last few years, Odets has insisted on a reevaluation of the entire effort—a call to arms with implications for all public-health campaigns. In a recent book, in impromptu jeremiads, and in a series of withering articles (one of them called "The Fatal Mistakes of AIDS Education"), he has argued that prevention organizations have failed even the basic requirements of a sustainable initiative: to identify appropriate target audiences, provide them with accurate information, and respect their right to weigh risk against benefit according to their own values. In doing so, he concludes, the groups have been guilty of ignoring the deepest root of gay men's unsafety: the psychological root, what they *feel*.

That Odets has been vilified for such conclusions is, in a way, just another sign of the brittleness of the gay community after sixteen years of AIDS. But public-health interventions are generally most necessary in exactly those communities most sensitive to criticism. In the gay community, that sensitivity has often resulted in the sacrifice of candor to political correctness. Until 1995, for instance, there was not a single AIDS-prevention program for gay men anywhere in the country specifically targeted to those who were uninfected—the only logical audience—for fear of offending infected men *by suggesting their condition was something to avoid.* And it is still taboo in AIDS circles to broach the subject of promiscuity. At one gay men's support group I attended, a twenty-year-old who described himself as promiscuous was hissed into rewording his own experience: "All right, *slutty,*" he said, to applause.

Promiscuity is famously defined as any amount of sex greater than what you are having. Admittedly, it's an unhelpful word. And yet, *promiscuous* is how many gay men describe at least a part of their lives. Some of them mean a kind of innocent, adolescent freedom, but what others really mean is *compulsive* sex—sex that cannot be credibly taken as political liberation or personal ecstasy because it does not bring joy, cannot be controlled, and is used, exactly like alcohol or drugs, to assuage a nonsexual need. Either way, these words are important in understanding AIDS, despite the inability of the AIDS establishment to utter them. Which is why, at a time when public-health interventions of all kinds seemed to be failing, I set out to talk to HIV-negative men who were having problems with unsafe sex: the ones who were floridly unsafe, the ones who slipped now and then, the ones who were so scared of being unsafe that they had no sex at all. I was hoping they would be able to answer the question that has bothered, even angered, me since 1991: Why are gay men—ordinary gay men, who appear to function normally and enjoy the pleasures of life—systematically killing themselves?

"I do fit the bill and am interested," came the E-mail response from Mark Ebenhoch—though at this point I still knew him only by his handle, Nailinch9. Sitting at my computer, I had posted messages on various electronic bulletin boards, explaining that I was looking for HIV-negative gay men willing to talk about their unsafe sexual experiences. I did wonder what kind of person would respond to such an inquiry, but Nailinch9 addressed this problem at once. "My reasons are simple," he wrote. "If there is a way to prevent this type of behavior and share it, maybe someone else would miss the selfish hell I've put myself through."

I had, through more traditional methods, spoken to many men who also seemed to fit the bill, but most of them insisted on anonymity. Some said they were ashamed of the way they were endangering themselves and did not wish friends or family to know the difficult truths of their lives. Others—many others—were tormented about what even *constituted* unsafe sex. Over the last few years they had slowly come to accept the idea that unprotected anal sex was virtually the only way they might contract AIDS; Gay Men's Health Crisis, in New York, had reviewed dozens of scientific papers and found only four reports of "individuals presumed to have been infected by HIV through oral sex" in the United States as of 1995. Then, in June, a report about oral transmission of an AIDS-like virus in six rhesus monkeys implied that the common wisdom was false. And though all of the major AIDS organizations dismissed that conclusion, the men I spoke to were left so confused that they could barely make rational decisions about safety at all.

Mark Ebenhoch was not confused. Though he knew better, he had been unsafe at least several dozen times since his first adult sexual experience with a male, last year. He was forthcoming about the other things in his life that may have influenced him. Alarmingly, he seemed to match, point by point, each of the predictors of risk that AIDS educators have identified, combining in one short story the factors I had been hearing about singly from dozens of other men. For my purposes he was, in a way, *too* good. For his own purposes he was, in a way, not good enough.

And goodness had much to do with it. Mark was born into a chaotic family that zigzagged between Ohio, Florida, Arizona, and California; his mother, he says, was constantly getting married—"like Elizabeth Taylor without the money." His father left when Mark was nine, after which Mark shut down emotionally and devoted himself to fabricating a demeanor of perfect obedience and normalcy. If this was at the expense of real feelings, so be it; feelings tended to get in the way. At ten, his mother has told him, he was molested by a man assigned to be a Big Brother; Mark himself remembers nothing of the incident except being forced to wear a pair of tiny blue-and-white Speedos. "Which was agony," he says. "I was extremely bashful and had very low self-esteem. I was short to begin with, and a late bloomer besides. At thirteen I still looked nine. Even now . . ."

Even now, at thirty-six, only the slightly toughened skin of a Marine and the weary cast of his gray-blue eyes contradict the general impression of extreme youth. When I meet him in person, on a scorching April Los Angeles day, he's wearing a white mesh tank top, skimpy white corduroy shorts, and strange, ill-fitting, orange-tinted sunglasses. He is thin—too thin—and pool-boy blond. Despite the gold hoop in his ear and the pink-triangle ring on his left pinky, he comes off a little blank: edging sometimes toward gruffness, sometimes toward warmth, but always watchful, as if on patrol.

What stability Mark has had in his life has come from the U.S.M.C.: "the most homophobic, macho service, which was part of what attracted me to it." After joining directly from high school in 1977, he spent twelve of the next eighteen years among "Uncle Sam's Misguided Children," either as a reservist or on active duty, including a stint as a Stinger antiaircraft gunner in the Gulf War. Between enlistments he took various jobs—purchasing agent, mechanic, long-haul trucker—before ending up in Hollywood as an assistant military advisor on such films as *Platoon, Forrest Gump,* and, most recently, *Sergeant Bilko.* Throughout it all, he was celibate and lonely, though in his command voice there is no trace of sadness. "So when I finally decided to come out, it felt like a Niagara Falls of relief. It's not like I didn't know about AIDS. We had an AIDS-awareness class every six months in the Corps. And, as a senior sergeant, when I knew the men were going out, I'd say, 'You know what's out there, you know what to do, just do it.' But when it came time for *me* to be safe, no one was there to say anything. Even if they had, I doubt I'd have listened. I was on a euphoric mission. 'I am going to experiment,' I said, 'and see what it's all about.' *I want I want I want!*

"Maybe I'm an extreme case," he continues, "but I've met plenty of people like me. Go down Santa Monica Boulevard and look in the bars: It's lost people. And people like us don't pay any attention to the posters and ads. Don't they get it? It's *hard* to be safe. Think of the situation if you're looking to meet someone. You have to put away a lot of alcohol in the first place, just to get up the nerve, and then your reasoning is off. Last time, I was so toasted, I remember the room spinning. Luckily I passed out so nothing happened. But you can't blame it all on alcohol, either. It's something within you that makes you go on these binges. You remember what it feels like when somebody wants you: You're a god. And then it's over and you're a heel again. Alcohol is a tool to free yourself to destroy yourself if you already want to. And no poster is going to solve that."

If Mark Ebenhoch exemplifies many of the cofactors for HIV risk—recent emergence from the closet, lack of financial and domestic stability, alcohol use, depression, compulsiveness, a history of sexual abuse—he is not necessarily typical. Most of the men I spoke to fell into more definable single categories of risk. One group, consisting mainly of men over forty, seemed to be pushed toward unsafety by the accumulated grief of sixteen years' devastation. Many suffer from survivor guilt, marked by depression, isolation, and sometimes even a subconscious desire to seek communion with their lost friends by courting the same fate. These men are often ridiculed as whiners, which reinforces their isolation. A letter last October to *The Bay Area Reporter* in San Francisco, responding to an article about the emergence of HIV-negative support groups, sarcastically suggested the formation of similar groups for men who felt neglected because they didn't have *breast cancer.* Such men were invited to seek further information by writing "Victims-Are-Us" in the "PoorMeBuilding" at "4 Crybaby Lane."

Young men get more sympathy, if not more actual support. Several expressed to me the feeling that they would get AIDS no matter what they did; why even try to be safe? For them, ghoulish as it sounds, contracting the disease seemed almost like a rite of initiation into the gay community. Others were just too ecstatic about coming out of the closet to think about the consequences of their newfound freedoms. These young men, like young men of every stripe, felt themselves to be immortal, or at any rate not subject to the biological facts that govern other lives. A twenty-one-year-old named Danny O'Toole told me that "practically everyone" he knows has a lot of unsafe sex, and that they justify it with all sorts of magical thoughts. "They seem to believe that just being in a relationship protects them from risk," he said, "even if the partner is HIV-positive. And others don't even bother to ask, thinking: 'If he isn't concerned, why should I be?'"

Older men in "serodiscordant" couples—in which one partner is HIV-positive and the other is not—sometimes don't want to face reality, either. They may already feel separated from one another by the difference in their status, and condoms seem to underline that. When *both* partners are uninfected, though there is of course no risk of transmission, fears about unsafety may arise anyway, in the form of questions about fidelity. One man I spoke to, who said he sometimes had sex outside of his long-term relationship, was afraid to tell his lover that they should consider using condoms. And another man, who was in a completely monogamous relationship, told me that, despite everything, he sometimes feared he was putting himself at risk. He had somehow acquired the belief that, whatever they might say and promise, gay men (like all men) were inherently untrustworthy.

It's not hard to see where he got that idea. The unwavering focus of safe-sex campaigns on eternal condom use—no matter what you think you know about your partner—has led Danny O'Toole, for instance, to a bleak conclusion: If you can't trust, you can't love, so why even bother trying to have a relationship? And while this is certainly a way of remaining uninfected, it isn't a very happy outcome of safe-sex education. Still, for some, it's better than trusting the inconstant compass of self-preservation; a man need not be permanently delusional, suicidal, alcoholic, or self-loathing to slip and make a fatal error. He need only be human.

"It's about love, finally, or what you think is love," Mark says. Several days after our first meeting, he is telling me about the most unsafe of his unsafe encounters. Like all gay men I have spoken to, but unlike any prevention poster, he sees his behavior in an emotional context. "I'd made a decision to come out publicly. So the night before, New Year's Eve, I'm at this bar, and there's this one very good-looking individual about my age or so—preppy, brown hair, and just cute, period. At two in the morning I make my attack, bum a cigarette. Alcohol wasn't a factor for me, but *he* was sloshed. And he was into poppers, which I'd never been introduced to until I went home with him. We did everything, I mean everything. And this went on for an entire weekend. Never thought about precautions. If we would have had to go through the whole nine yards of getting the condom and the lube and *talking* about it, you would have lost everything. This wild, instinctive, spontaneous, split-second fun would just . . . die. It's too much work. I mean, if you have to plan for three weeks to go on a camping trip for one day, that one day isn't worth it, right? Why even go?"

Mark isn't alone in his complaint. Most gay men (and straight men, for that matter) agree that condoms interfere not only with physical sensation but with the spiritual sensation of union. They may also make sex more real than one's romantic illusions can tolerate; just tearing the foil package makes some people feel they are admitting the specter of death into their bedrooms.

"Thinking back on it, I should have definitely said something. But at the time I thought: It doesn't make any difference *now* whether I try to be safe or not. There's no going back. Especially because I was falling in love. And, of course, *that's* when I begin to find out that he was a very unhappy person, extremely promiscuous all over the world. And that's when I finally go, *Oh my god.* I replayed the events over and over, looking to find out how many instances there could have been of transmission: Were there any cuts or injuries? It stopped all of my sexual activity—for a while."

I ask Mark if he's heard of a strategy called "negotiated safety," which is now a widely accepted approach to AIDS-prevention for gay men in Australia, Canada, and Great Britain. Instead of pushing "a condom every time," public-health officials ask gay men to talk about risks with their partners and to tailor their condom use to the individual circumstances.

Mark responds acidly, as if I haven't understood his point. "Things are happening so fast you're just not thinking about that. I'm sorry, if the world was a perfect place, yeah, but not everybody is going to be perfect."

It is not the answer I wanted, and Mark knows it. He looks rather forlornly around my cheerful hotel room. "A teacher in North Carolina who just bought a brand new condo, yes, he's going to have negotiated safety or whatever. People like me, who go to the bars every night, by definition don't have what they want in life. They can't find how the successful ones did it, because the successful ones are enjoying their success outside the bar scene. They get up on a Sunday and go to the rodeo or something and go to dinner and then go home to their lover. Where are the rest of us supposed to learn how to love right? Joe Mr. Straight Guy cruising down the street in his car with his *girlfriend* has society just pushing him up and up, but if you're gay they just push you the other way. Maybe I did it wrong, but I wanted to experience happiness. Isn't that what we all want? Someone who's there for you, even if just for a moment?"

Strangely, I'm reminded of the dilemma of poor, teenaged girls, for whom sex and even pregnancy may be a way of repairing, if only temporarily, a damaged sense of self-esteem. No wonder campaigns aimed at holding such girls to a vow of chastity—or that simply throw birth control at them—have so little chance of working; they are as misdirected as the safe-sex campaigns that have so far failed to reach Mark. Still, I make a little campaign of my own. "But don't you want to be safe," I ask, "so that you can try for that nice life you describe?"

"I can say that I would *like* to: that's the kind of answer you give yourself," Mark answers flatly. "But I don't know what I'm going to feel like next week after I get four or five rejections."

As the lilt of enthusiasm slowly fades, Mark's voice begins to resemble the other voices I've been hearing: the voices of men bewildered and pained by the untenable balancing acts of their lives. Listening to them individually, I had been able to think of unsafe sex as an individual problem; listening to them all combined in Mark's encompassing story, I begin to think of it as a problem of community. Not just the AIDS community, with its effective or ineffective messages, but the *gay* community, such as it is, which so fears the imposition of external values that it can barely promote any of its own.

"I regret a lot of things I did," he adds quietly. "But I regret that I have to be gay in a world that bashes you or gives you AIDS. I don't think I have it now, but I probably will eventually. And if I do, it'll be from hooking up with the wrong person, a lonely person, a person who doesn't feel he has any reason to care—someone like me."

A month earlier, Mark had rolled up his sleeve for an HIV test; to his surprise, he was still okay. Still, it can take up to six months for the antibodies to show up, so he was only slightly relieved. "I'll get tested again in June," he says. "And then we'll see."

"What the hell is this?" Walt Odets exclaims. A trim, handsome man with pale blue eyes and graying temples, Odets reminds me of Warren Beatty—but on speed. Right now, he's looking at an AIDS-prevention poster that features photographs of various enthusiastic people with this legend: "Can't be afraid . . . We have control." He almost blows up. "They waste millions of dollars on this and they have no idea what to say. 'We have control'? What does that mean? 'Can't be afraid'? Why not? Men *are* afraid, they *don't* have control. These messages are a complete denial of what is actually happening in men's lives!"

If Odets is a bit edgy, it's partly because he has never been in a sex club before. Indeed, he has only come to this one, in a bleak, industrial San Francisco neighborhood on a Friday night in February, to accompany his friend Ed Wolf, who works for San Francisco's AIDS Health Project. Wolf spends two evenings a month here at Blow Buddies, offering free, anonymous HIV testing and counseling to patrons; the club's owner has set him up in an unused space on the second floor, formerly a nursery school. Downstairs, though I am expecting a scene that would shame a Bosch etching of hell, the club seems anything but decadent. Rather, there is a frank acceptance of the mechanical nature of the enterprise. Explicit safe-sex warnings abound, and monitors, who strictly prohibit anal contact of any kind, lend the place a kind of kindergarten propriety. ("We just stay away from the heinie altogether," the owner has advised me.) I guess it's true, as many people have said, that AIDS is happening more in bedrooms than in bath houses: more for the hope of love than the always-reneged-upon promise of lust. Still, for all the constant palaver about the joys of anonymous sex, there is no joy here tonight. The customers—inside and especially in the long line outside—look anything but liberated; they seem grim, determined, ground down by grief.

No one has yet come upstairs for testing, and while Wolf sets out his fliers and forms, Odets paces the room, occasionally checking the Mickey Mouse clock. Wolf, though he works for one of the organizations whose efforts Odets once criticized, agrees with much of what his friend says and has the equanimity to tolerate the rest. "But the others," he whispers confidentially, "they *hate* him. You don't know!" In fact, I do: Odets has made such a pest of himself in San Francisco that none of the major AIDS organizations there will work with him. Instead he has consulted on projects for Gay Men's Health Crisis, three thousand miles away in New York.

It isn't hard to see why Walt Whitman Odets (named for the poet) rankles. Raised in Manhattan, he is anything but the laid-back Californian, and his habits, especially for a man whose mission is risk reduction, seem immoderate. At forty-nine, he smokes, drinks, scarfs down scrambled eggs and bacon, and rhapsodizes about his days flying planes and driving motorcycles. He is a daredevil, I come to realize, both physically and intellectually. But that doesn't mean he's wrong.

"Most prevention efforts have been based on risk elimination rather than risk reduction," he tells me during another of our talks over the course of a year. "But the question is whether one *ever* eliminates risk for things that are valuable. As a society we do all kinds of things that may or may not be in the interest of our long-term health because we consider them important. We *weigh* the risks against the value. If you say to a man: 'In order not to get HIV you are never going to have sex again without using a condom,' his response would be that that seemed impossible. But there's a difference between going out with a guy you've never met whose status you don't ask about, and a friend who you've known ten years who tells you he's negative. Education has refused to allow gay men even to *think* about that difference. It's like telling people that if they want to be safe drivers, they must always drive thirty-five miles per hour without regard to when, where, or road conditions. Which any sane person will instantly reject."

As it happens, this conversation is taking place in a cubicle at a Mercedes dealership, while Odets's car is serviced and a $175,000 black convertible revolves on a turntable behind us. The lone sign on the wall seems to be a relevant warning: "The State of California does not provide for a cooling-off period. All contracts are final."

But Odets is oblivious to his context. "We don't say to heterosexuals: 'A condom every time' for the rest of their lives. We expect them to enter relationships and dispense with condoms when their HIV-negative status is confirmed. But this is a possibility that by and large we deny to gay men. As a matter of national policy, negotiated safety is considered the primary means of prevention for heterosexuals. For gay men it's considered negotiated *danger*. It's a very old story, telling gay men how to have sex; publicly they're complying, privately they're doing something else. We're the only country in the Western world that is continuing to even *discuss* the issue of oral sex in gay men. Oral sex *can* transmit HIV, but the risk is comparable to everyday, ordinary risk in modern life, like driving a well-maintained car at moderate speeds on the superhighway with a lap belt and shoulder belt on. Not to acknowledge the low risk is to deny the *value* of sex between men. Of course, the educators don't mean any harm, and God knows they've been working longer than I have. They want to err conservatively, which is understandable. But if erring conservatively means giving instructions that we know will not be followed, is that the best approach to education?"

"How *would* you word the message?" I ask.

" 'As a sexually active adult there are many occasions during which you will probably have to use a condom to avoid transmission of HIV and there are many others where you won't.' That sounds like something a person could conceive of doing for sixty years."

"So why have prevention agencies avoided saying just that?"

"Partly, it's because education is still based on the feeling that we need an absolutely reduced task for gay men," Odets says. "A single clear message—which is patronizing. And partly, it's because the campaigns are constructed from an advertising point of view, like selling soft drinks. They show a poster and ask: 'Do you like this?' If no, they don't use it. Well, my question is: *Why* don't they like it? Is it because it's addressing something difficult and true? You *have* to say things that create anxiety; the anxiety is justly motivated. Instead we seem to produce comfy campaigns that leave people with a false sense of resolution and calm."

Like Odets, I have found some of these campaigns, particularly the ones that attempt to eroticize safer sex, coercive or coy. But I have to admit that I have been comforted by others. San Francisco's famous "Be Here for the Cure" series—which Odets has excoriated as dangerous—was beautiful and popular. Looking back on it now, though, I do wonder whom it was aimed at. Did it mean to tell men who were already infected that they should try not to die? Or uninfected men not to worry if they *did* contract AIDS? Odets has pointed out that the two groups need different kinds of support, and that you can't help protect the HIV-negative man unless you acknowledge that it is a disaster to become HIV-positive. "You have to understand that we were working in an environment in which there was a real fear of offending HIV-positive people," says Bill Hayes, who led the team that created the campaign. "But maybe we were overreacting. My own boyfriend, who has AIDS, doesn't feel the need to have his self-esteem supported by ad campaigns."

The unwillingness to distinguish between the two populations has produced what Odets calls a unique confusion in the gay community between the normally distinct categories of *carrier* and *public*. "HIV-negative men should not be thinking of themselves as carriers, or as destined to get HIV just because they're gay. By helping them think that way we make it more likely that this will come true. But," he adds darkly, "this confusion is part of a much larger mental-health problem. Partly it's a matter of the identification gay men already have with being dirty and defective."

Odets has often been criticized for drawing conclusions from his experience with patients in his private practice: twenty-five privileged psychotics, they're sometimes called. (In reality, there have been several hundred over the years, none psychotic.) Be that as it may, the HIV-negative men I spoke to about their unsafe sex adventures—few of whom were in any kind of therapy—all echoed at least some part of Odets's thesis. They feel their dilemmas to be essentially psychological. Some of the AIDS-prevention organizations, on the other hand, suffer from what has to be called an antipsychological prejudice: a disbelief, almost, in the power of the subconscious. Understandably eager to ingratiate themselves with the mainstream medical establishment on which they depend for funding, they have gravitated toward purely "medical" interventions: condoms, condoms, condoms. But what this approach fails to acknowledge is that people are strange. They react not only to rational thoughts but also to illogical feelings, and do what appear to be insupportable, destructive things.

"The truth is that the community is rife with self-hatred," says Odets, displaying the genius for provocation that got him into so much trouble. "There is no question you can ask that doesn't eventually go back to that. It's not necessarily conscious; it's a diffuse feeling about oneself. Which is why gay men have this profound need to be liked and do good; if I criticize the AIDS-prevention programs they feel as if I'm saying that we *haven't* done good, that we've failed again. The first failure, of course, is being homosexual. There's not a gay man alive who doesn't feel he's failed his family. And then we all got caught with our butts in the air by an epidemic caused by receptive anal sex, and we've beat a hasty retreat and been apologizing ever since."

Americans have difficulty discussing *any* kind of sex frankly (which may be why our teen pregnancy rate is double the rate in Canada, for instance). But anal sex, which for many gay men is the defining act of gayness, is virtually unmentionable—despite being common even among heterosexuals. As a result, potentially important research into the efficacy of the so-called female condom as a *rectal* condom during anal sex, or of newly developed vaginal microbicides as a means of protecting gay men, has largely been ignored. Odets would see this prudishness as another factor in gay men's self-loathing, another way they are "mangled" by a hateful society.

It's a strong word, and he uses it often; does Odets himself feel *mangled?*

"My father"—the playwright Clifford Odets—"was open and comfortable about homosexuality; but when he died . . ." Odets pauses for perhaps the first time; he was sixteen when his father died, still yearning for public approval. "I felt unprotected from the rest of the world's disdain."

Only a few days after returning from Los Angeles, I receive a series of breathless E-mails from Mark Ebenhoch. "I did something now that I'm in seriously deep," the first one begins. Feeling rather like the parent of an adolescent boy, I brace myself for the rest of the message. As it turns out, my fears are justified, for what Mark has done is the most dangerous thing I can imagine. He has fallen in love.

"I left you on Tuesday and I went to Apache Territory, the bar, to kinda think about what we discussed. As I was trying to get picked up by this guy I had been getting to know, another guy had been watching me the whole time. We played this staring game until I couldn't take it any more and went over to say hi. That's where it all started.

"We did nothing sexually on Tuesday. And Wednesday we went to the mountains . . . and the rest of the night was very very sweet. We were safe but . . ." And here Mark goes on to explain that his new friend has full-blown AIDS.

If any hardness lingered in my heart toward men who risk their lives for sex, Mark has finally worn it down to a core of helplessness. It would be easy to dismiss him as atypical; most gay men do not appear to be as child-like, as impractical, as self-destructive as he is. But of course Mark doesn't *appear* that way, either, thanks to the command voice and the other forms of camouflage he has perfected over the years. It's only when you get to know him that you see how far his life has come from what he meant it to be. And then you wonder how many other people are masking beneath a facade of daily competence a willingness to flirt with suicide. In this main trait, Mark is exactly like most gay men I spoke to about unsafe sex: He re-fuels himself over and over not so much from a love of life itself as from an apparently bottomless reservoir of hope for the companionship that makes life worth it.

"I hope I can hold on," one of the E-mails concludes. "I don't know where to go from here. Someday maybe it all will become clear. Thanks for the worry, but I'll survive (always have somehow) Mark."

The flier advertising the workshop was not like any I'd seen before. In it, three men, average-looking and fully dressed, sit around a table; one of them is thinking to himself: "If I tell my friends that I've had unsafe sex, they don't know what to do." Below the picture, the text describes a "free, confidential three-session workshop for HIV-negative gay men or gay men who haven't tested." Such men are invited to come talk about "testing, par-tying, and the sex you are having, what it means to you and what it may cost you."

It did not surprise me to learn that this GMHC flier was, in part, the result of a collaboration with Walt Odets. The tag line, "Staying negative—

it's not automatic," had the open-ended, non-prescriptive quality I'd so often heard him endorse. What *did* surprise me was how effective it was. Some two dozen men showed up at the sessions I attended, on Tuesday nights in mid-July, visibly relieved to be talking to one another in a non-commercial, nonsexual atmosphere. Usually safe, they were worried about the times they'd slipped, or about slipping in the future. Most agreed that residual feelings of shame over their homosexuality enhanced their risk; that they were confused and therefore highly anxious about the safety of oral sex; that they wanted to be in long-term relationships; and that the gay "community"—at least as it was most evident to them in the form of bars and phone-sex ads—was not helping them in their struggle to stay safe.

GMHC, which began its programs for HIV-negative men in the spring of 1995, considers them highly successful, as do I. Still, only a few other organizations have followed their lead. For many in the prevention business, profound questions remain about the validity of Odets's approach.

"It's a tricky issue," said David Nimmons, who with Richard Elovich helped develop the GMHC program. "Walt has argued very persuasively against lumping HIV-negative and HIV-positive men together, and I obviously agree. But that's not to say there isn't a *common* interest in keeping as many men uninfected as possible. Here's something uncanny: Men who test positive are likely to be *more* consistently adherent, as a group, to safe-sex practices than negative men. That's a hard act to explain if you follow the model of self-interest, which is what most of AIDS prevention has been based on. On the other hand, men who *should* have the motivation of self-interest—HIV-negative men—increasingly say that things are getting in the way of their following out that self-interest. It makes you want to look at other things, like altruism and communal continuity, that cut across the serochasm."

It is something of a surprise to hear a discussion of spiritual motivation from the head of the largest AIDS-prevention education program in the world; Nimmons (who has recently left GMHC) supervised a staff of fifty-one people and an annual budget of about $3.9 million. But, unlike many others in the field, Nimmons accepts the psychological nature of the epidemic. He understands that the early reductions in transmission were made only at a great cost in depression, anxiety, and despair—a cost being paid on a long-term installment plan. On the other hand, Nimmons would not go so far as Odets in targeting gay men's low self-esteem. "Low compared to what?" he asks. "Compared to women who are anorexic and bulimic because they need to fit an externally determined mold? Ours is a culture that instills self-loathing in *everyone,* particularly in minority groups. It's part of what keeps the power structure intact. I don't want to gainsay that it's there, but are all *your* friends shriveled in self-doubt and riven with anxiety? I resist strongly the idea that this is a characteristic of gay men. We don't have any more mental illness or psychopathology than anyone else.

"Now I don't want to be a cheerleader, either. Mental health and community health are intrinsic to effective long-term prevention. You can get all the condoms onto all the penises on the first pass. But you can't do prevention in a vacuum of meaning, ignoring the struggles that your target group is going through. I think we *would* do better to talk about values and heart and ethics. To talk about the things that really drive this behavior. A code of *omertà* is not helpful to anybody. We've been looking obsessively at monads and gonads: at people as individuals, not in relationships or communities, and at sexual acts instead of sexual values. That's where we have to go next—and we have to go there regardless of AIDS itself."

Regardless of AIDS itself. As I think about this phrase, I realize that what Odets (if not Nimmons) has been suggesting all along is that there is an epidemic beneath the epidemic we know about. Beneath and beyond. It predates AIDS and will probably outlast it and comes not from a virus but a vacancy. Like most minorities in America, gay men grow up feeling different, but uniquely they grow up both different and *alone.* They are unlike, and often cannot speak to, the families that raise them. They have no role models or society of peers with whom to practice their emergent personalities; no way to learn, innocently, the byways of sex and how to follow them to happiness. Odets puts it plainly: "Gay adolescents are subjected to developmental abuses that make adult relationships harder. Society has a lot of nerve subjecting them to this kind of abuse and then, when they come out the other end of the tube mangled at twenty-five, to accuse them of depravity."

If, as Odets says, gay men feel inordinately bad about themselves, many work doubly hard to make up for it by developing their capacities for empathy, decency, and loyalty. The epidemic has accelerated this process, or intensified its sublimations: Lo, we were actors, waiters, lawyers; now we're lay epidemiologists and social workers. We were pansies and perverts, now we're heroes on the six o'clock news. We are finally, if temporarily, accredited Americans, and part of the reason AIDS organizations have so entrenched themselves against the new realities is that hard-won halos are not easily discarded. But halos cannot ameliorate the underlying problem, which stems from how homosexuals are *hated.* And while other groups are hated too, the tragedy for gay men has been that the thing that makes them different (indeed, perhaps the only thing) is the thing that has bound them inextricably to the worst public health disaster of our era.

The problem, finally, isn't sex but love—and the six o'clock news doesn't want to talk about that. And while no one seriously argues that it is the job of public health to make gay men happy, ignoring the role that homophobia plays in the psychology of AIDS—or, for that matter, ignoring the role that joblessness plays in the psychology of drug addiction—means ignoring an element of disease at least as powerful as biology. If we care about public health, there is little choice but to care about people's feelings, too. As Thomas Delbanco, a professor of medicine at Harvard Medical School, points out, you can find tons of papers analyzing the public-health benefits of universal sigmoidoscopy to detect colon cancer—"but try to find one that tells you the best way to get a man or a woman to bare his or her bottom on a periodic basis to a large tube."

Delbanco, who was trained in an era when doctors were gods but now sees himself as a "hopefully expert adviser" to his patients, thinks it's time for prevention organizations to make the same kinds of attitude adjustments. It will not be easy. Public health has traditionally contented itself with maintaining quantity of life, assuming that *quality* of life will (or ought to) take care of itself. If AIDS teaches us anything, it's that the formula works the other way around. At the same time, we seem to get the prevention we deserve. Politicians want quick fixes because they're cheaper and catchier than long-term solutions. (When prevention works, it's invisible of course: you can't see it because it *prevents* something.) And we abet those politicians by clamoring, albeit fitfully, for war instead of change. Democracy be damned: we want drug czars, AIDS czars—as if behavior driven by feelings could be corralled by an attack of the cavalry.

In a country that has outgrown its ability to promote strong norms, or finds the very idea of norms too normative, public health must find new methods of intervening in dangerous private behavior. What would that intervention look like? Instead of Just Say No, drug prevention might include nuanced discussions about the relative risks of marijuana and harder drugs, just as Odets wants gay men to distinguish between different kinds of sex. Instead of promoting vows of chastity, pregnancy-prevention programs might ask a girl to envision the kind of life she wants before weighing how a baby could enhance, or ruin, it. What all such programs would rely on is candor: complete information, delivered in plain language, respectful of individual values—which seems obvious until you realize it's rarely done.

And the bitterest pill in prevention today is that the programs already exist. Largely unfinanced or ignored, they sit even now in bookcases and file drawers, waiting for political winds to shift while the epidemics rage.

Mark Ebenhoch's command voice, which hasn't worked any better for him than it has for AIDS educators, is almost completely gone now. Even over the phone, when I speak to him in mid-July, I can hear the change. His latest affair has ended unhappily and, he adds, almost as an afterthought, he has some news we have both been fearing for months: He is finally HIV-positive himself. A psychiatrist has put him on antidepressants. "Sometimes I think that if I had gotten help three years ago—emotional help, psychiatric help—I most likely wouldn't be positive now. I'd have had a clearer head. But really, it was my own fault. There's no other way around it."

As a person with HIV, Mark is suddenly eligible for the whole range of benefits provided by AIDS organizations—including the free counseling that might have helped him earlier. And the Veterans Administration provides him with a handsome monthly disability check. In a way, becoming positive has been a windfall; could Mark be forgiven a bit of cynicism? In a world where financing for AIDS research keeps increasing but agencies that serve gay youths go begging for pennies, should we be surprised if gay men wonder whether the disease is more important than they are? For AIDS will someday end. And when the promise of the protease inhibitors is fulfilled, when the vaccine arrives in our elementary schools, will anyone turn as feverish a light on what *else* is destroying gay men? Will anyone see it as their responsibility to help assuage the damage inflicted, and replayed night after night, upon boys whose only real desire was to be liked, to be loved, to be good?

But somehow Mark *isn't* cynical. "I have an upbeat attitude," he says. "With the news about the new drug treatments, I'm cautiously optimistic. And I'm letting go of a lot of things. Because of the medication I'm on I cannot drink alcohol; and I quit smoking cigarettes. I've completely stopped the promiscuity, too. I want to live well. I'm eating better. Believe it or not, I have a *date* tonight, not a pickup but a real date. With a guy I met through the Internet. I went into the Gay and Lesbian Bulletin Board—where I met you—and looked in the personals under HIV-positive. And I found a guy that was rather interesting. We're going to go out and have coffee and something to eat, and talk. And that's *it*. I want to find somebody who will"—he searches for the word he wants—"*belong* to me. And that means somebody HIV-positive now.

"In a way it's a relief," he says, echoing a sentiment I have heard too frequently from newly infected men. "I don't have to wonder anymore. That awful waiting is gone. So now, if I do find someone, the relationship can be one hundred percent real with nothing in the way. That's what I want: one hundred percent natural, wholesome and real. Maybe now that I'm HIV-positive, I can finally have my life."

4. GABRIEL ROTELLO

From his founding of *OutWeek* magazine to the recent publication of his book *Sexual Ecology: AIDS and the Destiny of Gay Men,* Gabriel Rotello has never shied from controversy. In this widely discussed opinion column from *The Advocate,* he calls for HIV-positive men to shoulder some of the responsibility for AIDS prevention.

To Protect and Serve

OF ALL THE FAULT LINES THAT DIVIDE THE GAY COMMUNITY— male and female, black and white, young and old, urban and rural—none is more frightening, disorienting, or enfeebling than the rift between the HIV-infected and the uninfected. Many HIV-positive men feel patronized, contagious, written off. Many HIV-negative men feel crushed by the endlessness of the epidemic and burdened with guilt for feeling that way. We rarely acknowledge this division, either personally or politically, but lately our denial is threatened by a contentious new debate about responsibility.

In the past, the notion of shared responsibility for AIDS in all its dimensions has been a healing principle: The healthy have by and large accepted an ethical responsibility to provide services for the afflicted, to protect them from stigma and blame, and to fight for a cure. Now some activists, me included, have begun talking about the responsibility of positive men to help protect negative men from infection. We've been prompted by reports that HIV transmissions are rising again in our community and by a simple biological truth that underlies those statistics: Each new infection results from a failure of both a negative man and a positive man to be safe.

This new call for responsibility has encountered a wall of fear, for a very understandable reason. Epidemics have almost always prompted an insidious search for scapegoats. The very names of many diseases contain germs of prejudice: Think of Asian flu, of German measles. The use of blame to gain distance from contagion seems hardwired into our fear of infectious illness. Within the gay world we have largely suppressed that impulse—so far, anyway—perhaps because we've realized that all gay men are collectively seen by most of the rest of society as sources of contamination, whether we're HIV-positive or not. Any impulse to apportion blame within the gay world has been far outweighed by the impulse to defend our collective selves from the larger blame bearing down upon us from the outside.

Now, however, with so many gay men becoming infected in the face of almost universal AIDS awareness, many activists are bracing for a panicked attempt to pin the blame on HIV-positive men and feel desperately that they must be prepared to resist any such attempt. Some have interpreted the new call for equal responsibility between positives and negatives as the beginning of that insidious internal scapegoating, the start of the blaming process they've been dreading.

I don't think it is. In fact, since many of those calling for a new commitment to responsibility are themselves HIV-positive, I think it's the opposite: an expression of community and solidarity between positives and negatives. Implicit in that expression is the hope that positive men will feel they have a stake in the gay future even if that future doesn't include an immediate cure.

But I do fear that the talk of balanced responsibility could result in a deep psychic split between positives and negatives if those making the call are not balanced in the way they frame the issues. So anybody talking about equal responsibility must start by acknowledging a few facts, among them these: Cohort studies consistently show that men who know they are HIV-positive are the *least* likely of all gay men to engage in risky behavior. By contrast, those who test negative often take their test results as proof that their past risky behavior was really safe and thus a license to engage in even more of it. And since at least 1989, psychological studies have reported that quite a few men who don't know their status—including, no doubt, some of the approximately two out of three HIV-positive men who don't know they are positive—deliberately avoid getting tested (or retested) because they want to continue having risky sex and feel that if they knew they were positive, they could no longer allow themselves that luxury. Apparently, for such men ignorance is, if not bliss, permission.

Given these facts, any implication that self-acknowledged positive men are largely responsible for the rising tide of new transmissions is not only unfair, stigmatizing, and inflammatory, it's downright inaccurate. Any call for equal responsibility must strongly emphasize the responsibility of the untested to get tested, of those having risky sex to get retested, and of those who are HIV-negative to continue looking out for themselves.

Yet that being said, it must also be said that some men who know they are positive do indeed have unsafe sex, do knowingly risk exposing others to HIV, and sometimes excuse their actions by arguing that negatives should take responsibility for themselves. Therefore, any call for truly equal responsibility must include the responsibility of infected men to avoid putting others at risk, even if those others are momentarily willing to let down their guard.

Gay men must strive not to allow our legitimate fear of stigma to blind us to the equally legitimate call for responsibility. AIDS places claims on us all: on the uninfected, to fight for the rights—and the lives—of the infected, and on the infected, to acknowledge their role in keeping the uninfected safe. Equal responsibility is not blame. It is a lifeline tenuously tossed across a canyon that already separates us, whether we admit it or not.

S. SCOTT O'HARA

Former porn star, *Steam* magazine editor, and perennial firebrand Scott O'Hara staunchly opposes any constraints on his sexual promiscuity—be they from the right wing or the gay community. Sex is inherently good, he contends, and even—especially—in the age of AIDS, should not be policed by anyone.

Talking with My Mouth Full

IT'S A CLICHÉ IN GAY CIRCLES, I KNOW. I'D JUST LIKE TO POINT out that for gay men, all through history, having our mouths full of dick has been a political statement like no other. In that sense, nothing's changed. Sucking dick is still the perfect expression of our First Amendment rights: It screams to the Authorities, Fuck You (and your little dog too)! It gives us the status of Outsider, the perspective necessary to comment on a sick society, and the detachment to realize that their world is not quite the utopia they seem to think it is.

I would like to state that I think heterosexuals who insist on monogamous relationships should be arrested and quarantined, so they can't infect the rest of us with their insanity. Monogamy is unnatural behavior, as any zoologist or anthropologist will attest, a curiosity of so-called Western Society, and one need only look at modern history to understand how unhealthy it is. But alas, since the folks in control these days are heterosexuals, and since it is socially unacceptable to promote promiscuity, my suggestions will probably not be adopted anytime soon.

Promiscuity is not a "right," exactly; it's an instinct. I don't maintain that people have a "right" to food or water or air; they *need* to pursue each of these, in whatever manner they can. (Air is generally considered to be free, but consider all those poor souls in Los Angeles and Mexico City who live without it.) And men are compelled by their natures to pursue sex, in whatever form pleases them, in as many venues as possible. (I'd rather not get into the debate over the putative differences between men's and women's sexualities, so I limit my remarks to men.) Monogamy is unnatural; it's a construct designed by society ostensibly to raise children, but what it raises more effectively is the level of social control and guilt. These social constructs are undoubtedly useful to priests and politicians, but they don't do anything for me. I believe in pleasure, not guilt. I don't wish to give anyone else guidance on how to live their lives. What works for Jesse Helms obviously would not work for me, and vice versa. So I don't claim that I have a "right" to sex. The Declaration of Independence didn't maintain that we're all entitled to happiness—merely the *pursuit* of happiness. I'm not gonna file a lawsuit against someone who refuses to have sex with me; I just deny that anyone has the right to declare that I MAY NOT have sex.

When I go out on a warm, summer, full-moon night, to Buena Vista Park (or Central Park, or Olin, Griffith, Volunteer, Pease, Overton, or Stanley Parks), sex is very definitely on my mind. I may or may not actually fuck; that part is irrelevant. (Really!) But I go there with intent—no, that's too strong a term—I go there with *interest* in fucking. It's not that I will be disappointed if I go home without shooting a load (or having one shot on me or in me); who could walk through Buena Vista Park on a warm and moonlit night and go home unsatisfied? There is a sense, when I'm in an environment so sensual, so welcoming, and yet so mysterious, that this is a place meant for sex; even the feel of the steps underneath my feet, the well-worn tree limbs that I lean against and bend over, the sensual caress of a warm breeze on my bared butt, conspire to give me a (mental) hard-on. Bedrooms are not meant for sex; bedrooms are meant for sleeping, reading, and many other things, but they do not arouse my libido. A park at night does that, and the world would be a better place if everyone would just acknowledge that essential attraction and get over their hang-ups.

For a humorous touch to all this, I should add that for the past several years, I've been largely impotent—with occasional notable exceptions. (If I could figure out what causes my periodic bouts of perfect potency, things might be much busier at Casa O'Hara.) When I talk about having unsafe sex in parks and bathhouses, I'm mostly speaking theoretically. In theory, yes, I believe that unsafe sex is good for me (and yes, I do get fucked regularly without condoms). In reality, I fuck fewer men than almost anyone I know, frequency of opportunity notwithstanding. Ah, irony.

I have AIDS. I've made a habit, some would say a career, out of announcing that fact at the top of my voice for the past couple of years. I talk about it at every available opportunity, because gay men (and especially positive gay men) have been beaten into submission over the past fifteen years. They've been convinced that positive men and attractive men are two incompatible groups; they've been convinced that positives never have sex (except for Gaetan Dugas and other Typhoid Marys). There is an image of the PWA: He has a gaunt face, staring eyes, stick-like limbs, and no dick. That's what we all tend to go through at the end of our lives, and that's the stage at which AIDS becomes visible. I am healthy; I'm not readily identifiable as a PWA until I take my clothes off, and even then, I often encounter guys who don't seem to know a lesion when they see one. That's why I've been so vocal about it: I want to change that stereotype. I also want to make it clear that having sex is not going to kill me. It seems much more likely to me, given my continued vibrant good health, that I will eventually be hit by the proverbial truck (probably while I'm on my motorcycle). I've had many worse things happen to me than being infected with HIV; most of them resulted from long-term relationships, which our society regards with benevolence.

Being positive, in the current climate of fear and anger, is the best thing that could possibly have happened to me. I look around me at the negative world, and I see men who are in the closet about their desires: mustn't admit to wanting to get fucked; mustn't admit to liking rimming; mustn't admit to drinking piss; mustn't admit to frequenting sex clubs or bath houses. It's as if AIDS has taken us back to pre-Stonewall days: It's okay to be gay, now, as long as you're in a monogamous relationship and you never, ever do anything the least bit interesting. And of course, there's an unhealthy slice of jealousy and anger built into that equation, too: they look at positives, who don't have to live by their rules, and I can understand why they'd be green-eyed. Having AIDS has, in the long run, given me back my sexuality and my voice. Not only has it given me freedom from that fear of death, it has given me license to say and do things—without censure—that wouldn't have been acceptable had I been negative. (And, you ask, what's Scott O'Hara doing using words like "acceptable"? All right, it's not exactly what I meant. "Effective" is closer. A negative, saying the same things I've said, would be scoffed at; a negative, doing the same things I'm doing, would be called irresponsible. And many have called me irresponsible, but just as many have called me courageous. I'm indifferent to what I'm called, so long as I'm called. Silence would wound me.) Because I know, first-hand, the advantages of being positive, I don't feel the need to warn people away from the virus. In fact, I admire those whose sense of self-esteem is high enough that they can distinguish between those desires that emanate from themselves, and those that are imposed upon them from outside. I know a man who recently seroconverted; he admitted to me, after a number of conversations, that he'd been trying to get AIDS for over a year, getting fucked, unprotected, by as many men as he could. I don't know all his reasons for doing so, but he had thought them through pretty rationally, and made his choice based on his own circumstances, rather than the dictates of our Professional Health Providers (who would undoubtedly be shocked and appalled by his irresponsibility). That indicates a fairly strong personality—one of the most attractive characteristics in a man. Is it any wonder that I find "irresponsibility" to be downright irresistible?

When I meet that man in the park (or at a bath house, or just walking down the street) and we have sex, what rationalization can society give for interfering in what is clearly a voluntary interpersonal transaction? When I fuck that faceless stranger in the bushes, in the moonlight, he and I both get pleasure from the act; the rest of the world, without extreme measures of surveillance, would never even know about it. I don't know how anyone can claim that we're harming society. The justifications for surveillance and punishment have changed many times over the centuries; the mere fact that the intent has never altered (stop the homosexual sex!) should alert the objective observer. I find it very difficult to accept the medical profession's advice about AIDS, in part because their advice—stop fucking!—is exactly the same thing that the various other erotophobes have been screeching for centuries. When the police departments and concerned citizens groups (mostly the former) start talking about the dreadful effects of sex in parks, they inevitably bring up the horror of having their children exposed to men fucking. They don't seem to realize that the problem isn't with the men; it's with the parents who haven't raised their children to live in the real world. If fucking is part of the world (and I guarantee that it always has been, and always will be), then it's a truly monstrous parent who keeps his or her children in the dark about it, or doesn't want them exposed to it. Sounds like real child abuse to me.

Sex is not safe. Sex *cannot* be safe. Trying to make it safe destroys the essence of it. But at the same time, neither is it harmful. Sound contradictory? Oh, come on—there are hundreds of similar cases in everyday life. Driving a motorcycle is not "safe"; neither is crossing the street in any major city, or whitewater rafting, or eating chocolate if you have diabetes. None of these things is inherently harmful; yet each of them can kill you, if you don't do it right. That's what my life has been about: teaching men how to do it right. Sex, that is. Oh, I don't believe that I know the One True Way of having sex; I don't prescribe positions and lotions like an advice columnist, and I don't even try to persuade straight men that "you gotta try everything once." But by acting in porn flicks, and doing so with a smile, I feel that I showed men the pleasure I was taking from my work. I wasn't exploited; I did it because I wanted to. By printing a magazine about sex, I hope I'm letting men know that they can talk about those subjects that the world considers too dark and dastardly for discussion. People may have printed horrified editorials about me, but no one's tried to assassinate me— yet. And by going out to parks at night (or, for that matter, in broad daylight) and fucking with strangers, I hope I'm reassuring my partners of the essential harmlessness of sex. Sex isn't the problem. The puritanical, power-hungry attitude of the police is the problem.

There are probably still people out there who don't understand what I mean when I say that AIDS has been good for me. I'm not saying that I'm grateful for the epidemic itself; believe me, I have a long list of dead friends and lovers, and I mourn them and wish they were here. I'm also confident that if the epidemic had not happened, we would be more sexually liberated today than we are, and that would be a good thing. But given the epidemic and the effect it's had on all of our lives, I am thankful to be in the middle of it. The life of a negative, at this point in our history, seems to me to be the most irrelevant and pointless of positions; the continual fear of conversion under which most of them live is equally distressing. It's not as if this were the bubonic plague. I've lived with this so-called fatal disease for years— probably about thirteen years, to be precise. I'm spotted like a dalmatian, which bothers neither me nor my sex partners, and I survived a bout with lymphoma, which is certainly not exclusive to HIVers. Otherwise, my life has never been better; and I feel that this "disease" has given me a heightened awareness of the beauty of life.

AIDS, if it is anything, is only a test. If this had been an actual emergency, I would be dead. No, this epidemic is a test of our wits and endurance and compassion. I don't believe in an omniscient teacher who's administering the test—I think it's basically self-graded—but I could point to a number of groups, primarily religious, who I think have failed dismally. I think they—and the people who maintain that we need to castrate ourselves to avoid risk—are the real losers in this war. We will probably all die, sooner or later; the important thing is what we do before that hypothetical date. And I know what I'll be doing. I'll be out there endlessly repeating the same old message, which I have learned to convey quite effectively with a mouth stuffed full of dick: Sex is good. Not "some sex is good." SEX, in and of itself, is good, positive, life-affirming, joyful, ecstatic, beneficial. And those who are out there trying to control my sex life, whatever the rationale, are "evil." Yeah, I know, that's the same thing that a lot of them are saying about me, and the word doesn't therefore have much objective meaning, except "antithetical to my own way of life." But when I signed on to that Declaration, I meant it. Liberty *is* a fundamental right, whether god-given or otherwise. It's worth fighting for, and that's what I'm doing. Fighting with my mouth full.

6. D. TRAVERS SCOTT

With legal gay marriage suddenly within the realm of possibility, gay men face with new urgency an age-old question: How can long-term relationships work? In this practical guide, twentysomething novelist and performer D. Travers Scott discusses a range of nontraditional variations on monogamy.

Flexible Fidelity

I CAME OUT AT FIFTEEN, IN 1985. WITH "MAKING LOVE" ON CABLE and AIDS in my face every day, I didn't feel alone in my queerness. I never "thought I was the only one." I had gay friends at school. They told me about bars, but I didn't share their taste for cruising. Wasn't that some tacky Al Pacino movie, anyway? I considered myself above bars, baths, and parks, which all just seemed so *seventies* (a grave insult in 1985). I must've radiated a prudish vibe: No one ever made a pass at me, neither my queer peers nor the high-school band instructor (whom several would publicly indict years later). I read *Maurice* and *Torch Song Trilogy* repeatedly, confident sex should be the ultimate physical expression of love. The times I lived in, plus a childhood divorce, small family, and some alternative parenting made me crave emotional stability. I dreamed of a steady, committed romantic partner.

I've had one for over seven years now. Dave is only five years older than I am, but his upbringing and experience afforded him very different romantic needs and expectations. An Iowan farmboy, rural isolation had left him craving queer contract. His mainstream, American Gothic childhood sent him searching for validation of his outsider identity. From interstate rest stops to Chicago's bustling Halsted Street, he looked for others like him—but not necessarily a husband. His large, nuclear family had loaded him with stability up to his eyeballs.

Although too young to buy alcohol when we began dating, I pushed Dave for committed monogamy. He clung to independence; I shot his bar friends dirty looks. After nine months, things got serious and Dave found himself considering our relationship exclusive as well, and for the next year or so we entered into monogamy. It was more difficult than I anticipated. Older gay friends warned, "Monogamy is a myth!" and espoused 1970s promiscuity-is-power politics. Sex rad ACT-UPpers sniffed at our bourgeois, patriarchal assimilation and didn't invite us to their leather-jacketed orgies.

But we needed strict limits and stuck to them. Our period of monogamy was a grounding time to focus exclusively on one another, bonding and meshing as a couple, building a foundation of security and trust. I felt frustrated that little of my (perceived) "gay community" respected that, yet simultaneously they painted a very cynical portrait of "open relationships." Options and advice seemed scarce.

There were negatives to being monogamous. Lust from and toward others continually reared its head, and what today are minor incidents—jerking off next to some guy in a public john, getting horned up and cruisey when together at a bar—precipitated huge fights. I also felt too young to be in a relationship sometimes—was I missing out on that wild-oat sowing I'd heard so much about? Our limits squeezed us tight like a balloon that could rupture from the slightest prick.

So we talked. Negotiation and communication became a continual process. Events such as drunk kissy-face with friends and a threesome—in which for once nobody got jealous and we all had a great time—spurred us to talk more about our sexual parameters. We talked and talked and talked (then fucked). We were both noticing increased interest in sex outside of our relationship. As people called us the single unit "DavenTrav," we risked voicing desires we feared our relationship couldn't fulfill. Sometimes we'd address issues before they came to a head; more often it was a hung-over, morning-after discussion of "about last night . . . ."

About this same time, we began extracting ourselves from queer nationalist direct-action groups. Although we were disillusioned with politics in general and identity politics in particular, the rhetoric of anti-assimilation had gotten us in the habit of scrutinizing the hetero-based presumptions undermining our lives. From the Radical Faeries we'd gleaned an appreciation for contrariness, contradiction, and paradox—the trickster spirit. From both of these arenas, plus sex radical and transgender cultures, and a dash of pomo art theory, we came to realize that monogamous/open was as false a dichotomy as straight/gay, male/female, etc. We could experiment with our relationship incrementally, exploring different shades on the spectrum rather than flipping an absolute coin.

If you're considering opening up your relationship, here's my first tip: New Orleans. Our second-anniversary trip there provided a fertile laboratory for kick-starting exploration and, again, communication and negotiation provided necessary lube. We found what worked: a bathroom three-way with a humpy Australian before an appreciative audience; an after-hours session with a bearish bartender atop a pool table. We found out what didn't work: solo tricking and bath house exploration. We took these experiences home and, as we continued sampling and assessing, realized the possibilities were limited only by imagination.

Any couple can tailor their relationship to their needs. We've shifted our degrees of monogamy sometimes as frequently as month by month. I've listed below several permutations we've discussed and sampled. Although roughly sequential in degree of exclusivity, I don't mean to imply they can't be refigured in many more ways, or that one stage necessarily follows another. We've found it necessary to increase our degree of monogamy in times when one or both of us felt unusually vulnerable, needy, or unstable. Ultimately, your relationship can be as flexible, idiosyncratic, and unpredictable as your libido.

- *Rose-Colored Monogamy.* No sexual or romantic contact with anyone outside relationship. Even appreciating the yardman's sweatpants is off limits. At my most extreme during this phase, I felt jealous of Dave's masturbating.

- *Pragmatic Monogamy.* Sexual exclusivity but tolerance for social kissing, affection, and flirtation, as well as open acknowledgment of desire. You can dish and rubberneck guys together, but not act on those desires.

- *Virtual Monogamy.* No physical sex outside relationship but porn, Internet, videos, phonesex, etc., are OK.

- *Expanded Monogamy.* Sexual exclusivity except for bringing home mutually agreed-upon and shared third parties.

- *Sleazy Monogamy.* No hardcore sex outside of relationship, only quick, anonymous, public jerk-offs to vent steam.

- *Out of Sight, Out of Mind.* When Dave won a three-month artist's residency, we faced our first major separation. We'd been monogamous at home but decided outside sex while separated could be OK. Distance somehow shunted the emotional reverberations, and we didn't have to finagle the awkward logistics of individual cruising despite sharing a home and preferred bars. When we had separate apartments, it was no biggie for one of us to spend the night at a bath house, but when living together the absence became more acute and required discussion beforehand. Now, things are looser at home but remain different than when we're separated: Neither of us minds the other bringing someone back to his hotel room, but we don't like whichever of us is at home to bring people back there. Sanctity of the hearth or something. It's completely illogical, given that the at-home person can go to someone else's house, and we've certainly sullied the family bed with strangers in threesomes, but one of the first things we learned in this process was respecting the illogic of emotions.

  - *Variation: Don't Ask, Don't Tell.* You may not want to tell each other about your separate activities until reunited, in order to avoid getting competitive and trying to outdo one another. On the other hand, your adventures might provide great phone-sex material.

- *Open, with Exceptions.* Full-fledged sex with others is OK, but you and your partner negotiate limits of intimacy to be respected. Sometimes Dave and I keep fucking as a special treat between us. You might want strict top/bottom arrangements with outside partners, or no experimenting with activities (dominance, watersports, fisting, etc.) not already established in your sexual repertoire. This could also include fetishes (transsexuals, amputees, redheads, etc.) one of you feels threatened by: At one point I wasn't comfortable with Dave fooling around with African-American guys. I feared they offered him some something I couldn't. Similarly, if one of you is bisexual, you might have different sets of limits for different genders. In any case, these exceptions have the potential to diminish as you feel more secure in your relationship. Or they may not—your brunette partner may retain for all his life a deep-seated insecurity button pushed by redheads, and request they always remain off-limits. It's absurd and illogical again, but much of a relationship involves accepting degrees of absurdity and illogic from one another.

- *Open but Anonymous.* Everything up to and including full-fledged hardcore sex is OK, allowing for bath houses and tricking, but only with strangers: no friends, no exes, no repeats, nothing prearranged.

- *Boomerang.* Do whatever you want, but always come home. Both partners agree never to make the other spend a night alone.

- *Anything Goes.* Complete and unrestrained whoredom.

When I'm explaining our current setup to a friend or potential sex partner, STDs invariably come up. For some reason, people tend to see a committed couple having occasional casual sex as riskier than promiscuous singlehood, as if there's an immediate correlation between transgression, or not following mainstream models, and risk. Although playing around as a couple intensifies some problems (crabs require very exact synchronization of first and follow-up medications), overall we've found we're safer in an open-ish relationship. When single, we had no other person to consider, love, and protect; no contract to honor. It was far easier to succumb to a self-destructive "what the fuck!" when it didn't affect the person you loved most in the world.

When opening up sexual parameters, it's vital to avoid presumptions regarding the safer-sex knowledge, beliefs, and practices of outside parties *as well as* your long-term partner. "I can't believe you deep-kissed him right after we ate tortilla chips!" is not a fun fight. Even if you've heard it all a hundred times, a safer-sex discussion group or workshop for mixed-status couples can help you reexamine issues, uncover new questions, and discover discrepancies in each of your thinking. Again, it's a spectrum, never as simple as "just use condoms." Consider: Condoms for fucking and/or getting fucked? What about with people of the same HIV status as you? Condoms for sucking and/or getting sucked? Withdraw before coming? Coming on face? Ass? Gloves, finger cots for fisting, finger-fucking? Dental dams or equivalent for rimming? Deep kissing, body kissing only?

A sexbuddy once said, "Isn't that the whole point of being in a relationship? So you can have sex without condoms?" Well, not quite, but I got the point. However, the condom-less monogamy scenario gets risky: It depends on any cheating partner immediately telling the other about it before they have sex. Monogamy requires either 100 percent monogamy or 100 percent honesty to truly work. I don't trust absolutes. I trust a negotiated shade of gray eminently more than a relationship that's monogamous in theory only, both partners too guilt-ridden to confess and potentially infecting each other.

If you do explore opening up your relationship, here are a few practical tips we've picked up:

- You are living in a sexphobic, homophobic, Puritan-based culture. You will feel shame, guilt, and anger. Sometimes feelings arise from legitimate regret or anxiety that needs to be explored. However, they can also be post-climax blues, hangover-induced stress, or mere knee-jerk societal reflexes. Be prepared and listen equally to your heart and mind.

- Clarify what constitutes "cheating." In a somewhat-open relationship, it may seem obvious that outside sex does not constitute infidelity. What does, then? Agree on what constitutes a breach of loyalty. Secrecy? Repetition? Platonic dating? Emotional commitments? Know before something unexpected happens. Above all, don't misuse your sexual liberty as a justification for behavior damaging to your relationship.

- Beware the tendency to sublimate emotion onto an outsider. Exceptionally good or atypical sex with a new stud can provide a ripe screen on which to project issues or needs not being met by your main man. Talk to your partner about any sudden, intense emotions toward a fuckbuddy. Displaced needs are far more likely—and easily dealt with—than love at first fuck.

- If unsure whether an activity falls within your relationship's limits, you can always take a rain check. A postponement is merely frustrating; a "mistake" can require major healing. Trust your partner and your ability to communicate rather than risk hurting him. However, remember you can't anticipate everything. Surprises will happen. I went home with a fresh-scrubbed little prepster, fully expecting I'd play the tough guy. To my surprise, he smacked me around and put me through my paces with a finesse that went beyond what Dave and I were at the time comfortable with. Soon afterwards I told Dave. Although initially he felt a little threatened, the event ultimately led us to new awareness and perspectives in our own sexual relationship.

- If you feel very jealous, stop. Jealousy is perhaps immature, petty, and irrational, but it is a real, painful feeling. Don't discount it just because you think you should be above it. You may rationalize a certain behavior as OK, but emotions aren't so neat. If something feels wrong, don't force it. The right time will come. You may wake up one day and your heart will have caught up with your mind (or vice versa).

- Talk! Every major problem we've had since opening up our relationship has been due, on some level, to a lack of communication. Even simple, innocent forgetfulness can appear to be secrecy and cause huge traumas. Imagination tends to be worse than the truth, so keep the truth in the open. And not just once—you and your partner's needs and desires will continually change back and forth; you'll need to frequently check in and tweak your agreements.

The first time you kissed, groped, fucked, sucked or did whatever with someone of the same sex, you chose to live on your heart's terms rather than society's. Queer communities and legal protections often add more confusion than support when they seem primarily interested in laying down sets of rules customized for us, but modeled after old ones. Being not-straight taught me that the old rules don't work. I'm uninterested in new, tailored versions.

My lover and I have forged our relationship one step at a time, like spelunkers in a dark cave. With role models scarce and vastly dissimilar, we drifted, climbed, and tumbled through most every color in the monogamy spectrum. Heterosociety's Ozzie & Harriet map had a clear destination, but we charted a map of possibilities, one that said, "You can go here—or try this—or try it like that—or do this."

Although our monogamous period was necessary and beneficial in many ways, the openness of our current relationship has definitely helped us grow and stay together. Beyond scratching our numerous and sundry sexual itches, our outside sex has given us enriching information and experiences we've brought back into our relationship. As our sex life is not forced to carry the entire weight of our every desire, fantasy, and impulse, we've become much less stressed and self-conscious. Our sex life remains hot, vibrant, and unpredictable. The negotiation and communication skills we've learned have been useful in many other aspects of our relationship. Finally, the risk-taking and vulnerability we've shared through our sexual license has fostered more trust, intimacy, openness, and growth as a couple.

Popular *Out* magazine columnist Michelangelo Signorile has a knack for touching the gay community's most sensitive buttons. Here, the author of *Queer in America* and *Life Outside* writes about balancing a committed relationship with the desire to appear sexy and available.

Sex and the Not-So-Single Guy

HOW DAVID AND I MET IS, SOMEWHAT EMBARRASSINGLY, A CHELSEA cliché. That is, we met in Chelsea, the overexposed New York gay ghetto of choice these days. I first saw him one afternoon at the Big Cup, a coffeehouse where men nurse one cappuccino for hours while relentlessly cruising and hoping to meet a dream date—or whatever. He wouldn't look at me, as he was enamored of someone else (who, predictably, wasn't paying him too much attention). And before I could do a cartwheel to get his attention, he was out the door, on to his next appointment.

A few nights later, I spotted him at Food Bar, an effusively queer restaurant down the street where they blare house music at you while you eat your Vietnamese spring rolls. I was at the bar, and he was sitting with a friend in a booth in the corner. I asked Kenny, the maitre d', if he knew him. No, he said, but he advised me to move quickly because a man across the room had just sent his telephone number over there. I took Kenny's advice, and after some eye contact and a coy smile, I was sitting with David, chatting for hours. (His friend soon left.) As if to complete our hokey yet hopelessly romantic encounter, we spent the rest of the night walking around Chelsea, kissing, holding hands and, well, just being silly.

I tell this story because, celebrating our one-year anniversary together, it suddenly dawned on me that while I used to have a lot of experiences similar to this one when I was single (even if they went nowhere after the night was over), I clearly haven't had one—with a stranger, that is—since we've been together. Of course, the relationship has its own, greater rewards: the kind of experiences you can only have with someone you know intimately, a good deal of fun, and just plain hot, times. But when you're in a couple—whether it's two men, two women, or one of each—it's impossible to have a connection with a stranger in which the possibilities are endless. Even someone in the most open of relationships knows that a prospective sex partner can never be Prince or Princess Charming, because Charming is already waiting back home.

And yet, for gay men in particular, so much of our interaction—indeed, much of gay culture itself—is based on being single and available for . . . whatever. Certainly the most visible aspects of the gay male community—the gay ghettos with their clubs and nightlife and bar rags filled with hot, pumped men—are all about being unattached and ready-to-roll. It's my impression that lesbians have a greater unity between the coupled and the single, but with Clit Clubs and sex clubs of their own these days, there's certainly an element of single-gal glorification going on. In contrast, the most visible aspects of straight culture, from sitcoms to stump speeches, are focused on promoting and serving "the family." Perhaps we're rebelling against that, going off in the opposite direction and glorifying "the individual," but just as the traditional family system greatly influences how heterosexuals (and the rest of us) order our lives, the gay male focus on singledom affects in a big way how gay men interact on a daily basis.

"I come to every social event, every party, every gay anything with the idea that I'm going to be looking at hot men, that they're going to be looking at me, and of course I want them to think they can maybe have me, and, yes, that gives me an ego rush," a West Hollywood man tells me while we're sitting by the pool at the Wyndham Hotel in Palm Springs on the day before Easter. It's the weekend of the White Party, one of many "circuit" parties around the country that attract thousands of gay men from around the world. In this case, we've taken over three hotels in the middle of the desert, to cavort and play. The actual White Party is on Saturday night, but there are parties all weekend (including the pool bash we're attending) at which hundreds of near-naked, muscled guys dance and swim in the 95-degree dry heat. It will be three days of this—sun, drugs, sex, and parties day and night—all those things that epitomize the stereotype of the single gay life.

"Of course I feel that way here, at something like this," the West Hollywood man continues, "because, well, that's what this is all about—seeing and being seen. But honestly, I feel this way *all the time*—when I go to the video store, when I get my clothes out of the dry cleaners, and definitely in the supermarket. I want men to think I'm available—even if I'm not, even if I'm involved with someone. I mean, it's part of the allure. I don't buy it when people say that being in a relationship makes you more attractive and more desired because you're 'unattainable.' That may be true, but being unavailable also means you are 'off the shelf,' 'not for sale,' and 'out of commission.' And who the hell wants to be any of those things?"

While his sentiments are somewhat extreme, I know what he means. Both here in Palm Springs, as well as in my day-to-day life in New York, I find myself meeting men and having conversations and, strangely, not mentioning up front that I have a lover, even when it seems appropriate. "Do you have a boyfriend?" they inevitably ask. Then a bell goes off. I know that as soon as I answer this question our entire interaction will change. It has little to do with wanting to have sex with someone; often I'm not even attracted to these men. Rather, as the West Hollywood guy says, it's about "allure," which is ultimately about power. Gay men, all too often it seems, are not much different from straight men in that we're just as insecure at seeming powerless. And in much of the gay male world, there are only two kinds of power: money and sex. If you don't have money, which most men don't, and if you are, for whatever reason, "off the shelf" when it comes to sex and romance, you can feel a bit invisible.

For me at least, that feeling is inescapable, simply because my being "unavailable" is omnipresent in my own mind; I find, even at this male-muscle extravaganza in Palm Springs, I can't just feel single, no matter how hard I may try—even though David is a million miles away and I might not always bring him up in conversation. I'm only kidding myself, I realize, if I think I can just make believe that I'm making the kind of connection with men I could make when I was single. Again, it's not about actual sex: I know I could have all the sex I wanted and still not feel single—

even if I make myself physically available, I'm not available emotionally. It's like being a kid in a candy store and realizing that you don't really crave candy that much anymore—it may look tasty, but you're just not hungry, even though you may still want to be.

The reason I'm in Palm Springs in the first place, believe it or not, is for work: I'm covering the White Party weekend, interviewing men about their experiences for a book I'm working on. In the past I reveled in such work: Part of the way I've gone about studying and writing about the gay world, in fact, has been to immerse myself in it deeply, often letting loose. But in Palm Springs I enjoy myself to a point and then just find I'm kind of bored; it becomes a chore to go to every happening event, and suddenly my work seems a lot like, well, work. I'd rather be with David, doing something that a lot of single people would consider dull.

Much as we in the gay world pretend we're all one big happy community, there really is a difference between the single and the coupled, and it can create a subtle tension, especially between friends. I have one friend in particular whom I've been close to for seven years, and we've never been single—or coupled, for that matter—at the same time. When I was single, he was in a relationship. Now he's single, and I'm coupled. When I was single, I used to bring him out with me, to parties, bars, and nightclubs, and he'd go home within fifteen minutes. Now I'm the one who's never in the mood to go out. Our entire friendship, it seems, has been about meeting for coffee in the afternoon, talking on the telephone—and going our separate ways at night.

Of course, provided your single friends actually like your lover (which is another issue entirely), you can all hang out together; some of my single friends spend a lot of time with David and me. But I'm always subtly aware that some of them are looking at us and wishing they were coupled, which makes me kind of uncomfortable. In fact, that's something I now find interesting about many (though certainly not all) of my single friends: their unwavering desire to be coupled. Because the lament I hear from many (though certainly not all) of my coupled friends is that they long for the freedom and visibility they had when they were single.

The truth is, we all want both. We want the freedom of singledom, and we want the security of coupledom. Some couples find interesting ways to give themselves at least the illusion of both: At the White Party I meet and interview several couples, some together for years, who do the party circuit together. For some, it works, keeps them socially active, and even enhances their relationships; for others, it's a recipe for jealousy, disaster, or sheer boredom (since they feel there's nothing there for them)—and no handbook can tell you which will be the case with your relationship.

Whatever way each of us navigates either coupledom or singledom, however, the fact remains: We all need to rethink how we interact with each other, and how we view each other, whether we're single or coupled. In the meantime, I'm content with being considered "off the shelf," if that's what having a great guy to go home to means.

8. BERNARD COOPER

Known for his prose mastery and the unflinching honesty of his self-examination, Bernard Cooper is one of America's most talented writers. This excerpt from his acclaimed memoir collection *Truth Serum* reveals how he and his lover Brian's sex lives changed after Brian learned he was HIV-positive.

If and When

AIDS TURNED DESIRE INTO CHALLENGE, A DARE. DESIRE WAS THE haven at the center of a maze, and I had to wend my way down misleading paths and into plenty of dead ends in order to return there. Along the way, there sometimes seemed to be no boundary between public and private fear; reading an interview with someone who insisted they'd contracted AIDS through a mosquito bite, or hearing about someone who sued their HIV-positive doctor for failing to disclose his serostatus, would leave me uncertain and churning for hours. If everyone else was this afraid of AIDS, maybe I should be terrified, too. AIDS might be more contagious than I thought. What I knew to be proven fact and what I worried might be true wrestled together like hulking bears. The only advantage to these psychological grudge-matches was that they left me so drained I finally gave in to a kind of exhausted abandon. Fine, I would think, drinking Brian's kiss when he walked through the door, if this is lethal, it's how I want to go.

For a while, any obvious attempts at safer sex—trying fellatio with condoms, for example—with its fumblings and apologies and nervous laughter, reminded us we were a sero-different couple. Donning that condom was a little like wearing an asbestos suit and trying to forget you're walking through fire. Our self-consciousness became a third party who crawled into bed with us, cajoling and cheering and shouting directions; however well intended, its presence between the sheets was distracting.

It took several months after we'd taken our HIV tests for our sex life to return to normal. I realize that many people entertain grave doubts as to the normalcy of same-sex relationships in the first place, and in some sense, it was precisely my internal arguments with such people that helped restore my sex life with Brian. *How can you two still have sex?* an imagined skeptic would ask me. *How can you play Russian roulette with your life now that you know your partner is positive?* He's been positive all along, I'd remind them, and I've stayed negative. Slowly, deliberately, I'd explain to them the rules of safer sex, citing statistics and going so far as to list a few of the specialties on the menu—frottage, massage, mutual masturbation—that don't put one at risk. By convincing them I knew what I was doing, I gathered the broken bits of my conviction. Wouldn't the skeptics be asking the very same questions about our physical involvement if AIDS didn't exist? *How can you have sex with a man? You're ruining your life!* Listen, I'd say when no other argument worked, I'd rather be dead than to be alive and afraid of having sex with my lover.

Refusing to treat Brian like a pariah set me apart from the guests on talk shows who announced, with what I couldn't help but see as a kind of fearful zeal, that celibacy was the only answer. In the face of AIDS, they sternly advised, run the other way. In an attempt to single-handedly dam the tide of human sexual response, some of them suggested AIDS was proof that sex outside of marriage is wrong. But if married couples also got AIDS, weren't they saying that sex itself is wrong? The more I heard about the infamy of sex, the more determined I was to have it, to cultivate my craving for Brian.

That I found him beautiful made this easier. Once the shock of his testing positive began to fade, I could see him as he hoped to see himself: the same man as before, infected with a virus. I'd watch him emerge from the shower; wiping the misted mirror, he'd appraise his wet reflection. More persuasive than debates with imaginary foes, stronger than my fear of infection, there existed the pull of my lover's body, irresistible, definitive.

Disease might make him a ragged, abject man, but every fear about what might befall him was countered by the memory of sex: the heat of his thighs as he straddled my stomach, sweat beading on his shoulders and chest. When I asked myself, as Brian had once asked me, if I'd rather be free of our relationship, I'd think about drawing him down to the bed, and the answer no would always come back with the same unvarying odds as an echo.

Brian felt the burden of responsibility when it came to making love. "I'd die if you got it," he once confessed. But the less I worried, the more he relaxed, and the more he relaxed, the less I worried. The knot of inhibition loosened. We enjoyed testing our return to sex, scientists who performed the same experiment again and again just to rejoice in the unchanging outcome. Raising an eyebrow or staring at each other an instant too long became a signal to rush into the bedroom. To try another impromptu reunion. To see if we could hold onto caution and throw it to the wind.

If I thought about AIDS while we made love, for the most part those thoughts were fleeting, as remote and muffled as sounds from the street. Sex became an empirical matter: I concentrated on the things I could see— Brian's ribs, the small of his back, the arch of his ass as he lay on his stomach— instead of on the things I couldn't—platelets, bacteria, virus. While our hearts were racing, skin hot to the touch, the visible world of weight and shape took precedence over the realm of minutiae. For a few blessed seconds we tensed in release, hurling away from worry.

In the aftermath I sometimes went into the bathroom and rinsed with mouthwash or took a shower, refusing to scold myself or wonder if Brian might be insulted. Hundreds of other couples, positive or not, did the same after sex. A few precautionary rituals, necessary or not, were preferable to the hypochondria that had once overwhelmed me, and in the end they seemed no more unusual than loosening my belt after a good meal.

Padding back into the bedroom, I'd find Brian petting Zack, who'd leapt on the bed for scraps of affection. "We love you, too," Brian would assure him. "But in a different way." The dog crooned and twisted in the blanket, nose pressed against the embers of our scent.

PART TWO Spirit

INTRODUCTION

How could gay men not be concerned with matters of the spirit? Growing up in a world that tells us we do not belong, we are forced to turn inward and to contend with those fundamental conundrums at the heart of every faith: Who am I? Where do I fit? What is true?

Religion, in its essence, is much less about answers than questions—and gay men are consummate questioners. Our very existence is an insistent challenge to conventional wisdom. One might even classify our presence a miracle, "an event which appears unexplainable by the laws of nature and so is held to be supernatural or an act of God" (*American Heritage Dictionary*).

In many traditional cultures, including some Native American tribes of the Midwest, this was precisely the way gay people were viewed. Because they were clearly different, those whom we would now call gay men often held the position of priest or shaman, serving as bridges between the explicable and the inexplicable, the known and the unknown, this world and the next. Their differentness was special, holy, to be revered.

But in the dominant strains of Western religion, differentness was seen as sinful and excoriated. Considering same-sex love to be dangerously destabilizing to the familial and social norms they sought to enforce, established religions singled out gay people for particularly harsh condemnation. Gayness was godless, an abomination.

Given this history, it's easy enough to understand why early gay liberationists made the rejection of religion one of their fundamental tenets. Organized religion was (and to a large degree still is) the very seat of gay men's oppression. Thus, in the revolutionary context, a "gay religious person" seemed as much of an impossibility as a "gay Republican." To the extent that gay liberation itself became something of a dogma, any desire for reconciliation with traditional dogmas was the highest form of blasphemy.

Not all gay men felt this way, of course. Some—such as those in the gay Catholic group Dignity and gay Jewish groups like Boston's Am Tikva—sought ways to unite their sexuality and their conventional faiths. Others became involved in the Metropolitan Community Church, a specifically gay ecumenical denomination. Others still immersed themselves in non-Western spiritual ideologies.

But by and large, the gay culture that developed in the decades after Stonewall was explicitly anti-religious. For a gay man to speak publicly about his spiritual concerns was as unseemly as a priest discussing his homosexuality.

Recently, though, as millennial fervor sweeps the globe and people of all backgrounds ask the "big questions" with renewed urgency, the gay community, too, seems to be exhibiting a marked increase of interest in things spiritual. Witness the overflow of recently published books like Brian Bouldrey's *Wrestling with the Angel: Faith and Religion in the Lives of Gay Men,* Mark Thompson's *Gay Soul,* Will Roscoe's *Queer Spirits,* and Lev Raphael's *Journeys and Arrivals: On Being Gay and Jewish.*

Perhaps even more telling is the best-seller status in gay bookstores of the numerous titles dealing explicitly with homosexuality and the Bible: Daniel Helminiak's *What the Bible Really Says About Homosexuality,* Chris Glaser's *The Word Is Out: The Bible Reclaimed for Lesbians and Gay Men,* Peter Gomes's *The Good Book,* and Jim Hill and Rand Cheadle's *The Bible Tells Me So.*

If the transgressive move a quarter-century ago was for gay men to reject religion, now the radical development may in fact be their turning back in large numbers to traditional faith communities. This return has been facilitated in part by the increasing openness of some fellowships to the participation of gay members. Some Protestant and Jewish congregations have even ordained openly gay clergy and sanctioned same-sex marriages.

There are still many gay men who, because of bitterness or simply lack of interest, remain estranged from organized religion. A community that cuts across all lines in society will of course include its fair share of atheists, agnostics, and iconoclasts. But it is now no longer possible—for religious conservatives or gay radicals—to claim that homosexuality and spirituality are necessarily at odds.

The following writers attest to the diversity of ways in which gay men manifest their spiritual natures.

The section begins with Frank Browning's "American Religion, Gay Identity," in which he contends that the process of coming out is, in this country, a fundamentally spiritual phenomenon. Comparing personal accounts of coming out to religious conversion testimonials, he notes that the gay rights movement acts much of the time like a proselytizing faith community, spreading the good news that it's possible to be "born again." Thus, in Browning's view, far from being un-American—as the McCarthyites of the religious right would charge—the struggle for gay liberation is perfectly exemplary of our national experiment, which since colonial days has been about linking personal and communal salvation in a New Jerusalem.

Browning's notion of gayness as a kind of American civil religion is broader than any particular faith; nonetheless, many gay men remain deeply committed to their formal denominations. Bruce Bawer is one prominent thinker who identifies and writes explicitly from the point of view of a "gay Christian." As such, he is critical of both the so-called Christians who, in the name of religion, have waged war on homosexuality, and of a gay subculture that is still overtly hostile to organized Christianity. In "The Fundamentals of Faith," Bawer insists that Christianity in its *true* form has plenty of room for gay people and should be prescribed as an antidote to the bastardized version practiced by bigoted zealots. After all, he points out, Jesus' message was about love, compassion for outsiders, and a new understanding of the word *family*.

Andrew Sullivan is another writer who struggles to reconcile his life as a believing Christian with his life as a gay man. "Alone Again, Naturally" is notable for Sullivan's rigorous philosophical critique of the Catholic Church's position on homosexuality. Confronting the Church on its own terms, he debunks various arguments against gayness and posits an alternative understanding based on the naturalness of homosexuality. But perhaps even more notable is Sullivan's frankness about the impossibility of settling these questions. The Church, he admits, is a human institution, just as contradictory as human life itself. And faith, he says, like sexuality, is inherently mysterious and inexplicable.

Writing from an Orthodox Jewish perspective, Rabbi Yaakov Levado also finds himself coming up against inherent contradictions. Rabbi Levado is firmly committed to a life following Halacha, or Jewish law, but he is equally sure of his God-given homosexuality. Conceding that a strict reading of the Torah prohibits male-male intercourse, he wonders if it is nonetheless possible to find a "halachic" way for gay men to love each other and celebrate their sexuality. In "Gayness and God," he offers no firm answers, but the crucial beginning of a dialogue. His heartfelt, creative wrangling with biblical texts is nothing if not quintessentially Jewish.

While Bruce Bawer, Andrew Sullivan, and Rabbi Levado all seek inclusion and acceptance in their traditional organized religions, other gay men have turned elsewhere to fulfill their spiritual longings. Recent years have seen an explosion of interest in "alternative" spiritualities—

some entirely new (or New Age), and others based on ancient beliefs of native peoples.

Harry Hay's "Remarks on Third Gender" are an angry challenge to Western religion and culture which, with their rigid dichotomies, have alienated him and like-minded individuals. Hay calls for a "leap of consciousness" that would allow gay men to reclaim a visionary "Third Gender" role similar to that of shamans and berdaches in Native American societies.

Mark Thompson also takes his cues from shamanic tradition. In "Making a New Myth," Thompson suggests that gay men serve as mediators in the transition to a new epoch that will move us beyond either/or dialectics. Like indigenous cultures' soul guides who are symbolically dismembered and then resurrected, he says, gay men share the experience of being wounded. And if, following the archetype of the wounded healer, we learn to claim and make use of the harm that's been done to us, we can catalyze widespread spiritual change. We must reinvent our own myths, Thompson asserts, and in doing so offer the hope of rejuvenating society as a whole with our new vision.

Surely the greatest collective wounding gay men have endured—and the greatest challenge to our faith—is AIDS. Like Jews who wondered if there could be a God after Auschwitz, many gay men—seeing lovers and friends stolen by the plague, or themselves facing disease and early death—have found themselves questioning the existence of God and the meaning of existence.

Craig Lucas's "Postcard from Grief" is a wrenching account of despair written shortly after his lover's death. Lucas rages at politicians, at think-positive friends, and at life itself, refusing to be consoled. The depth of his sorrow, he says, is something no religion or philosophy can touch. As painful as it is to hear, his mourning cry is a searing reminder of how gay men's spirits have been tested by recent events.

Mark Matousek is a writer who tumbled into despair when he learned of his own HIV-positive diagnosis. Seeking solace in the face of his mortality, he sampled a wide variety of spiritual alternatives. In an excerpt from his book *Sex Death Enlightenment,* he recounts his experiences with options ranging from Zen Buddhism to Twelve-Step programs to Indian faith healers. Although he finds some help in his quest, Matousek realizes that in the end only he can be responsible for his own enlightenment.

The kind of reflection exemplified by Mark Matousek's saga is common to people who learn they have a fatal illness and feel their time on earth is short. Countless gay men, upon learning they were HIV-positive, have prepared themselves to face death. But what happens when what seemed an imminent death sentence suddenly becomes a long-term manageable illness? What happens if there's a cure?

The recent advent of protease inhibitors and other AIDS "miracle drugs" brings these questions to the fore. There is still much debate about protease inhibitors—which are not universally effective, nor universally available, nor a "cure"—but a large number of men who had been gravely ill are now, aided by the new drugs, recovering their health and may live for years. One would think this is cause for celebration—and it is—but for men who had already adjusted to the idea of dying soon, it can also be bewildering and problematic. In "Heaven Can Wait," Alec Holland tells of reacting to his HIV-positive diagnosis with a devil-may-care attitude: spending his savings, bungee-jumping from a bridge. But now, given the success of his protease regime, he is rethinking his outlook. For the first time in years, he sees a future not in some distant afterlife but in life here on earth.

Mark Doty, too, had considered giving up on life—not because of his own health status but because of his lover Wally's death from AIDS. In "Consolations," he describes punching through to the other side of grief and reawakening his faith in the continuity of existence. Without forgetting the past, he finds inspiration in the boundless possibilities of the future.

The section ends with "A Prayer," from acclaimed playwright Tony Kushner. Kushner's moving address is part elegy, part political manifesto, part supplication. He expresses our collective hope for a life in the next millennium free from all that currently oppresses us.

9. FRANK BROWNING

Following up on his controversial book *The Culture of Desire,* Frank Browning's *A Queer Geography* explores the effects of sexuality and culture on the gay psyche. This probing chapter links the notion of "coming out" to the distinctly American quest for spiritual rebirth.

American Religion, Gay Identity

WHENEVER I ENCOUNTER QUEER PEOPLE FROM OTHER LANDS— Brazil, Italy, northern Europe, especially East Asia—I almost always find a fascinated amusement with the communitarian spirituality of the American gay movement. They are not startled to find a spiritual element in homosexuality: The notion of special powers being linked to a body with special capacities, of Neapolitan *femminielli,* of Zuni berdache, of Indian *hijras,* of Candomblé spiritual leaders in Brazil, is nearly universal. What surprises them is how American gay activism has cast a spiritual, often almost religious, character over what is essentially a *civic* movement for human rights. "How is it," one of my Italian friends asked me, "that a country premised on the separation of politics from religion should build a movement for sexual freedom that is so full of spiritual overtones? You talk about coming out like your preachers talk of being born again."

Village Voice writer Richard Goldstein addressed that question several years ago in an essay he called "Faith, Hope and Sodomy." Recounting the last century's treatment of homosexuality as first a crime, then a psychosis, then a politics, Goldstein argued that it was precisely America's peculiar history of politics and religion that has shaped the gay project: "What sprouted at Reading Gaol, from the depths of Oscar Wilde's despair, has taken root in the American dream. A condition has become a community: A movement is becoming a faith." Goldstein's musings drew heavily on Harold Bloom's remarkable book *The American Religion.* Like many students of American culture, Bloom reminds us how profoundly American life continues to be shaped by our religious origins, how suffused in religion we are even in our most secular concerns. "Freedom," he writes, "in the context of the American Religion, means being alone with God or with Jesus, the American God or the American Christ. In social reality, this translates as solitude, at least in the inmost sense. The soul stands apart, and something deeper than the soul, the Real Me or self or spark, thus is made free to be utterly alone with a God who is also quite separate and solitary, that is, a free God or God of freedom."

Nearly four centuries after the pastoral utopians settled in Virginia and the Protestant radicals dropped anchor off Provincetown, our most fundamental understanding of personal freedom and common spiritual being still echoes our ancestors' project. The sermons and debates that launched the American errand in the wilderness recur, altered and in new language in today's critical debates: in our search for a proper relation to the environment, in our struggles over property rights versus public welfare, in our anxieties over a stagnated national vision and moral renewal. Our sense of sexuality and identity is no less weathered by that past; indeed, I think, the very notion of a "sexual identity" owes much to the peculiar notion of American identity itself, an identity that arose from our first and most radically utopian enterprise among the Puritans of the Massachusetts Bay Colony.

Puritans, for most of us, have become a pejorative metaphor for the loathing of pleasure. The metaphor is apt. The Massachusetts Puritans abhorred the worldly body as an evil thing, "a varnisht pot of putrid excrement," in the words of the famed colonial poet and missionary Edward Taylor. To ridicule the Puritans as grim prudes alone, however, is to miss their importance for America as a nation and for Americans as individuals— hetero, homo, or otherwise. The central contest in the American psyche then and now, the Puritans well understood, is between individual and community—in ecclesiastical terms, between the *exemplum fidei* and the *sola fides:* to see each person, each soul, as the individual expression or example of the godly community (the community of saints) even though each individual's experience of God was absolutely internal unto herself. Socially and politically, the Puritans were a repressively communitarian people, even communistic in their insistence that individual ambitions and prerogatives must be subjected to the values of community welfare. Yet the communitarian dream was continually shaken. Since the true church was to be found not in a building administered by a hierarchy but within the spiritual communion of saints touched by God, the potential for individual heresy was constant. Innumerable crises and heresies did break out as the Puritans went about constructing a New Jerusalem of the New World. Most centered on the individual's capacity for direct experience of God, his ability to make personal spiritual communion, and to find redemption (what we might call wholeness) within that communion—a belief that the Calvinist insistence on predestined election strictly precluded.

The idea of the New World has become such a commonplace to us from our elementary school history books, we forget how potent, how radical, a notion it was. This New World was not merely a new geography where the Pilgrims could be free from "religious persecution." As historian Sacvan Bercovitch writes, the New World was *providential.* The existence of a New World was demonstrable evidence of "God's overarching, inviolable plan" in which every individual, every community, every event, occupied its own place "within the scheme of salvation." Man in the New World—and it was always *man*—was both the guardian of God's handiwork and the reflection of Christ's will. He and His kingdom were one. There could be no separation of self from the noble experiment, from the mission of God. If the pioneer's fortune fell, it was because he had separated himself from God's mission, and he had to be "reawakened" to reclaim his mission. If John Winthrop's "city on a hill" declined, it was because "the city"—the community—had lost its unity with the redemptive mission. Each new mission, each new utopian expansion and rebirth, religious or secular, became an exercise in the recovery of that singular idea of self and mission. That idea, deeply buried in the bedrock of our national myth, cycles over and over through our cultural, historical, and spiritual lives without respect to ideology or ethnicity.

Self and common destiny came to be interlocked for the emerging Americans in ways their European cousins could not conceive. Across the Atlantic, French, Spanish, and British rulers had only begun to define their own ideas of nationalism in rivalries over territory and in internal conflicts among monarchs, nobles, and traders. The ordinary subjects of the kingdom could hardly see themselves as a people united in a transcendent vision that would enable them to divine their common future according to the laws of providence. The king—and if not their king, another country's king—was the final authority against whom one carved out a space of freedom. God and the crown were all-powerful forces outside the individual's personal life. They were forces to be feared and revered, forces from which a stableman or a shopkeeper or a noble might win redemption.

Yet finally in neither the Protestant nor the Catholic cosmology did most humans see themselves as possessing God. Certainly they did not see themselves as manifest evidence of God's mission. At best they were foot soldiers in battles beyond their understanding, and they had learned well that the churches were firmly aligned with the competing political powers. Only radicals—Enthusiasts, Levelers, Diggers, mystics who claimed guidance from an "inner light"—dared to find God inside themselves. The notion of finding God inside yourself, of actually being a part of God, was breathtakingly dangerous to Church and Crown alike. Such people were heretics—as much to the Puritan radicals in the New World as to the entrenched authorities of the Old World.

If the Puritans succeeded in suppressing the "inner light" heretics on theological grounds, however, they still were captive of the Calvinist commitment to individual enterprise. Possessed by the certainty that America was God's kingdom, they came to see it as their duty to exploit the kingdom and make it fruitful, for in its fruitfulness was the evidence of its godliness. Successful personal enterprise was a sign of God's providence. Lacking the restrictive power of the Crown or of a universal Church, and confronted with the boundless opportunity of the frontier, the young Americans were let loose to construct the freest, most rugged commercial markets in the world. By the time the Revolution had succeeded, and the Lockean ideas of a secular state had helped bring about a government divorced from any single religion, the Puritan vision of an ecclesiastical America had lost out to the deeper force of individualism that lay at its core.

"Commerce, commerce, commerce!" exclaimed a prominent European traveler as he sent back reports of the young American republic in the 1820s. A century earlier the great revivalist preacher Jonathan Edwards had written in *Images or Shadows of Divine Things:* "The changing of the course of trade, and the supplying of the world with its treasures from America is a type and forerunner of what is approaching in spiritual things, when the world shall be supplied with spiritual treasures from America." Independent and prosperous, the New Americans understood well that the source of their treasure was nothing less than nature herself. Prosperity linked them to the resources of resplendent nature. Both stewards and exploiters of the godly kingdom, the New Americans were more still: They were of this boundless natural frontier. As it flourished, they flourished. Its destiny was their destiny. As they were of God, so was it. There sprang, in Sacvan Bercovitch's phrase, "the myth of America," giving birth to an American Adam in spiritual unity with the place of his making. Even, finally, for those who were not properly Christians, the unity of God, man, and nature had become inseparable. Or as Emerson, the greatest of our nineteenth-century philosophers, saw it, "The continent we inhabit is to be physic and food for our mind as well as our body. . . . The Genius or Destiny of America is . . . a man incessantly advancing, as the shadow on the dial's face, or the heavenly body by whose light it is marked. . . . Let us realize that this country, the last found, is the great charity of God to the human race."

Emerson, the transcendentalist, saw in the secular transformation of the Puritan project a rebirth of human possibility that exceeded the strictures of Christianity or politics. The American Adam, what he called "the young American," would regenerate the whole of mankind, become "the home of man" where "new love, new faith, new sight shall restore [creation] to more than its first splendor." Out of the Puritan mission had emerged the fundamental faith that remains with us today: self-reliance.

There in that essential regeneration of the world is what Harold Bloom calls the true "American Religion"—the religion of gnosticism, at once experiential and absolutely internal, inside each individual, containing God and contained by God. Bloom, too, turns to Emerson and his famous Harvard "Divinity School Address" and his vision of Christ as the "one man [who] was true to what is in you and me. He saw that God incarnates himself in man, and evermore goes forth anew to take possession of his World." In the American Religion, God does not create man, Bloom argues, because we are older than creation; we are God in that God inhabits our truest spiritual reality. The act of making America, therefore, is and has been an act of spiritual imagination whereby we save ourselves *and* the world—at least all that world that would join us in realizing our rebirth. To realize the rebirth as a personal rebirth of the God within us is the essence of the *American* journey, or as Bloom puts it, "*Awareness,* centered on the self, is *faith* for an American." Bloom traces the rise of what he calls the ecstatic, gnostic religion throughout the nineteenth century in the triumph of the born-again Southern Baptists, the Mormons, the Seventh-Day Adventists, African-American Pentecostalists—all of whom in different ways experience God directly within themselves. To quote the gospel lyrics, "He walks with me and He talks with me, and He tells me I am His own."

The whole of Christianity, of course, is dedicated to a theology of personal salvation. What Bloom points out is the American genius for finding the divine within the realization of personal identity. The Puritans, the Calvinists, the genuine Presbyterians or Methodists, the Catholics could never honestly reduce God to the expression of essential personal identity: but that is exactly what happened to my Kentucky neighbors when finally, during campground revivals, they were "saved" and declared themselves "born again." They experienced a euphoric, ecstatic communion with God in which was revealed their innermost self, a self that could not be seen by the unsaved, a "little me" inside the "big me" in African-American parlance, that led them to know that they had been saved and had joined the kingdom of God. In their salvation lay all salvation; the surviving dictum of the American vision is universal redemption: A reborn America will bring about the rebirth of all humankind.

That was—and remains—the essential errand in the wilderness: a New Jerusalem that will be a light unto the darkened world. To make that reborn self real was no less than to realize, to *become aware* of, the identity of the newly reborn soul. Unlike the conventional Christians, Bloom notes, the American Religionist *experiences* awareness directly—in trances, in tongues, in dances, in visions. The body, however denigrated it may be in sermon, is present at the emergence:

> The American finds God in herself or himself, but only after finding the freedom to know God by experiencing a total inward solitude. Freedom, in a very special sense, is the preparation without which God will not allow himself to be revealed in the self. And this freedom is in itself double; the spark or spirit must know itself to be free both of other selves and of the created world. In perfect solitude, the American spirit learns again its absolute isolation as a spark of God floating in a sea of space. . . . Salvation, for the American, cannot come through the community or the congregation, but is a one-on-one act of confrontation.

Change the words *American* to *gay man* and *God* to *sexual identity.* Only when he has permitted himself the freedom to see and experience his sexual identity free of the identities foisted upon him by the world will the gay man's true identity be revealed to him. Then he will understand his innermost being, his identity, as an emanation of the force of nature (love [God]) that permeates the universe. I use *gay man* consciously here because the ecstatic revelatory language of "coming out" seems so overwhelmingly male in the American experience. While the great majority of contemporary lesbian writers and activists speak of the importance of being "out," women's coming-out stories seldom seem to carry that explosive, almost evangelical power that marks the declarations of American gay men. From porno stories to high polemics, the parallels in language and emotion between stories of coming out and being born again are so stunning as to be unmistakable.

One of the plainest, most powerful, most poignantly spiritual coming-out stories I have ever heard is recorded by Steven Zeeland, who for many years has been interviewing soldiers, sailors, and Marines about their same-sex experiences. Alex was a twenty-one-year-old Marine corporal, half-German, half-Native American, from northern Wisconsin. He was at Camp Pendleton, California. Alex told Zeeland that he was attracted to women and started having sex with women at age nineteen, but he generally felt empty and degraded by the experience.

> ALEX   My sexuality awakened pretty late. There were sexual desires, but that was always limited just to dreams, or very brief daydreams or fantasies.
>
> ZEELAND   What were they like?
>
> ALEX   [Pause] Earlier, it was—it was just me having sex with a hole. Just a hole. A human hole, but . . . it didn't have any gender. . . . They were just sex. Dry; no intimacy, no caring. Then there was coming, and that was it.

Later during Marine boot camp, Alex's fantasies turned toward older, very masculine men, but still he had no sex with men. At Camp Pendleton he developed a deep attachment to a fellow Marine, a buddy who shipped out to Somalia in 1992.

> ALEX   I knew that I would have laid down my life for him. I was pretty sure that he would have done the same for me. We'd confide in each other. And when he went to Somalia, part of me—it was the closest thing I've ever felt to somebody like a lover, or mate, leaving. I was pretty tore up, because he was going off somewhere

and there were people already getting killed. I volunteered, but my gunny said that I couldn't go because I was too important to be sent away.

ZEELAND Did you have any further experiences with women?

ALEX During that time? Yeah. . . . There's only one word to describe them. Bad. There were three or four instances, and each one was just as bad as the first time I had it. . . . I do still sleep with women, sometimes. And I've refined that now, to where it's on a personal basis. I sleep with women if they're nice. And it's actually nice to sleep with women, too, because they're a lot more feminine . . . But it still doesn't compare to sex with other men.

I came out in May of '93. I was in an adult bookstore downtown. I had never been in one before. They had all these girlie magazines, and I was looking through them. And then I noticed one next to it that was a gay magazine. I picked it up and went around to the other side, where you could see everybody that was coming in. There weren't that many people in the store. I started reading it, and my blood started rushing to my head. I started getting very sexually aroused. I had never felt such a rush of anything before. I bought a magazine that was wrapped in plastic; on the cover it had a big guy with boots on a forklift. I also grabbed a copy of [a local gay newspaper], too.

On the way back I was starting to think of what I actually did, that I had got a gay magazine, and I started punishing myself or whatever. How could I ever expect to be normal if I was to read things like this? I saw it sitting next to me, and it was inciting me to think even worse thoughts about me. And then something inside of me kind of stood up, and I started saying to myself, "This is me!"

Soon this voice in me became overpowering, and I just started feeling happy about myself, happy to just be me. I was laughing and yelling in the car, "I'm gay! I'm gay! I'm gay!"

I was euphoric. I suppose people going by—well, people do weirder things in cars, but I didn't care what other people thought. That was my gay . . . release. I knew that I was gay and I was going to be happy that I was gay because I had desired to have sex with males more than with females. I would say that that was the happiest moment in my life.

Like Bloom's gnostic Christians who fill up Baptist churches all over the South, Alex experienced an ecstatic conversion, an awakening that filled him with joy. His awakening, like that of the evangelicals, was not precisely about redemption. It was more like the Good News that comes of looking into your heart and finding Jesus' truth, that He is Love and He is ever present. The American Jesus, Bloom writes, is an agent of salvation insofar as he is the revealer of truth. He is "not so much an event in history for the American Religionist as he is a knower of the secrets of God, who in return can be known by the individual. Hidden in this process is a sense that depravity is only a lack of saving knowledge. Salvation through knowing the knowing Jesus is a reversal wholly experiential in nature, an internalization of a self already internalized."

Being born again and coming out are ultimately acts of solitude that require public declaration. At its vital moment, each is a totally internal experience of awareness, later amplified and made communal by sharing the good news with those others who have had the same experience and know within themselves how the truth has saved them. Each is a linkage of sublime awareness and spiritual union with others. Spiritual union, however, remains the required second step to awareness, as much for the newly out gay man as for the saved evangelical as for Emerson's young American who through "new love, new faith, new sight" would restore the world to "its first splendor." Evangelicals render their gnostic truth as preachings; gay activists render the revelations of identity into polemical manifestos. At the polemical level, nothing exceeds Michelangelo Signorile's "Queer Manifesto" in *Queer in America:*

Everyone must come out of the closet, no matter how difficult, no matter how painful.

We must tell our parents.

We must tell our families.

We must tell our friends.

We must tell our coworkers. . . .

Badger everyone you know who is closeted—your friends, your family members, your coworkers—to come out. Put pressure on those in power whom you know to be queer. Send them letters. Call them on the phone. Fax them. Confront them in the streets.

Tell them they have a responsibility: to themselves, to you, to humanity.

Tell them they have to face the truth. And tell the truth yourself.

No Mormon missionary, no Jehovah's Witness, no Southern Baptist preacher could speak more clearly, more passionately, about spreading "the Good News" of Jesus' personal salvation for all those who will be saved and born again. About sexuality, homosexuality, there is only one truth, and we must tell it, all together, and to each other, until no one is left who knows it and has not revealed it and been made free by it. As a strategy of spiritual politics, Signorile's manifesto is mint American: It is the same strategy the Mormons and the Witnesses and the Baptists have employed for nearly two hundred years in their bids to link collective personal identity with self-revealed spiritual truth. It works because it inspires us, and it inspires us because it touches a chord deep within our national myth regardless of our attachment to any formal religion: We can be free only when we have spoken to and confessed our identity with our one true and hidden self, a self that is nothing less than the manifestation of the American quest.

The dilemma for "gay Americans," no less than for the Puritans three centuries ago, is how to imagine a psychic identity that nurtures both personal liberation and common purpose. To the extent that our quest for personal identity isolates and individualizes us, we lose the strength of a common movement. But a fixed-movement identity can all too easily lead us into a spiritual stagnation where we are nothing more than demographic consumer niches. The trick in our complex world of contending identities is to move instead toward dynamism, toward an identity of becoming.

The identity of becoming acknowledges that "coming out" is a fluid, continuous experience, more akin to Heraclitus' river, which can never be touched, because during the time it takes to dip your hand into it and pull it out, it has moved somewhere else. Both eros and love are not knowable, not capable of being fixed, any more than the force of the river, even the Mississippi River with all its engineered locks and dams, can be contained. The paradox of the Heraclitean river, of course, is that even though it cannot be touched, it forms the very definition of place. By its course it orders the land it divides, and more, it provokes those who live on that land to Promethean daring. It challenges them to snare its power for transportation, snatch its fish for sustenance, drain its water for irrigation—all the while risking death by drowning.

I linger on the metaphor of river as identity because it seems to speak to the dilemma we face now, at the end of the millennium, in our yearning for community and liberation. Like the river, we cannot retreat. That is the route of sentimentality, along which we would wistfully and hopelessly search, like the pope's speechwriters, for the nostalgic, small-town communities of our grandparents. The answer to the barrenness of the consumerized, zip-code-organized gay communities identified by bars, buns, and boutiques is not a homo shtetl marked by its own codes of fearful self-preservation.

If, on the other hand, we dare to see "coming out" as a simultaneous "going in" to the uncharted potential relationships we contain, then we may find in our sexualities a new method for finding community. Then "queerness" becomes a tool of navigation, an interrogatory technique for revealing the queerness in others, establishing spiritual and communitarian bonds with and among others too mysterious for the reductionist moguls of marketing to comprehend. Our charge, engineered at once through confrontation and seduction, is genuinely shamanic: It is not to protect ourselves but to subvert certainty and to destabilize power; it is not to build new families, but to open up and nurture the queer spaces already inside them; it is not to retreat into our own safe space but to discover, protect, and electrify the queer zones in calcified, dispirited communities everywhere. Our mission is, in the very best sense, spiritual: It is to provoke passion where planners, preachers, and commodity marketers have done their best to deaden it.

10. BRUCE BAWER

Bruce Bawer's *A Place at the Table* established him as the most prominent gay voice dissenting from queer progressive ideology. In the following article, one of his regular columns from *The Advocate*, he writes as a practicing Episcopalian of the ways in which antigay fundamentalism betrays the true spirit of Christianity.

The Fundamentals of Faith

YOU DON'T HAVE TO BE A GAY CHRISTIAN TO BE APPALLED BY THE 1996 Republican presidential hopefuls, but it sure doesn't hurt. At the Louisiana GOP convention, shown on C-SPAN in late January, Phil Gramm, Alan Keyes, and Pat Buchanan alternated between self-righteous Bible-thumping and vicious jabs at gay men and lesbians, among others. You'd have thought they were running for ayatollah. Even more grotesque than their ritual juxtaposition of pietism and thuggery was the audience's enthusiastic response: The nastier the digs, the wilder the applause.

Experiencing such spectacles as a gay Christian, I find myself doubly pained. It hurts to see self-styled Christians preaching antigay hate in God's name; it also hurts to know that such high-profile rhetoric has made *Christian,* in the standard gay lexicon, a synonym for *bigot.* Yet while 700 Club types have done a zealous job of making Christians look like creeps, I think it would serve our movement well for us to recognize that, as a human institution, the Church has never been any less diverse than, say, the lesbian and gay community.

At one extreme are Christians in whose minds the Church stands, above all, for eternal law, institutional order, and final judgment. Such folks staged the Inquisition and cited biblical "proof texts" to support slavery ("Slaves, obey your masters") and the subjugation of women ("Let your women be silent in the churches"). Barely a century ago in the American hinterlands, they retreated from modern scientific advances into a bizarre new set of apocalyptic doctrines and a severe biblical literalism that in 1920 won them the label "fundamentalist." Today those backwoods doctrines, slickly repackaged for the TV age by Pat Robertson and his ilk, draw millions to churches that claim to preserve "old-time religion" in the face of threatening social change. Yet what they're really doing is deep-sixing the ancient gospel message of nonjudgmental love and highlighting, in its place, a disagreeable habit of attaching God's name to their basest prejudices.

Then there are other Christians—people for whom the Church serves as a vehicle through which to emulate the ministry of Jesus, a revolutionary for whom love always transcended law. Such Christians spearheaded abolitionism, marched for civil rights in the 1950s, and today labor for such causes as—yes—gay equality. It's unfair to them, and strategically counterproductive, to glibly scorn their faith. A far more fair and fruitful approach, it seems to me, would begin with the recognition that the Christian Coalition's take on gay issues (among others) is not, in any legitimate sense, Christian at all. Indeed, I think it's about time that instead of bashing religion we started vigorously pointing out to the large nonfundamentalist Christian mainstream just how outrageously the religious right has perverted the Christian message.

First, since Christianity is, above all, about love, it's unchristian to disdain any kind of love. Fundamentalists often deem gay sex the most heinous of sins, while rarely acknowledging (and never honoring) gay love; by contrast, the gospels make it clear that Jesus didn't identify sin with sex, gay or otherwise, and that what mattered to him was not what people did in bed but how they treated one another.

Second, it's unchristian to demonize anybody. Many fundamentalists,

along with fellow-traveling Catholics such as Buchanan, unctuously identify themselves with God and equate gays with the devil. This is not Christian thinking: Christianity demands that you regard yourself in the same
way you do others. "Judge not, lest ye be judged," said Jesus, who frater-
nized with lepers, whores, and sundry outcasts.

Third, it's unchristian to fetishize the so-called "traditional family."
The religious right consistently yokes God and family, depicts the family as
critically endangered by gay rights, and denies that a family can consist of,
say, a gay or lesbian couple. This attitude would certainly not have been
shared by Jesus, who told his followers, "You must hate your parents."
Jesus! This in-your-face activism was shocking. But in a clannish society
where blood ties were all, he wished to emphasize that the keys of the kingdom lie not in glorifying those ties but in expanding one's understanding of
the word *family*. If Jesus were walking our streets today, one wonders, what
would the TV preachers make of his "family" of twelve men? John's gospel
has the crucified Jesus saying to Mary, apropos of his beloved disciple:
"Mother, behold your son." His point: Love alone makes a family.

When it comes to Christianity and homosexuality, a few things seem
clear. If more self-styled Christians truly *were* Christian, then Christianity
would be the chief bulwark of gay men and lesbians in the face of societal
anathematization, rather than the bigots' principal tool. Further, we *do*
have allies in all but the most far-out churches, and everything should be
done to work with them and not against them. Finally, if we respond to
religious-right attacks with a conspicuous respect for the real meaning of
Christianity, we can go a long way toward helping the majority of Christians, who are neither antigay fundamentalists nor pro-gay activists, to see
us, the religious right, and the likes of Gramm and Buchanan for what we
all really are—and toward reminding them what are, and aren't, the proper
fundamentals of their faith.

II. ANDREW SULLIVAN

In his five-year stint as editor of *The New Republic,* Andrew Sullivan earned a reputation as an intellectual wunderkind. This essay, like his best-selling book *Virtually Normal,* combines personal experience with political philosophy to challenge the Roman Catholic Church's opposition to homosexuality.

Alone Again, Naturally

In everyone there sleeps
A sense of life lived according to love.
To some it means the difference they could make
By loving others, but across most it sweeps
As all they might have been had they been loved.
That nothing cures.

PHILIP LARKIN, "Faith Healing"

I.

I CAN REMEMBER THE FIRST TIME WHAT, FOR THE SAKE OF ARGU-
ment, I will call my sexuality came into conflict with what, for the sake of
argument, I will call my faith. It was time for communion in my local
parish church, Our Lady and St. Peter's, a small but dignified building
crammed between an Indian restaurant and a stationery shop, opposite a
public restroom, on the main street of a smallish town south of London
called East Grinstead. I must have been around fifteen or so. Every time I
received communion, I attempted, following my mother's instructions, to
offer up the sacrament for some current problem or need: my mother's
health, an upcoming exam, the starving in Bangladesh or whatever. Most
of these requests had to do with either something abstract and distant, like
a cure for cancer, or something extremely tangible, like a better part in the
school play. Like much else in my faith-life, they were routine and yet not
completely drained of sincerity. But rarely did they address something that
could unsettle the comfort of my precocious adolescence. This time, however, as I filed up to the communion rail to face mild-mannered Father
Simmons for the umpteenth time, something else intervened. Please, I remember asking almost offhandedly of God, after a quick recital of my
other failings, help me with *that*.

I didn't have a name for it, since it was, to all intents and purposes,
nameless. I don't think I'd ever heard it mentioned at home, except once
when my mother referred to someone who had behaved inappropriately on
my father's town rugby team. (He had been dealt with, she reported darkly.)
At high school, the subject was everywhere and nowhere: at the root of
countless jokes but never actualized as something that could affect anyone
we knew. But this ubiquity and abstraction brought home the most important point: Uniquely among failings, homosexuality was so abominable
it could not even be mentioned. The occasions when it was actually discussed were so rare that they stand out even now in my mind: our Latin
teacher's stating that homosexuality was obviously wrong since it meant
"sticking your dick in the wrong hole"; the graffiti in the public restroom
in Reigate High Street: "My mother made me a homosexual," followed
closely by, "If I gave her the wool, would she make me one too?" Although
my friends and family never stinted in pointing out other faults on my part,
this, I knew, would never be confronted. So when it emerged as an irresistible fact of my existence, and when it first seeped into my life of dutiful

prayer and worship, it could be referred to only in the inarticulate void of that Sunday evening before communion.

From the beginning, however—and this is something many outside the Church can find hard to understand—my sexuality was part of my faith-life, not a revolt against it. Looking back, I realize that that moment at the communion rail was the first time I had actually addressed the subject of homosexuality explicitly in front of anyone; and I had brought it to God in the moments before the most intimate act of sacramental communion. Because it was something I was deeply ashamed of, I felt obliged to confront it; but because it was also something inextricable—even then—from the core of my existence, it felt natural to enlist God's help rather than his judgment in grappling with it. There was, of course, considerable tension in this balance of alliance and rejection, but there was also something quite natural about it, an accurate reflection of anyone's compromised relationship with what he or she hazards to be the divine.

To the outsider, faith often seems a kind of cataclysmic intervention, a Damascene moment of revelation and transformation, and no doubt, for a graced few, this is indeed the experience. But this view of faith is often, it seems to me, a way to salve the unease of a faithless life by constructing the alternative as something so alien to actual experience that it is safely beyond reach. Faith for me has never been like that. The moments of genuine intervention and spiritual clarity have been minuscule in number and, when they have occurred, hard to discern and harder still to understand. In the midst of this uncertainty, the sacraments, especially that of communion, have always been for me the only truly reliable elements of direction, concrete instantiations of another order. Which is why, perhaps, it was at communion that the subject reared its confusing, shaming presence.

The two experiences came together in other ways, too. Like faith, one's sexuality is not simply a choice; it informs a whole way of being. But like faith, it involves choices—the choice to affirm or deny a central part of one's being, the choice to live a life that does not deny but confronts reality. It is, like faith, mysterious, emerging clearly one day, only to disappear the next, taking different forms—of passion, of lust, of intimacy, of fear. And like faith, it points toward something other and more powerful than the self. The physical communion with the other in sexual life hints at the same kind of transcendence as the physical communion with the Other that lies at the heart of the sacramental Catholic vision.

So when I came to be asked, later in life, how I could be gay and

Catholic, I could answer only that I simply was. What to others appeared a simple contradiction was, in reality, the existence of these two connected, yet sometimes parallel, experiences of the world. It was not that my sexuality was involuntary and my faith chosen and that therefore my sexuality posed a problem for my faith; nor was it that my faith was involuntary and my sexuality chosen so that my faith posed a problem for my sexuality. It was that both were chosen and unchosen continuously throughout my life, as parts of the same search for something larger. As I grew older, they became part of me, inseparable from my understanding of myself. My faith existed at the foundation of how I saw the world; my sexuality grew to be inseparable from how I felt the world.

I am aware that this formulation of the problem is theologically flawed. Faith, after all, is not a sensibility; in the Catholic sense, it is a statement about reality that cannot be negated by experience. And there is little doubt about what the authority of the Church teaches about the sexual expression of a homosexual orientation. But this was not how the problem first presented itself. The immediate difficulty was not how to make what I *did* conform with what the Church taught me (until my early twenties, I did very little that could be deemed objectively sinful with regard to sex), but how to make who I *was* conform with what the Church taught me. This was a much more difficult proposition. It did not conform to a simple contradiction between self and God, as that afternoon in the communion line attested. It entailed trying to understand how my adolescent crushes and passions, my longings for human contact, my stumbling attempts to relate love to life, could be so inimical to the gospel of Christ and His Church, how they could be so unmentionable among people I loved and trusted.

So I resorted to what many young homosexuals and lesbians resort to. I found a way to expunge love from life, to construct a trajectory that could somehow explain this absence, and to hope that what seemed so natural and overwhelming could somehow be dealt with. I studied hard to explain away my refusal to socialize; I developed intense intellectual friendships that bordered on the emotional, but I kept them restrained in a carapace of artificiality to prevent passion from breaking out. I adhered to a hopelessly pessimistic view of the world, which could explain my refusal to take part in life's pleasures, and to rationalize the dark and deep depressions that periodically overwhelmed me.

No doubt some of this behavior was part of any teenager's panic at the prospect of adulthood. But looking back, it seems unlikely that this pattern had nothing whatsoever to do with my being gay. It had another twist: It sparked an intense religiosity that could provide me with the spiritual resources I needed to fortify my barren emotional life. So my sexuality and my faith entered into a dialectic: My faith propelled me away from my emotional and sexual longing, and the deprivation that this created required me to resort even more dogmatically to my faith. And as my faith had to find increasing power to restrain the hormonal and emotional turbulence of adolescence, it had to take on a caricatured shape, aloof and dogmatic, ritualistic and awesome. As time passed, a theological austerity became the essential complement to an emotional emptiness. And as the emptiness deepened, the austerity sharpened.

II.

In a remarkable document titled "Declaration on Certain Questions Concerning Sexual Ethics," issued by the Vatican in 1975, the Sacred Congregation for the Doctrine of the Faith made the following statement regarding the vexed issue of homosexuality: "A distinction is drawn, and it seems with some reason, between homosexuals whose tendency comes from a false education, from a lack of normal sexual development, from habit, from bad example, or from other similar causes, and is transitory or at least not incurable; and homosexuals who are definitively such because of some kind of innate instinct or a pathological constitution judged to be incurable."

The Church was responding, it seems, to the growing sociological and psychological evidence that, for a small minority of people, homosexuality is unchosen and unalterable. In the context of a broad declaration on a whole range of sexual ethics, this statement was something of a minor digression (twice as much space was devoted to the "grave moral disorder" of masturbation); and it certainly didn't mean a liberalization of doctrine about the morality of homosexual acts, which were "intrinsically disordered and can in no case be approved of."

Still, the concession complicated things. Before 1975, the modern Church, when it didn't ignore the matter, had held a coherent view of the morality of homosexual acts. It maintained that homosexuals, as the modern world had come to define them, didn't really exist; rather, everyone was essentially a heterosexual and homosexual acts were acts chosen by heterosexuals, out of depravity, curiosity, impulse, predisposition, or bad moral guidance. Such acts were an abuse of the essential heterosexual orientation of all humanity; they were condemned because they failed to link sexual activity with a binding commitment between a man and a woman in a marriage, a marriage that was permanently open to the possibility of begetting children. Homosexual sex was condemned in exactly the same way and for exactly the same reasons as premarital heterosexual sex, adultery, or contracepted sex: It failed to provide the essential conjugal and procreative context for sexual relations.

The reasoning behind this argument rested on natural law. Natural law teaching, drawing on Aristotelian and Thomist tradition, argued that the sexual nature of man was naturally linked to both emotional fidelity and procreation so that, outside of this context, sex was essentially destructive of the potential for human flourishing: "the full sense of mutual self-giving and human procreation in the context of true love," as the encyclical *Gaudium et Spes* put it.

But suddenly, a new twist had been made to this argument. There was, it seems, *in nature,* a group of people who were "definitively" predisposed to violation of this natural law; their condition was "innate" and "incurable." Insofar as it was innate—literally *innatus* or "inborn"—this condition was morally neutral, since anything involuntary could not be moral or immoral; it simply was. But always and everywhere, the activity to which this condition led was "intrinsically disordered and [could] in no case be approved of." In other words, something fundamentally in nature always and everywhere violated a vital part of the nature of human beings; something essentially blameless was always and everywhere blameworthy if acted upon.

The paradox of this doctrine was evident even within its first, brief articulation. Immediately before stating the intrinsic disorder of homosexuality, the text averred that in "the pastoral field, these homosexuals must certainly be treated with understanding and sustained in the hope of overcoming their personal difficulties. . . . Their culpability will be judged with prudence." This compassion for the peculiar plight of the homosexual was then elaborated: "This judgment of Scripture does not of course permit us to conclude that all those who suffer from this anomaly are personally responsible for it. . . ." Throughout, there are alternating moments of alarm and quiescence; tolerance and panic; categorical statement and prudential doubt.

It was therefore perhaps unsurprising that, within a decade, the Church felt it necessary to take up the matter again. The problem could have been resolved by a simple reversion to the old position, the position maintained by fundamentalist Protestant churches: that homosexuality was a hideous, yet curable, affliction of heterosexuals. But the Church doggedly refused to budge from its assertion of the natural occurrence of constitutive homosexuals—or from its compassion for and sensitivity to their plight. In Cardinal Joseph Ratzinger's 1986 letter, "On the Pastoral Care of Homosexual Persons," this theme is actually deepened, beginning with the title.

To non-Catholics, the use of the term "homosexual person" might seem a banality. But the term "person" constitutes in Catholic moral teaching a profound statement about the individual's humanity, dignity, and worth; it invokes a whole range of rights and needs; it reflects the recognition by the Church that a homosexual person deserves exactly the same concern and compassion as a heterosexual person, having all the rights of a human being, and all the value, in the eyes of God. This idea was implicit in the 1975 declaration, but was never advocated. Then there it was, eleven years later, embedded in Ratzinger's very title. Throughout his text, homosexuality, far from being something unmentionable or disgusting, is discussed with candor and subtlety. It is worthy of close attention: "[T]he phenomenon of homosexuality, complex as it is and with its many consequences for society and ecclesial life, is a proper focus for the Church's pastoral care. It thus requires of her ministers attentive study, active concern and honest, theologically well-balanced counsel." And here is Ratzinger on the moral dimensions of the unchosen nature of homosexuality: "[T]he particular inclination of the homosexual person is not a sin." Moreover, homosexual persons, he asserts, are "often generous and giving of themselves." Then, in a stunning passage of concession, he marshals the Church's usual arguments in defense of human dignity in order to defend homosexual dignity:

> It is deplorable that homosexual persons have been and are the object of violent malice in speech or in action. Such treatment deserves condemnation from the Church's pastors wherever it occurs. It reveals a kind of disregard for others which endangers the most fundamental principles of a healthy society. The intrinsic dignity of each person must always be respected in word, in action and in law.

Elsewhere, Ratzinger refers to the homosexual's "God-given dignity and worth"; condemns the view that homosexuals are totally compulsive as a "demeaning assumption"; and argues that "the human person, made in the image and likeness of God, can hardly be adequately described by a re-ductionist reference to his or her sexual orientation."

Why are these statements stunning? Because they reveal how far the Church had, by the mid-1980s, absorbed the common sense of the earlier document's teaching on the involuntariness of homosexuality, and had had the courage to reach its logical conclusion. In Ratzinger's letter, the Church stood foursquare against bigotry, against demeaning homosexuals either by antigay slander or violence or by progay attempts to reduce human be-ings to one aspect of their personhood. By denying that homosexual activ-ity was totally compulsive, the Church could open the door to an entire world of moral discussion about ethical and unethical homosexual behav-ior, rather than simply dismissing it all as pathological. What in 1975 had been "a pathological constitution judged to be incurable" was, eleven years later, a "homosexual person," "made in the image and likeness of God."

But this defense of the homosexual person was only half the story. The other half was that, *at the same time,* the Church strengthened its condem-nation of any and all homosexual activity. By 1986 the teachings condemn-ing homosexual acts were far more categorical than they had been before. Ratzinger had guided the Church into two simultaneous and opposite di-rections: a deeper respect for homosexuals, and a sterner rejection of al-most anything they might do.

At the beginning of the 1986 document, Ratzinger bravely confronted the central paradox: "In the discussion which followed the publication of the [1975] declaration . . . an overly benign interpretation was given to the ho-mosexual condition itself, some going so far as to call it neutral or even good. Although the particular inclination of the homosexual person is not a sin, it is a more or less strong tendency ordered toward an intrinsic moral evil and thus the inclination itself must be seen as an objective disorder." Elsewhere, he reiterated the biblical and natural law arguments against homosexual relations. Avoiding the problematic nature of the Old Testa-ment's disavowal of homosexual acts (since these are treated in the context of such "abominations" as eating pork and having intercourse during men-struation, which the Church today regards with equanimity), Ratzinger focused on St. Paul's admonitions against homosexuality: "Instead of the original harmony between Creator and creatures, the acute distortion of idolatry has led to all kinds of moral excess. Paul is at a loss to find a clearer example of this disharmony than homosexual relations." There was also the simple natural law argument: "It is only in the marital relationship that the use of the sexual faculty can be morally good. A person engaging in homosexual behavior therefore acts immorally." The point about procreation was strengthened by an argument about the natural, "complementary union able to transmit life," which is heterosexual marriage. The fact that homosexual sex cannot be a part of this union means that it "thwarts the call to a life of that form of self-giving which the Gospel says is the essence of Christian living." Thus "homosexual activity" is inherently "self-indulgent." "Homosexual activity," Ratzinger's document claimed in a veiled and ugly reference to HIV, is a "form of life which constantly threatens to destroy" homosexual persons.

This is some armory of argument. The barrage of statements directed against "homosexual activity," which Ratzinger associates in this document exclusively with genital sex, is all the more remarkable because it occurs in a document that has otherwise gone further than might have been thought imaginable in accepting homosexuals into the heart of the Church and of humanity. Ratzinger's letter was asking us, it seems, to love the sinner more deeply than ever before, but to hate the sin even more passionately. This is a demand with which most Catholic homosexuals have at some time or other engaged in anguished combat.

III.

It is also a demand that raises the central question of the two documents and, indeed, of any Catholic homosexual life: How intelligible is the Church's theological and moral position on the blamelessness of homosexuality and the moral depravity of homosexual acts? This question is the one I wrestled with in my early twenties, as the increasing aridity of my emotional life began to conflict with the possibility of my living a moral life. The distinction made some kind of sense in theory, but in practice, the command to love oneself as a person of human dignity yet hate the core longings that could make one emotionally whole demanded a sense of detachment or a sense of cynicism that seemed inimical to the Christian life. To deny lust was one thing; to deny love was another. And to deny love in the context of *Christian* doctrine seemed particularly perverse. Which begged a prior question: Could the paradoxes of the Church's position reflect a deeper incoherence at their core?

One way of tackling the question is to look for useful analogies to the moral paradox of the homosexual. Greed, for example, might be said to be an innate characteristic of human beings, which, in practice, is always bad. But the analogy falls apart immediately. Greed is itself evil; it is prideful, a part of Original Sin. It is not, like homosexuality, a blameless natural condition that inevitably leads to what are understood as immoral acts. Moreover, there is no subgroup of innately greedy people, nor a majority of people in which greed never occurs. Nor are the greedy to be treated with respect. There is no paradox here, and no particular moral conundrum.

Aquinas suggests a way around this problem. He posits that some things that occur in nature may be in accordance with an individual's nature, but somehow against human nature in general: "For it sometimes happens that one of the principles which is natural to the species as a whole has broken down in one of its individual members; the result can be that something which runs counter to the nature of the species as a whole, happens to be in harmony with nature for a particular individual: as it becomes natural for a vessel of water which has been heated to give out heat." Forget, for a moment, the odd view that somehow it is more "natural" for a vessel to exist at one temperature than another. The fundamental point here is that there are natural urges in a particular person that may run counter to the nature of the species as a whole. The context of this argument is a discussion of pleasure: How is it, if we are to trust nature (as Aquinas and the Church say we must), that some natural pleasures in some people are still counter to human nature as a whole? Aquinas's only response is to call such events functions of sickness, what the modern Church calls "objective disorder." But here, too, the analogies he provides are revealing: they are bestiality and cannibalism. Aquinas understands each of these activities as an emanation of a predilection that seems to occur more naturally in some than in others. But this only reveals some of the special problems of lumping homosexuality in with other "disorders." Even Aquinas's modern disciples (and, as we've seen, the Church) concede that involuntary orientation to the same gender does not spring from the same impulses as cannibalism or bestiality. Or indeed that cannibalism is ever a "natural" pleasure in the first place, in the way that, for some bizarre reason, homosexuality is.

What, though, of Aquinas's better argument—that a predisposition to homosexual acts is a mental or physical *illness* that is itself morally neutral, but always predisposes people to inherently culpable acts? Here, again, it is hard to think of a precise analogy. Down syndrome, for example, occurs in a minority and is itself morally neutral; but when it leads to an immoral act, such as, say, a temper tantrum directed at a loving parent, the Church is loath to judge that person as guilty of choosing to break a commandment. The condition excuses the action. Or, take epilepsy: If an epileptic person has a seizure that injures another human being, she is not regarded as morally responsible for her actions, insofar as they were caused by epilepsy. There is no paradox here either, but for a different reason: With greed, the condition itself is blameworthy; with epilepsy, the injurious act is blameless.

Another analogy can be drawn. What of something like alcoholism? This is a blameless condition, as science and psychology have shown. Some people have a predisposition to it; others do not. Moreover, this predisposition is linked, as homosexuality is, to a particular act. For those with a predisposition to alcoholism, having a drink might be morally disordered, destructive to the human body and spirit. So, alcoholics, like homosexuals, should be welcomed into the Church, but only if they renounce the activity their condition implies.

Unfortunately, even this analogy will not hold. For one thing, drinking is immoral only for alcoholics. Moderate drinking is perfectly acceptable, according to the Church, for non-alcoholics. On the issue of homosexuality, to follow the analogy, the Church would have to say that sex between people of the same gender would be—in moderation—fine for heterosexuals but not for homosexuals. In fact, of course, the Church teaches the opposite, arguing that the culpability of homosexuals engaged in sexual acts should be judged with prudence—and *less* harshly—than the culpability of heterosexuals who engage in "perversion."

But the analogy to alcoholism points to a deeper problem. Alcoholism does not ultimately work as an analogy because it does not reach to the core of the human condition in the way that homosexuality, following the logic of the Church's arguments, does. If alcoholism is overcome by a renunciation of alcoholic acts, then recovery allows the human being to realize his or her full potential, a part of which, according to the Church, is the supreme act of self-giving in a life of matrimonial love. But if homosexuality is overcome by a renunciation of homosexual emotional and sexual union, the opposite is achieved: the human being is liberated into sacrifice and pain, barred from the matrimonial love that the Church holds to be intrinsic, for most people, to the state of human flourishing. Homosexuality is a structural condition that restricts the human being, even if homosexual acts are renounced, to a less than fully realized life. In other words, the gay or lesbian person is deemed disordered at a far deeper level than the alcoholic: at the level of the human capacity to love and be loved by another human being, in a union based on fidelity and self-giving. Their renunciation of such love also is not guided toward some ulterior or greater goal— as the celibacy of the religious orders is designed to intensify their devotion to God. Rather, the loveless homosexual destiny is precisely toward nothing, a negation of human fulfillment, which is why the Church understands that such persons, even in the act of obedient self-renunciation, are called "to enact the will of God in their life by joining whatever sufferings and difficulties they experience in virtue of their condition to the sacrifice of the Lord's cross."

This suggests another analogy: the sterile person. Here, too, the person is structurally barred by an innate or incurable condition from the full realization of procreative union with another person. One might expect that such people would be regarded in exactly the same light as homosexuals. They would be asked to commit themselves to a life of complete celibacy and to offer up their pain toward a realization of Christ's sufferings on the cross. But that, of course, is not the Church's position. Marriage is available to sterile couples or to those past child-bearing age; these couples are not prohibited from having sexual relations.

One is forced to ask: What rational distinction can be made, on the Church's own terms, between the position of sterile people and that of homosexual people with regard to sexual relations and sacred union? If there is nothing morally wrong, per se, with the homosexual condition or with homosexual love and self-giving, then homosexuals are indeed analogous to those who, by blameless fate, cannot reproduce. With the sterile couple, it could be argued, miracles might happen. But miracles, by definition, can happen to anyone. What the analogy to sterility suggests, of course, is that the injunction against homosexual union does not rest, at heart, on the arguments about openness to procreation, but on the Church's failure to fully absorb its own teachings about the dignity and worth of homosexual persons. It cannot yet see them as it sees sterile heterosexuals: people who, with respect to procreation, suffer from a clear, limiting condition, but who nevertheless have a potential for real emotional and spiritual self-realization, in the heart of the Church, through the transfiguring power of the matrimonial sacrament. It cannot yet see them as truly made in the image of God.

• • •

But this, maybe, is to be blind in the face of the obvious. Even with sterile people, there is a symbolism in the union of male and female that speaks to the core nature of sexual congress and its ideal instantiation. There is no such symbolism in the union of male with male or female with female. For some Catholics, this "symbology" goes so far as to bar even heterosexual intercourse from positions apart from the missionary—face to face, male to female, in a symbolic act of love devoid of all non-procreative temptation. For others, the symbology is simply about the notion of "complementarity," the way in which each sex is invited in the act of sexual congress—even when they are sterile—to perceive the mystery of the other; when the two sexes are the same, in contrast, the act becomes one of mere narcissism and self-indulgence, a higher form of masturbation. For others still, the symbolism is simply about Genesis, the story of Adam and Eve, and the essentially dual, male-female center of the natural world. Denying this is to offend the complementary dualism of the universe.

But all these arguments are arguments for the centrality of heterosexual sexual acts in nature, not their exclusiveness. It is surely possible to concur with these sentiments, even to laud their beauty and truth, while also conceding that it is nevertheless also true that nature seems to have provided a spontaneous and mysterious contrast that could conceivably be understood to complement—even dramatize—the central male-female order. In many species and almost all human cultures, there are some who seem to find their destiny in a similar but different sexual and emotional union. They do this not by subverting their own nature, or indeed human nature, but by fulfilling it in a way that doesn't deny heterosexual primacy but rather honors it by its rare and distinct otherness. As albinos remind us of the brilliance of color; as redheads offer a startling contrast to the blandness of their peers; as genius teaches us, by contrast, the virtue of moderation; as the disabled person reveals to us in negative form the beauty of the fully functioning human body; so the homosexual person might be seen as a natural foil to the heterosexual norm, a variation that does not eclipse the theme but resonates with it. Extinguishing—or prohibiting—homosexuality is, from this point of view, not a virtuous necessity but the real crime against nature, a refusal to accept the pied beauty of God's creation, a denial of the way in which the other need not threaten but may actually give depth and contrast to the self.

This is the alternative argument embedded in the Church's recent grappling with natural law, that is just as consonant with the spirit of natural law as the Church's current position. It is more consonant with what actually occurs in nature; seeks an end to every form of natural life; and upholds the dignity of each human person. It is so obvious an alternative to the Church's current stance that it is hard to imagine the forces of avoidance that have kept it so firmly at bay for so long.

IV.

For many homosexual Catholics, life within the Church is a difficult endeavor. In my twenties, as I attempted to unite the possibilities of sexual longing and emotional commitment, I discovered what many heterosexuals and homosexuals had discovered before me: that it is a troubling and troublesome mission. There's a disingenuous tendency, when discussing both homosexual and heterosexual emotional life, to glamorize and idealize the entire venture. To posit the possibility of a loving union, after all, is not to guarantee its achievement. There is also a lamentable inclination to believe that all conflicts can finally be resolved; that the homosexual Catholic's struggle can be removed by a simple theological *coup de main;* that the conflict is somehow deeper than many other struggles in the Church— of women, say, or of the divorced. The truth is that pain, as Christ taught, is not a reason to question truth; it may indeed be a reason to embrace it.

But it must also be true that to dismiss the possibility of a loving union for homosexuals at all—to banish from the minds and hearts of countless gay men and women the idea that they, too, can find solace and love in one another—is to create the conditions for a human etiolation that no Christian community can contemplate without remorse. What finally convinced me of the wrongness of the Church's teachings was not that they were intellectually so confused, but that in the circumstances of my own life—and of the lives I discovered around me—they seemed so destructive of the possibilities of human love and self-realization. By crippling the potential for connection and growth, the Church's teachings created a dynamic that in practice led not to virtue but to pathology; by requiring the first lie in a human life, which would lead to an entire battery of others, they contorted human beings into caricatures of solitary eccentricity, frustrated bitterness, incapacitating anxiety—and helped perpetuate all the human wickedness and cruelty and insensitivity that such lives inevitably carry in their wake. These doctrines could not in practice do what they wanted to do: They could not both affirm human dignity and deny human love.

This truth is not an argument; it is merely an observation. But observations are at the heart not simply of the Church's traditional Thomist philosophy but also of the phenomenological vision of the current pope. To observe these things, to affirm their truth, is not to oppose the Church but to hope in it, to believe in it as a human institution that is yet the eternal vessel of God's love. It is to say that such lives as those of countless gay men and lesbians must ultimately affect the Church not because our lives are perfect, or without contradiction, or without sin, but because our lives are in some sense also the life of the Church.

I remember, in my own life, the sense of lung-filling exhilaration I felt as my sexuality began to be incorporated into my life, a sense that was not synonymous with recklessness or self-indulgence—although I was not immune from those things, either—but a sense of being suffused at last with the possibility of being fully myself before those I loved and before God. I remember the hopefulness of parents regained and friendships restored in a life that, for all its vanities, was at least no longer premised on a lie covered over by a career. I remember the sense a few months ago in a pew in a cathedral, as I reiterated the same pre-communion litany of prayers that I had spoken some twenty years earlier, that, for the first time, the love the Church had always taught that God held for me was tangible and redemptive. I had never felt it fully before; and, of course, like so many spiritual glimpses, I have rarely felt it since. But I do know that it was conditioned not on the possibility of purity but on the possibility of honesty. That honesty is not something that can be bought or won in a moment. It is a process peculiarly prone to self-delusion and self-doubt. But it is one that, if it is to remain true to itself, the Church cannot resist forever.

This essay by an Orthodox rabbi

discussing his gayness sparked

heated debate when it appeared

in the Jewish intellectual journal

Tikkun. The author, who writes

under a pseudonym, wrestles

with his seemingly conflicting

identities.

12. RABBI YAAKOV LEVADO

Gayness and God

I AM AN ORTHODOX RABBI AND I AM GAY. FOR A LONG WHILE I DE-
nied, rejected, railed against this truth. The life story that I had wanted—
wife, kids, and a family, a home of Torah and *hesed*—turned out to be an
impossible fantasy. I have begun to shape a new life story. This essay is part
of that life story, and thus remains unfinished, part of a stream of consciousness rather than a systematic treatise.

It is hard to say how or when I came to know myself as a gay man. In
the beginning, it was just an array of bodily sensations. Sweaty palms, warm
face, and that excited sort of nervousness in your chest that you get when
in the company of certain people occurred without understanding. The arrival of the hormonal hurricane left me completely dumbfounded. Just
when my body should have fulfilled social expectations, it began to trans-
gress them. I had no physical response to girls. But I was physically pulled,
eyes and body, toward guys. I remember my head turning sharply once in
the locker room for an athletic boy whom I admired. At the time, I must
have noticed my body's involuntary movement, but it meant nothing to

me. I understood nothing. How could I? I had no idea what it meant to be homosexual. *Faggot* or *homo* were words reserved for the boys hounded for being passive, or unathletic. None of this said anything about sexual attraction. There were no categories for this experience, no way to explain the strange muscle spasms, the warm sensation on my face, or the flutter in my chest. Not until years later, after countless repetitions of such events, did it slowly, terrifyingly, breathe through to my consciousness.

When other boys were becoming enraptured by girls, I found my rapture in learning Torah. I was thrilled by the sprawling rabbinic arguments, the imaginative plays on words, and the demand for meaning everywhere. *Negiah,* the prohibition to embrace, kiss, or even touch girls until marriage was my saving grace. The premarital sexual restraint of the Halacha was a perfect mask not only to the world but to myself.

My years in yeshiva were spectacular, in some measure because they were so intensely fueled by a totally denied sexuality. There were many *bachurim* (students) in the yeshiva whose intense and passionate learning was energized with repressed sexual energy. For me, the environment deflected sexual energy and generated it as well. The male spirit and energy I felt in yeshiva was both nourishing and frustrating. I do not know if I was alone among my companions or not. From those early years, I remember no signs by which I could have clearly read my gayness or anyone else's. I only know that I was plagued with stomachaches almost every morning.

Later, on one desperate occasion, beset with an increased awareness of my attraction to a fellow yeshiva student, I visited a sage, Rav Eliashuv, who lives in one of the most secluded right-wing Orthodox communities in Jerusalem. He was old and in failing health, but still taking visitors who daily waited in an anteroom for hours for the privilege of speaking with him for a few minutes. Speaking in Hebrew, I told him what, at the time, I felt was the truth. "Master, I am attracted to both men and women. What shall I do?" He responded, "My dear one, then you have twice the power of love. Use it carefully." I was stunned. I sat in silence for a moment, waiting for more. "Is that all?" I asked. He smiled and said, "That is all. There is nothing more to say."

Rav Eliashuv's words calmed me, permitting me to forget temporarily the awful tensions that would eventually overtake me. His trust and support buoyed me above my fears. I thought that as a bisexual I could have a wider and richer emotional life and perhaps even a deeper spiritual life than is common—and still marry and have a family.

For a long while I felt a self-acceptance that carried me confidently into rabbinical school. I began rabbinical training with great excitement and a sense of promise. At the center of my motivations were those powerful rabbinic traditions that had bowled me over in my early adolescence. I wanted more than anything else to learn and to teach Torah in its full depth and breadth. I finished rabbinical school, still dating and carefully avoiding any physical expression and took my first jobs as a rabbi. There were many failed relationships with wonderful women who could not understand why things just didn't work out. Only after knocking my shins countless times into the hard wood of this truth was I able fully to acknowledge that I am gay.

It has taken a number of years to sift through the wreckage of "my life as I wanted it" to discover "my life as it is." It has taken more time to exorcise the self-hatred that feeds on shattered hopes and ugly stereotypes. I am still engaged in that struggle. I have yet to receive the new tablets, the whole ones, that will take their place in the Ark beside the broken ones. Rav Nachman of Bratzlav teaches that there is nothing so whole as a broken heart. It is in his spirit that I continue to try to make sense of my life.

Although much has changed in the past few years as I have accepted my gayness, much remains the same. I am still a rabbi, and I am still deeply committed to God, Torah, and Israel. My religious life had always been directed by the desire to be a servant of the Lord. None of that has changed. The question is an old one, merely posed anew as I strive to integrate being gay into my life. Given that I am gay, what is it that the God of Israel wants of me?

Of course, many will hear this as an illegitimate question—fallacious in thinking that the God of Israel can somehow accept and move beyond my gayness. Leviticus 18:22 instructs: "Do not lie with a male as one lies with a woman, it is an abhorrence." I do not propose to reject this or any text. For the present, I have no plausible halachic method of interpreting this text in a manner that permits homosexual sex.

As a traditionalist, I hesitate to overturn cultural norms in a flurry of revolutionary zeal. I am committed to a slower and more cautious process of change, which must always begin internally. Halacha, the translation of sacred text into norm, as an activity, is not designed to effect social revolution. It is a society-building enterprise that maintains internal balance by reorganizing itself in response to changing social realities. When social conditions shift, we experience the halachic reapplication as the proper commitment to the Torah's original purposes. That shift in social consciousness in regard to homosexuality is a long way off.

If I have any argument, it is not to press for a resolution, but for a deeper understanding of homosexuality. Within the living Halacha are voices in tension, divergent strands in an imaginative legal tradition that are brought to bear on the real lives of Jews. In order to know how to shape a halachic response to any living question, what is most demanded of us is a deep understanding of the Torah and an attentive ear to the people who struggle with the living question. Confronting new questions can often tease out of the tradition a *hiddush,* a new balancing of the voices and values that have always been there. There is no conclusive *psak halacha* (legal ruling) without the hearing of personal testimonies, and so far, gay people have not been asked to testify to their experience. How can halachists possibly rule responsibly on a matter so complex and so deeply foreign, without a sustained effort at understanding? Whatever the halachic argument will be, we will need to know much more about homosexuality to ensure that people are treated not merely as alien objects of a system but as persons within it. Halachists will need to include in their deliberations the testimony of gay people who wish to remain faithful to the Torah. Unimagined strategies, I believe, will appear under different conditions. We cannot know in advance the outcome of such an investigation. Still, one wonders what the impact might be if Orthodox rabbis had to face the questions posed by traditional Jews, persons they respect and to whom they feel responsible, who are gay.

There is one quasi-halachic issue I must address—that of choice. One of the mitigating factors in halachic discourse is the presence of free will in matters of law. A command is only meaningful in the context of our freedom to obey or disobey. Thus the degree of choice involved in homosexuality is central to the shaping of a halachic response. There is indeed a certain percentage of gay people who claim to exercise some volition in their sexual choices. But for the vast majority of gay people, there is no "choice" in the ordinary sense of the word. Gay feelings are hardwired into our bodies, minds, and hearts. The strangeness and mystery of sexuality is universal. What we share, gay or straight, is the surprising "queerness" of all sexual desire. The experience of heterosexuals may seem less outlandish for its being more common, but all sexual feeling is deeply mysterious, beyond explanation or a simple notion of choice.

The Halacha addresses activities, however, not sexual identities; thus, in halachic Judaism there is no such thing as a gay identity—there are only sexual impulses to control. The tradition describes all sexual desire as *yetzer ha'ra* (evil impulse), rife with chaotic and destructive possibilities. Heterosexual desire is redeemed and integrated back into the system through a series of prescriptions and prohibitions that channel sexuality and limit its range of expression. Confined within marriage, giving and receiving sexual pleasure, even in non-procreative ways, is raised to the level of mitzvah.

Homosexual desire, in contrast, is not seen as redeemable and thus remains an implacable *yetzer ha 'ra* that needs to be defeated rather than channeled. In this argument, gay people are treated as people with a dangerous and destructive sexual desire which must be repressed. The spiritual task of a gay person is to overcome that *yetzer ha 'ra* which prods one to have erotic relations with members of the same sex.

The unfairness of this argument begins with the recasting of homosexuals as heterosexuals with perverse desires. The Torah is employed to support the idea that there is only sexuality, heterosexuality. God confirms heterosexual desire, giving heterosexuals the opportunity to enjoy love and companionship. With the impossibility of another sexuality comes the implicit assumption that gay people can "become" straight and marry and indeed should do so.

This has in fact been the ordinary state of affairs of many, if not most, gay men and women throughout history. I know a number of gay (or bisexual) men who have married and sustain relationships with their wives. Of course, most have had an affair at some point which did not end their marriage. Two gay rabbis I know were married and are now divorced, and a third remains happily married, surviving recurrent bouts of depression and emotional exhaustion. What disturbs me most in this sometimes heroic attempt at approximating the traditional ideal is the cost to the heterosexual spouse. While in my first rabbinical post, I decided to come out to an older rabbi and seek his advice. He counseled me to find a woman and marry. I asked him if I was duty-bound to tell her about my attractions to men and my general sexual disinterest in women. He said no. I was shocked to hear that it was all right to deceive a woman who could very easily be damaged by such a marriage. It made no sense to me. Surely some heterosexual women might be willing to marry a gay friend who could provide children and be a wonderful father. There have been rare instances of gay women and men who have worked out marriages where the "uninterest" was mutual. I struggled for a number of years to find such a woman, gay or straight, with whom to begin a family. Sometimes I still torment myself to think that this is all possible—when it is not. I still feel ripped apart by these feelings—wanting a woman at the Shabbat table and a man in my bed. If I am judged for some failure, perhaps it will be that I could not choose the Shabbat table over the bed, either for myself, or for the forlorn woman, who, after dinner wants the comfort of a man who wants her back.

Having rejected this option, the standard Orthodox position is to require celibacy. Many recent articles and responsa regard gay sex as indistinguishable from adultery, incest, or bestiality. The heterosexual is asked to limit sexuality to the marital bed, to non-relatives, to human beings; the homosexual is asked to live a loveless life. I have lived portions of my adult life as a celibate clergyman. While it can have spiritual potency for a Moses or a Ben Azzai, who abandoned sexual life for God or Torah, it is not a Jewish way to live. Always sleeping alone, in a cold bed, without touch, without the daily physical interplay of lives morning and night—this celibate scenario is life-denying and, for me, has always led to a shrinking of spirit. What sort of Torah, what voice of God would demand celibacy from all gay people? Such a reading of divine intent is nothing short of cruel.

Many gay people now and in the past have been forced to purchase social acceptance and God's love through a denial of affection and comfort, and, worse, a denial of self. Today many simply leave Judaism behind in order to salvage a sense of dignity and to build a life. This understanding of homosexuality provides no legitimized wholesome context for sexuality; no *kedusha* and no *kedushin*.

I have come to understand my gayness as akin to my Jewishness: It is integral to my sense of self. Others may misunderstand and even wish me harm, but from myself I cannot hide. I did not choose it, and yet now that it is mine, I do. It is neither a mental illness nor a moral failing, but a contour of my soul. To deny it would be self-defeating. There is nothing left to do but celebrate it. Whether in or out of the given halachic rubric, I affirm my desire for a full life, for love, and for sexual expression. Given that I am gay, and cannot be otherwise, and given that I do not believe that God would demand that I remain loveless and celibate, I have chosen to seek a committed love, a man with whom to share my life.

But so little of life is carried on in the bedroom. When I indeed find a partner, what sort of life do we build together? What is it that the God of Israel wants of me in regard to family and community? Struggling with God and with Torah as a gay person was just the beginning. To be Jewish is to be grounded in the continuity of the Jewish people as a witness—a holy people, a light amongst the nations—a blessing to all the families of the earth. How does a gay person help to shape the continuity of the Jewish people? The carrying forth of the Jewish people is accomplished by marriage and procreation. It is both a tool of the Abrahamic covenant and its most profound meaning statement.

We are a people on the side of life—new life, more life, fuller life. The creation story invited the rabbis to read God's blessing of "be fruitful and multiply" as a command to have two children, a male and a female. Every Jewish child makes the possibility of the Torah's promise of a perfected world more real, more attainable. Abraham and Sarah transmit the vision by having children. Often the portrayal of blessing includes being surrounded with many children. Childlessness is a punishment and curse in the tradition, barrenness a calamity.

Gay life does not prevent the possibility of producing or raising Jewish children, but it makes those options very complicated. Being gay means that the ordinary relationship between making love and having children is severed. There is a deep challenge to the structure of Judaism, since its very transmission is dependent on both relationship and reproduction. For Jews who feel bound by *mitzvot*, bound by the duty to ensure that life conquers death, the infertility of our loving is at the core of our struggle to understand ourselves in the light of the Torah.

This problem, among others, lies at the root of much of the Jewish community's discomfort with gay people. To a people that was nearly destroyed fifty years ago, gay love seems irresponsible. Jews see the work of their lives in light of the shaping of a world for their children. By contrast, gay people appear narcissistic and self-indulgent. Gay people's sexuality is thus a diversion from the tasks of Jewish family and the survival that it symbolizes, and is perceived as marginal to the Jewish community because we are shirkers of this most central and sacred of communal tasks.

This challenge also has a moral chord which strikes deep into the problems of gay subculture. The tradition understood parenting as one of the major moral crucibles for human development. No judge could serve without first being a parent for fear that without the experience of parenting one could grasp neither human vulnerability nor responsibility. Being heterosexual carries one down a path that demands years of selfless loving in the rearing of children. While not all straight couples have children, and some gay couples become surrogate or adoptive parents, the norm is shaped less by choice and more by biology. Given that gay people do not fall into childbearing as an ordinary outcome of coupling, how do we find our place in the covenant? And what of the moral training that caring for children provides, how do we make up for that? Is there another job to be done that requires our service to God and to the Jewish people? Of all the problems entailed in gay sexuality, this one looms for me, both spiritually and emotionally.

Although there is no obvious biblical resource for this dilemma, there are biblical writers who struggled to address God's will in very new social circumstances. Isaiah was one such writer who bridged the worlds before and after the Exile. Some familiar passages have become charged for me with new meaning. In these verses, Isaiah is speaking to his ancient Israelite community and trying to convince them that God's covenantal plan for Israel is larger than they think. The covenant begins with Abraham and Sarah but has become much more than a family affair. He speaks to two obvious outsider groups in chapter 56, the *b 'nai ha 'nechar*, the foreigners of non-Israelite birth, and the *sarisim,* the eunuchs:

> Let not the foreigner say,
> Who has attached himself to the Lord,
> "The Lord will keep me separate from His people";
> And let not the eunuch say,
> "I am a withered tree."

In the Talmud, a eunuch is not necessarily a castrated male, but a male who is not going to reproduce for various reasons *(Yevamot* 80b). Why does Isaiah turn his attention here to the foreigners and the eunuchs? In the chain of the covenantal family, the foreigner has no past and the eunuch no future. They both seem excluded from the covenantal frame of reference. It is this "exclusion" that the prophet addresses:

> For thus said the Lord:
> "As for the eunuchs who keep my sabbaths,
> Who have chosen what I desire
> And hold fast to My covenant—
> I will give them, in My House
> And within my walls,
> A monument and a name
> Better than sons or daughters.
> I will give them an everlasting name
> Which shall not perish."

The prophet comforts the pain of eunuchs with the claim that there are other ways in which to observe, fulfill, and sustain the covenant. There is something more permanent than the continuity of children. In God's House, the achievement of each individual soul has account. A name in the Bible is the path toward the essence, the heart of being. It is passed on to progeny. But there is another sort of name, a name better than the one sons or daughters carry. The covenant is carried forward by those who live it out, in the present. Loyalty to the covenant is measured in God's House in such a way that even if one's name is not passed on through children, an eternal name will nonetheless be etched into the walls. Isaiah offers a place to the placeless, an alternative service to the person who cannot be part of the family in other ways:

> As for foreigners
> Who attach themselves to the Lord,
> to be His servants—
> All who keep the sabbath and do not profane it,
> And who hold fast to my covenant—
> I will bring them to my sacred mount
> And let them rejoice in my house of prayer.
> Their burnt offerings and sacrifices
> Shall be welcome on My altar;
> For My House shall be called
> A House of prayer for all peoples.
> Thus declares the Lord God, Who gathers the dispersed of Israel:
> I will gather still more to those already gathered.

So inclusive is God's plan for Israel in the world that any foreigner can join. The notion of conversion, so obvious to us now, was a striking innovation for the generation of Isaiah. Conversion is about rewriting the past. Like adoption, conversion redefines the meaning of parents and family. Birth and lineage are not discarded. The central metaphor for Israel is still family. But Isaiah and later tradition open up another avenue into the covenant. Those with no future are promised a future in the House of the Lord; those with no past are nevertheless included in Israel's destiny.

God can only require the doable. A foreigner cannot choose a different birth, or the eunuch a different procreative possibility. Gay people cannot be asked to be straight, but they can be asked to "hold fast to the covenant."

God will work the story out and link the loose ends as long as we hold fast to the covenant.

Holding fast to the covenant demands that I fulfill the *mitzvot* that are in my power to fulfill. I cannot marry and bear children, but there are other ways to build a family. Surrogacy and adoption are options. I have a number of friends, gay and lesbian, who have found ways to build wonderfully loving families. If these prove infeasible, the tradition considers a teacher similar to a parent in life-giving and thus frames a way that the *mitzvah* of procreation can be symbolically fulfilled.

A special obligation may fall upon those who do not have children to attend charitably to the needs and the protection of children in distress. However, childlessness offers more than a call to activism and philanthropy in the defense of children. It can be received as way to live with unusually open doors. I have always felt that the open tent of Sarah and Abraham was loving and generous in the extreme because they were, for the bulk of their lives, childless. With no children upon whom to focus their affection, the parents par excellence of the covenant spent lifetimes parenting other people's grown children.

Holding fast to the covenant demands that I seek a path towards sanctity in gay sexual life. The Torah has much to say about the way people create *kedusha* in their sexual relationships. The values of marriage, monogamy, modesty, and faithfulness which are central to the tradition's view of holiness need to be applied in ways that shape choices and life styles.

Holding fast to the covenant means that being gay does not free one from the fulfillment of *mitzvot*. The complexities generated by a verse in Leviticus need not unravel my commitment to the whole of the Torah. There are myriad Jewish concerns, moral, social, intellectual, and spiritual, that I cannot abandon. Being gay need not overwhelm the rest of Jewish life. Single-issue communities are political rather than religious. Religious communities tend to be comprehensive of the human condition. The richness of Jewish living derives in part from its diversity of attention, its fullness.

For gay Orthodox Jews, this imagination of engagement between ourselves and the tradition is both terribly exciting and depressing. Regretfully, the communities that embrace us, both gay and Jewish, also reject us. The Jewish community wishes that we remain invisible. The gay community is largely unsympathetic and often hostile to Judaism. There are some in the gay community who portray Judaism as the original cultural source of homophobia. More often, the lack of sympathy toward Jewish observance derives from the single-mindedness of gay activism. Liberation communities rarely have room for competing loyalties.

Gay synagogues have filled a void for many, providing a place of dignity in a Jewish community. This work is part of a movement toward a fuller integration in the larger Jewish community for which most gay Jews long. Gay-friendly synagogues may well point the way, modeling a community of families and singles, young and old, straight and gay that is in spirit much closer to my hopeful future imagination than anything yet.

Gay Jews who wish to be part of an Orthodox community will find very few synagogues in which there is some level of understanding and tolerance. Some gay Jews attend Orthodox services and remain closeted in their communities. It is crucial that Orthodox rabbis express a loving acceptance for known gays in their synagogues even if public legitimation is now impossible. Attacks on homosexuality from the pulpit are particularly painful to those who have remained connected to the traditional synagogue, despite the hardships.

For the present, in regard to sexual behavior, I personally have chosen to accept a certain risk and violate the Halacha as it is presently articulated, in the hope of a subsequent, more accepting halachic expression. I realize that this is "civil disobedience." It is not the system itself which I challenge but its application to an issue that has particular meaning for me and for those like me. There is always the possibility that I am wrong. Ultimately, the halachic risks that I take are rooted in my personal relationship with God, Whom I will face in the end. It is this faith that makes me both confident and suspicious of myself.

I have, admittedly, a rather privatized form of community. I am closeted and have chosen to write this essay in anonymity to preserve what is still most precious to me: the teaching of Torah and caring for my community of Jews. What concerns me most is neither rejection by the Orthodox community, nor the loss of my particular pulpit. Were I to come out, I suspect that the controversy would collapse my life, my commitments, my identity as a teacher of Torah, into my gayness. Still, the secrecy and the shadowy existence of the closet are morally repugnant and emotionally draining. I cannot remain forever in darkness. I thank God that for the time being, the Torah still sheds ample light.

I have a small circle of friends, gay and straight, men and women with whom I share a sense of community. We are looking for other tradition-centered Jews who can help build a place that embraces both the Torah and gay people. Not a synagogue, not a building, but a place for all the dispersed who are in search of community with Israel and communion with God. In this place, this House of the Lord, now somewhat hypothetical and private, and soon, I pray, to be concrete and public, those of us who have withered in the darkness, or in the light of day have been banished, will discover our names etched upon the walls.

Postscript

I wrote "Gayness and God" only four years ago, and while it may appear insignificant to those who live in more open societies, much has changed in the Orthodox world in that short span of time. Four years ago the closet was darker and the door shut tighter for most traditional Jews. Social attitudes in the Orthodox community toward homosexuality have moved in two opposing directions due to the greater social acceptance in the larger society. The most important change is that in the past four years the topic has been raised repeatedly in articles, conferences, and newsletters. In short, as homosexuality, as an issue, has come out of the closet, things are worse and better.

Anti-homosexual rhetoric in the Orthodox community has become more shrill over the last few years, with various leaders and writers using gay liberation as a symbol of social and familial disintegration and expressing shock and horror at Reform Judaism for its acceptance of gay commitment ceremonies and gay rabbis. But the effect of the rhetoric has often been to the advantage of those pressing for gay inclusion. A gay and lesbian student organization established by a few graduate students in a professional school associated with Yeshiva University drew public outrage from religious authorities, university students, and community members. The president of the university, Norman Lamm, chose to put the issue to bed by claiming that public funds necessary for the university depended upon a liberal policy in regard to student associations. The public debate has invited Orthodox rabbis to speak from the pulpit on the issue, mostly in unaccepting ways, and be confronted later by parents of gay children and by gay Jews themselves who take the opportunity to come out to their rabbis.

Gay traditional Jews have not come out en masse, but they have begun in larger numbers to make themselves present to each other. Today there is a Gay and Lesbian Yeshiva Day School Alumni group that meets monthly in New York City, has a membership of nearly a hundred people, and even has a web site. Until recently, it was impossible to speak about AIDS prevention in the Orthodox community for fear that any talk was an incitement to promiscuous gay sex. Now there is an AIDS Hotline for Orthodox Jews which especially targets the Haredi neighborhoods of Brooklyn and Queens. Until recently it was common for Jewish hospital groups in religious communities to actively avoid visiting Jewish AIDS patients. Today there are Orthodox synagogues in Manhattan and Queens that have special *Bikkur Holim* groups that deliver meals and visit Jewish AIDS patients.

Fifteen years ago the boundary issue was feminism. Orthodoxy surely constructed its difference in a number of ways, but anti-feminism was a difference that proved evocative both theoretically and pragmatically for its constituents. Until the line was drawn openly, it could not be contested. Once the conversations about women's roles were engaged, everyone was led into consideration and dialogue. This past February one thousand people gathered for a conference on Orthodoxy and Feminism. It used to be an oxymoron to say that one was an Orthodox feminist. It no longer is. Today the line in the sand for many, the boundary case that distinguishes the halachic Jew from the rest, is homosexuality. While the issues are potentially more explosive and the concerned parties much less numerically significant, still engagement begins a conversation. Public formulation actually works to problematize the issues and raise to consciousness the human concerns that expand the possibilities.

After I wrote "Gayness and God" I received many letters, mostly from Orthodox or once-Orthodox gay men and lesbians grateful for the attempt to make sense of their experience. I met Jews who had been self-accepting homosexuals in their college years and in their thirties were turning toward observance and Torah study as much deeper resources of humanity and identity than those which they had found elsewhere. I received letters from a number of Orthodox rabbis, all but one sincerely engaging if not supportive. I was showered with support from family and friends.

Recently, one Orthodox rabbi was asked by a group of young leaders about his stance on homosexuality. In the public forum he said that only a few years before he knew exactly what he thought about homosexuality and would easily articulate his halachic position. He now admits that he is humble before a profound human dilemma and prefers less rhetoric and more understanding. He doesn't know what he thinks, nor is he quite sure what to say, and that is how he responds when asked.

It takes great faith to stand at the threshold of another human being and really listen. It takes great courage to do so before a person whose inner life is terribly alien, whose experience touches dark fears, or whose commitments seem to shape a threatening ideological frame to thousands of years of tradition. It is much easier, safer, to have the procrustean bed already made. It is true that in most settings those beds are ready made with all the proper arrangements for stretching our legs or cutting off our feet. Most Orthodox rabbis are not like my rabbi-friends or the rabbi mentioned above.

Often over the past twenty years I have wanted to storm the heavens, to demand of God an explanation, a reconciliation, a response. In the language of Judith Plaskow, I am standing again at Sinai, insisting to be heard and to hear anew. One of my dearest colleagues is an Orthodox rabbi schooled in black-hat yeshivot and a psychologist. A few years ago he accosted me as we walked in New York City to a kosher diner. He told me that he'd had enough of my self-doubt and that he didn't even see how I could make do with mere self-acceptance. "You have no choice," he said, "but to celebrate your gayness." I began to cry on Thirty-seventh Street not knowing what had burst in me. Later I understood my response as surprise. For years my Orthodox compatriots, friends, and family had accompanied me to this Sinai not by the force of a rational argument or a textual proof but by having come to share my demand for sense, my longing for wholeness. I had just not thought to look behind me.

13. HARRY HAY

Harry Hay, the gay-liberation pioneer who founded the Mattachine Society in 1951, continues as the millennium draws near to buck conventional wisdom. Building on Native American concepts, he insists in this speech that gay people are neither male nor female, but a separate, spiritual, "Third Gender."

Remarks on Third Gender

IT IS TIME FOR US TO REJECT THE *LIE* BY WHICH ORGANIZED RELI- gions have attempted to obliterate us for two millennia. Sexual orientation isn't the *only* difference between Us and the Heteros. As a result of the way we had been malignantly demeaned and diminished over the centuries, *it is the only difference LEFT* between Us and the Heteros. It's time we took a leaf from the lessons Third Gender brothers in other cultures have to teach us in how to re-earn the respect and gratitude of our Hetero Communities for the *different people that we are*—as well as for the talents and gifts we bring to share. In other parts of Earth, in the Third and Fourth Worlds, sedentary village cultures and quasi-civilized tribes—some of which rose to city-state status and then subsided again, some whose traditions still pertain today—noticed that though most men seemed naturally inclined to be competitive, to be warriors, hunters, and fathers, always there were those some who seemed to be *men not for killing and men not for war.* These ones were gentler types—they seemed to want to celebrate their brothers rather than to compete with them. These ones seemed to have particular powers of insight—they could distinguish between the seen and the unseen; they could sense the anguish in someone's heart and so act out stories or songs that magically dispelled the torment. In later centuries this would be called Theatre. They could mediate between the known and the unknown, and seemed not always so awed or terrified of the dread Supernaturals that they couldn't talk to them, or send messages to the shadowy Powers beyond the sky. In later centuries, this would be called prayer, and the agency bringing not only rain but many other needed changes of circumstances would be known as Temple.

Because these brothers' contributions were essential to the cultural and spiritual well-being of the people, these different gentle ones were treasured—they would be seen as men of a different Gender. If warriors and husbandmen were men of a First Gender, then these Differents would be men of a Third Gender—and so they are still perceived, *and loved and treasured,* by the largest tribe of Native Americans in the American Southwest today, the Diné, whom the whitemen call Navajo. The Diné say, "When all the *nádleehé* [third-gender men and women] are gone, that will be the end of the Navaho."[1] And, equally, such different gentle men are seen among the largest tribe in West Africa, the Hausa, as spirit mediators, while in Hawaii, contemporary inheritors of the traditional *mahu* role are playing a role in reviving the ancient art of hula dancing.[2] In smaller, more compact Native American communities such as Zuni, in western New Mexico, the supernatural counterpart of the *lhamana,* Kolhamana, traditionally represented the balancing of men and women.[3]

We Third Gender men of Indo-European stock equally have similar talents and treasures to share. Living in the cracks of Hetero Western World sidewalks for a millennium, we actually have learned a great deal, should we finally begin to put it to use. Because we Queers need nothing from either Hetero men or Hetero women, we have learned to see them as *they would like to be seen*—in makeup, in hairdress, in design, and in tailoring, for instance. Because we Queers need nothing from either Hetero men or Hetero women that we couldn't just as easily supply one another, we have learned over the centuries *to listen to them nonjudgmentally.* And this talent, now, can stand us in very good stead for its many modern uses and applications.

Over the centuries, listening to and observing Western World parliaments, we may have learned that for any self-loving, self-respecting minority, the so-called Democratic process is never more than a tyranny of the majority. In the twenty-first-century world, when most urban areas in America will be aggregates of plural societies, it would be unconscionable for minorities to be always *competing with* one another and even more infuriating to have them always *voting against* one another. The only possible form of governance shall have to be an advance of political consciousness, in the electorate, to the recognition that, henceforth, they must learn to function and govern by means of the consensus process. The key to functioning by consensus is learning *to listen to one another nonjudgmentally!* Radical Faeries have discovered that, by learning to slip the nonessential Hetero-male ego, we can really listen to one another with our inner ears. Listening with inner ears to discern principles held in common, community councils or coalitions might be enabled to collectively develop mutually respectful agreements on issues. To facilitate governing by the process of mutually respectful sharing consensus, Radical Faeries and, if they were of a mind, all gay brothers and sisters, exercising their innate inclinations to process in subject-subject consciousness, might make a major contribution to society by helping to create the most politically healthy of all possible communities. If Third Gender men and women could become facilitator-specialists in such governing processes, we might discover a loving appreciative need for us.

We need to make the leap in consciousness for a second reason, as well—to reclaim our own sense of an ancient and historical legitimacy, parallels to which are continually being held open for us to duplicate by our brothers of the Third and Fourth Worlds. We made a wrong assessment of the strength we would garner as a result of claiming minority status. When our Gay Liberationist Zappers hit the bricks in the 1970s shouting "We're a minority—and we got rights just like every other minority," we hadn't reread our history books very carefully. When "the huddled masses yearning to be free" emigrated to the United States in the nineteenth century to earn a place for themselves in the bright and beckoning American Dream, they all, naturally, brought gifts to trade—gifts the United States was hungry for—huge quantities of raw labor power. What had *our* Gang brought?

Well, as a matter of fact they hadn't, consciously, brought anything—

just their noisy deviant sexuality, which three-quarters of the country took one look at and said, "We don't like it, and it's *wrong* anyway." Of all the minorities who came petitioning for the privileges of first-class citizenship, *we* alone hadn't thought to bring anything to share *or* trade. (As a matter of fact, we had, innately, brought tons of talent and treasures to share. But, liberated young gays pouring out of our closets, we just hadn't thought about anything further than getting *out*. Truth to tell, in our middle-class arrogance we just *hadn't thought!*)

But the notion of developing Third Gender is ready and willing to pay off. I spoke to a very politically involved Black Hetero friend in recent times and mentioned that I felt it might be time for us gays to reclaim our Third Gender responsibilities, and he said, "Third Gender responsibilities? You've never said that before. That makes good political sense—that socially communicates something. Third Gender men are respected as valuable persons in a number of tribal societies."

At this point in time, I don't suppose we can expect the "bottom-line-driven" Western World Heteros, still mired in their almost obsolete and quite lethal subject-object consciousness, to be panting to discover how we Queers are necessary to *their* survival. But, to an ever-growing number of them, it is now becoming recognized that we who belong to the Third Gender carry a capacity for being able to leap to and develop a new and vitally needed social consciousness—what Radical Faeries know as subject-subject consciousness—within which the collective functioning by sharing consensus is *the natural way to go.* It could be that we are expecting too much for the Heteros to comprehend how much they need to learn to survive themselves!

So it is now that I am proposing that we take a hand-up example from our potential allies in the Third and Fourth Worlds, whose cultures may well be overtaking, and even outnumbering, our Hetero Western so-called Free World sensibilities in the not-too-far distant first decades of the twenty-first century. I propose that we gay men *of all colors* prepare to present ourselves as the gentle, noncompetitive Third Gender men *of the Western World* with whole wardrobes and garages crammed with cultural and spiritual contributions to share.

In the November 8, 1992, "Opinion" section of the *Los Angeles Times,* columnist Richard Rodriguez said, "There is a great moan in the American heart. Something is wrong with the way we live. We have lost the knack, or the gift, of intimacy. We do not know how to love one another." I would submit that the American Gay/Lesbian Community, having shouldered almost entirely by itself the mobilizing of American cities to confront and contain the pandemic of AIDS—*with little help from criminally insensitive Congresses and three Administrations*—has rekindled vast surges of community groups reaching out with love to one another on a scale not seen in decades.

Equally would I submit that Third Gender Faerie men, in addition to forming superlative support groups for their own ailing brothers and lovers, are developing through their many Gatherings across both the United States and Canada (not to slight "far Australia") whole new dimensions in the perceptions and sharings of intimacy. It is time for us Third Gender folk, actually, *to rejoice in the gifts we bring!* And, so saying, in such an endeavor—as my Hetero Black Friend and well-wisher suggested earlier—we even might, in collective Gala, discover new Faerie ways to make such contributions both substantive and politically creative.

Notes

1. Hill, Willard W., "The Status of the Hermaphrodite and Transvestite in Navaho Culture," *American Anthropologist* 37 (1935): 274.
2. Robertson, Carol E., "The Māhū of Hawai'i," *Feminist Studies* 15(2) (1989): 313–26.
3. Roscoe, Will, *The Zuni Man-Woman* (Albuquerque: University of New Mexico Press, 1991).

14. MARK THOMPSON

Mark Thompson's anthologies *Gay Spirit* and *Gay Soul* blazed the trail into gay men's open discussion of spirituality. This essay, adapted from his book *Gay Body,* draws on "shadow theory" in suggesting that gay men "own" their emotional wounds and transform them into opportunities for healing.

Making a New Myth

THE REAL PROMISE OF BEING A QUEER MAN IN AMERICA TODAY IS that we are dynamic in a deadened world. Having given birth to ourselves, we also have the chance of giving birth to a new myth. Nothing should be more important to us right now than to follow its call. Finding the meaning of who we truly are requires no less than this.

It is important to realize how integral myths are to our lives, for they are the building-blocks of daily reality. Myths are the metaphors of the collective unconscious, and are ideally meant to instruct, inspire, and transform. They are distilled over time and by numerous retellings until only the universal remains. Like a river flowing to the sea, a myth is destined to become part of a greater whole as it wends its way through history.

But because we cannot see the myths that substantiate our lives any more than a fish can notice the water in which it swims, finding the source of our beliefs is an often elusive task. Still, if they are to continue to serve us meaningfully, myths must be refreshed or translated into modern metaphorical language and then read anew. The notion of a modern homosexual—or "gay person"—is one myth that warrants our re-examination.

Like a brick through glass, gay liberation's fiery first years rudely assailed society's homophobic assumptions. Drawing energy from concomitant struggles for peace and justice, queer revolutionaries generated new ideology to counter the old dogma of sin and sickness. But as important as messages of pride and self-determination are, the notion of a "liberated" gay person is still an historical construction spun from the same basic system of values which oppress us. The falsity of that underlying invention has kept us false to ourselves to this day.

The word *homosexual* was coined more than a hundred years ago by a European physician, during a time when many forms of human experience were being categorized and contained. As if the seizing and maiming of the earth wasn't enough, the vast and still uncharted landscape of the soul had to be dissected, too. Needless to say, those responsible were sexist, racist men intent on propagating a patriarchal order in which sex, women, and nature are seen objectively; as objects and therefore as exploitable commodities.

In a world ruled through the reapportionment of language, words themselves become powerful political tools: If you name something, you control it, or at least have a way of defining its life energy. Therefore, to be a homosexual was to suffer the fate of being a "bad" heterosexual. In this way, we became a deviation of a correct model: a perversion to cure or extinguish.

The populist slogan, "Gay is good," is a bald rebuttal to the construct of a good-versus-bad sexual identity. Still, the very idea of that "goodness" remains within the domain of the central governing myth of homosexuality itself. Communicating the truths of so-called gay people, a people whose place in the world has been largely self-won and whose culture today is undeniably real, does not rectify the problem. Resolving the paradox of what we've been labeled and who we might intuit ourselves to actually be is one of the great moral challenges yet before us. We must always be rejuvenating the language of self.

Sorting out fact from fiction, true meaning from a false myth, is trickier than it would first appear, however. Where and to whom do we look for answers? The morally charged dynamic of good or bad is just one dualism that gay people find themselves dangled between. The argument of nature versus nurture is also waged about our lives. Are we "essentially" gay—that is, born this way? Or has our identity as homosexuals been "made," mandated by society as a means to control its gender-variant members?

I believe answers exist outside the argument of nature versus nurture, labels of either one thing or only another. It is simply shortsighted, for instance, to identify too closely with the various forms of homosexuality on the planet that have preceded our own. Although the sentimental assumption of shared behavior across time and various cultures may soothe the itch for self-knowing, it can hardly remedy the deeper question.

The idea of same-sex love as a cultural creation, a juncture of polymorphous sexuality and historical circumstance, also offers only part of the solution. How ironic that the discourse about homosexuality—and *which* homosexuality, at that—is mired in the very system of perception which oppresses us. As long as the critical queries about our lives—Who are we? Where did we come from? What are we for?—remain in orbit around the false myth of the homosexual, we'll be at loggerheads in the dialectic of good/bad, hetero/homo, born this way/constructed.

The accepted role of shamans in various indigenous cultures offers one clue about who we may really be, as tenuous as that comparison may seem at first. Shamans are initiated into their work as mediators, healers, and soul guides through a ritual descent into the underworld, where they are symbolically dismembered and their bones scraped of flesh. Shamans are mortally wounded, and thus after their resurrection are endowed with the capacity to perceive the wounds of others.

What queer man who has struggled to gain consciousness about his true self has not felt the scrape of flesh from bone? It is a soul-making process sadly without context, an experience perhaps not even wanted, but one most of us go through nevertheless. When we descend through the wound, a part of who we think we are—or have been taught to be—dies as a result. Through this transmutational act, the archetype of the wounded healer is brought to the fore. And so, too, discovery of the gifts and powers that await those who live out its myth. Claiming the wound is our spiritual occasion: the royal road to coming out inside as the transformers, healers, and workers of wonder we have the potential to be.

Queer people are harbingers of a new way of seeing and being in the world: an ascending consciousness that will help carry the world of the old, dying myths we now live in toward a more inclusive reality. As traditional systems of belief are forced to change, gay and lesbian people will play a vital role in effecting that change.

When acting from our authentic selves, we evolve definitions of family, community, caregiving, of culture itself, even as that change continues to be resisted with an equal force. Before we can realize this potential, however, there is much inner work to do.

If being gay has taught me anything, it's that pride alone is not enough. Indeed, I now wonder, when does too much pride become hubris: a preening satisfaction with the self which ultimately defeats it? To come out to a world of gay affect is hardly a salvation when the inner world has been as devastated as it's been in nearly every queer life. What we can't see is exactly what hurts us the most. Not claiming the wound means abandoning it to shadow, and thus we are fated for failure time and again—until what is hidden is *seen*.

The gay pride movement has worked hard in rebuking bad fathers: from the sins of the patriarchy to the deficiencies of personal dads who didn't provide the nurturing we needed. Those bad fathers live within us still, but we're too shielded against the rage and pain all that poor parenting wreaked to see it. We look for this lost love in others who are similarly wounded and therefore are just as blind, only to wonder why it so often doesn't work out. And we clamor for acceptance by using the very myth that was devised to demonize us while secretly asking: Is that all? Bad fathers, bad myth: it's no wonder that we're so confused.

It is no longer enough to bargain for small favors: a bit of ghetto sidewalk, a new way to name the same old lie. Advancing conditions in the modern West have allowed us to come out at this moment in time yet have also defined us in the process in ways we have scarcely begun to know.

Gay men today are poised on the edge of two ways of being. We've endured as acquiescent sons of the matriarchal age, which historically ended more than four thousand years ago. At the same time, we're the sons of thoughtless fathers, whose current patriarchal age of miracles has been born out of plunder and destruction on a scale previously unimagined. Further familiarity with the Great Mother is not necessary; we bear her gifts and injury alike. Our task is to find the Good Father and realize his favor within ourselves. And then, ultimately, for each other.

Perhaps we gay men stand on the frontier of some enlightened place now forming, a new epoch fusing the matriarchy and patriarchy into a more androgynous wholeness. Two epochs of the world, two realms of the soul, out of balance and lacking unity—except in the lives of those who already exist between them.

If there is a New Age dawning, who would be better harbingers of it than members of the world's first postmodern tribe? It is a tribe with no land to call its own, consisting of queer folk who have crafted themselves from particles of worlds now disappeared and ebbing.

Seekers without portfolio, we queer men are no strangers to the wilderness. But finding our way home means leaving false sentiment behind: regret for fathers we never knew, longing for mothers who know us too well.

A queer soul in-the-making requires authenticity, relationship, delight, and eros. Only by risking to come out inside can we ever hope to keep on evolving our own myth.

15. CRAIG LUCAS

Best known for his screenplay for the breakthrough AIDS film *Longtime Companion,* Craig Lucas has experienced the tragedy of the disease in his own life. He wrote this raw and angry testimonial less than a year after his lover's death.

Postcard from Grief

MY LOVER DIED THIS YEAR ON JANUARY 5TH. WE WERE TOGETHER for eleven years. He was forty. His name was Timothy Scott Melester. He was a surgeon and an AIDS educator.

I find my way by sticking to simple declarative sentences: hand-holds over the swampy, rocky terrain of my terror and grief. After the initial crush of letters and flowers, phone calls and devotional meals, I went into a mania of work—writing plays and screenplays, attending rehearsals, traveling, seeing friends, tackling projects. I went through all of Tim's belongings and gave many of them away. I took off my wedding ring.

Now, seven months after the fact, the layers of shock are beginning to fall away and I am left with a feeling for which nothing in my life has prepared me: not religion, not politics, not philosophy. I have stopped running, and the waves are breaking over me in no regular pattern, each one bringing new sensations and stripping me further of my illusions: I know nothing about who I am, where I am going, what I believe, what I want. Tim was my anchor: his battle to live was my battle.

My closets and bookshelves are filled with his notes and textbooks from medical school. What happened to all that learning and effort? Where did it go? The four languages he taught himself to speak, and the two dead ones he learned to read—all the facts, the growing up, the struggle and ultimate joy of coming out to his friends and family, all the music he listened to, all the novels he devoured: Where are they now? So much wisdom and beauty and pain—vanished. Friends put me in touch with a medium and she convinced me that his spirit was present. Every word she spoke on his behalf was plausible. She knew countless things she couldn't have known. So perhaps our spirits do go on. Still I can't touch him, I can't kiss him, I can't suck, fuck, and hold him. He can't reach up and stop me from picking my nose.

Nothing makes any sense to me. I have stopped reading the *New York Times:* It's all gossip, fashion, and obscene cruelty I have no power to change. In the months since Tim died, the world is still obsessed with O. J. Simpson. I turn on the TV less than once a week, and I want to vomit.

I talk to Tim. Out loud. I attend my support group, and continue to write, and to see friends. Others who are grieving share their experiences with me—online, in person, even by snail mail. The depth of their despair is the air I breathe. Here are other things I enjoy: Sad music. Sex of almost any kind—cyber, phone, video voyeurism, even real and true in-the-flesh sex. Nature—watching the sunset, walking in a garden, on the beach, playing with my dogs. They understand my grief perfectly, it would seem, and when I cry, they grow still and pensive, put their faces on my knee, and wait for me to come out of it. Which is more than most people can do. A very few friends and colleagues are able to listen when I howl, to be present and hold my hand, or make me laugh. But the most common response to my litany of boundless sorrow is, "So what does your shrink say?" Anyone who says that to me can expect to be deleted from my address book. Grief is not a pathology. It is the body's natural response to devastation. Anyone who can formulate a stiff upper lip is, to me, already dead. I mourn for them. Go away if you can't stand my grief. It's nowhere near over.

My rage is boundless, too. I want Bill Clinton to lose in the next election and I am going to actively campaign against him. I will consider voting for anyone who steps forward and says that Bill Clinton has failed miserably; he is a cowardly fuck who can't even be bothered to file a brief in the Supreme Court opposing Colorado's Amendment Two and should be dragged through the streets of every city and town, like Mussolini, weeping while we pelt him with rotten *fruit* to remind him of who elected him.

That's just the tip of the iceberg. Don't tell me I'm lucky to be alive, to be HIV-negative. Don't tell me that life is beautiful. Don't tell me that I have a lot to offer. To whom? A nation that wants to lower taxes on the rich as it abandons the poor and disenfranchised to further deprivation? A culture that accepts a filthy, reactionary piece of crap like *Pulp Fiction* and calls it Art?

Here's what I understand: people who tear at their flesh and throw themselves in the grave. People who join monasteries and spend the rest of their days praying for peace. Terrorists.

Maybe I'll come out of this and be utterly ashamed to have confessed to the depths of what I am experiencing. Maybe, someday, I will marry another wonderful man and we'll adopt a child and name him Tim. Or maybe I will decide that the countless deaths I have witnessed are too much for me, that the consolations of sex and music and art and love and community are not enough in the face of this idiot culture, this drug-besotted land of ours, filled with death and indifference. And I will join my loved ones "before my time." Don't ask me what my shrink says.

People who are not grieving say, "Don't get depressed, *organize*!" Of course they're right. I hope to be back in the ranks of the mentally balanced. But I do not believe I can get there without being here first. So here I am. This is my postcard from Grief. Don't write. Wish I weren't here.

Mark Matousek ditched his job at Andy Warhol's *Interview* magazine to pursue a quest for meaning in his life—a quest made all the more urgent when he received an HIV-positive diagnosis. This chapter from his memoir *Sex Death Enlightenment* finds him feasting on a smorgasbord of spiritual choices—and unsatisfied by them all.

Sex Death Enlightenment

THE TERROR BROUGHT ON BY THE KNOWLEDGE OF THE VIRUS CIRCU-lating in my bloodstream came in waves. I would ignore it for as long as possible, then it would catch up with me, crowding everything else out of my mind, forcing me to look at it squarely. Any attempt to avoid the anxiety only made it worse. I knew I had to go through it, not around or over it—straight through—to really *feel* the sensation of panic in my body—and let the virus become my teacher. The only problem was *how* to do this.

I tried everything.

Zen: During Sunday meditation sessions at the Zen Mountain Monastery in Mount Tremper, New York, I sat miserably staring at the wall while a bald nun walked around whacking people on the shoulder blades. Periodically, in an unbelievably shrill voice—like an insane dybbuk—she would shriek, *"Wake uppp!!!"* I counted my breaths and hated the rigidity, the dynastic name-dropping, the bowing and the scraping. When it was over, I watched the *roshi,* an ex-sailor covered with tattoos, zoom around the grounds on a golf cart, smoking Benson and Hedges.

Vipassana: I enrolled in a nine-day silent *vipassana*—or mindfulness—meditation retreat, at Southern Dharma, a rustic center in the Smoky Mountains of North Carolina, led by John, an American who'd been a Buddhist monk in Thailand. After two days, I was twitching and squirming on my pillow like someone with Saint Vitus's dance. Sitting perfectly still on a hard cushion in a cold room for fourteen hours a day might be the path to our true nature, as John advised, but after several days of this, I wasn't sure I wanted to find mine.

On the last day, John asked what the word *discipline* meant to us. "Hitler," said a middle-aged man with a Brooklyn accent. "Attila the Hun," seconded a grandmother with white hair. So much for the enlightened mind, I thought.

Immortalism: I sat in a room while a preacher who called himself Reverend Matt jumped around the stage of the Radiant Light Ministry in San Francisco, wearing leather pants and a Hawaiian shirt, exhorting a crowd of New Age dykes and queers—who screamed out and cheered him on like a rock star—that if they just *breathed* enough, rebirthing themselves through all the negativity inside their bodies, they could live forever. "Death is just an old *idea*," Matt insisted. "It's all in your mind, people!" I left before the end of the lecture.

Yoga Retreats: Cabbage soup at six o'clock in the morning under the dining room photograph of a master yogi holding his own intestines in his hands. Though I knew that self-disembowelment was not the goal of this practice, I was intimidated anyhow. The daily regime involved four hours of twisting, breathing, contorting myself into unnatural positions in a drafty room. Extreme hunger and stiffness, leading to stiffness and extreme hunger. Early escape while the teacher was sleeping.

Kundalini Initiation: For $125 each, twenty other people and I sat with a woman in Santa Fe, chanting Sanskrit and meditating, then receiving instruction on the two hours of daily practice required at home for the serpent energy to blast up our spines and open our crown chakras. When the ceremony was over, this gentle lady placed a red rose on top of my head, which I balanced as best I could, walking back to my seat in front of the other initiates. Ten days later I burned out.

Hermitage: For two summers, I lived alone in a ten-by-fifteen-foot cabin in the woods outside Woodstock, reading Thoreau and Annie Dillard, trying to commune with nature. I hoped that through sheer isolation, removed from city distractions, I would be forced to settle down and *see* in the Zen way—the trees, the woodchuck, the stream trickling in the distance. What I saw, in actuality, was that I was going berserk.

Twelve Steps: For several months, I attended meetings of Sex and Love Addicts Anonymous, where visitors introduced themselves with multihyphenated labels ("Hi, I'm Louise, a recovering daughter of an alcoholic-incest-survivor-romantic-compulsive-bulimic") and told long sad stories about their erotic mishaps, counting the days they had abstained. I was turned off by the recovery-speak and never got past the First Step.

These experiences left me frustrated. I longed for holy company, the direct hit of an enlightened master to recharge my batteries and restore my faith.

I heard about a woman saint, Amritanandamayi Ma—or Ammachi (Little Mother)—who was scheduled to give *darshan* in New York. That evening, Carole and I arrived early at the Universalist Church on Central Park West and took our places on the floor along with several hundred other people. Men and women in saris and white dhotis prepared the stage for Ammachi's arrival; there were tamburas and a sitar to accompany the singing of devotional *bhajan* hymns, and a chubby Indian man with thick glasses overseeing the whole affair, checking mikes, smiling at the crowd as they assembled.

While we waited for Ammachi's entrance, I read up on who she was. Her story was archetypal—for a saint. Born into a poor village family forty years before, she'd had visions from an early age, repeating the names of Hindu deities until her family began to think she was mad. One night when Ammachi was ten, she went out walking on the beach near her village and, chanting the name of Krishna, fell senseless for an entire night. When she awoke, she was quite a different girl, transformed by this experience into a teacher. Since that time, she had lived at her ashram in

Kerala—which had thousands of visitors every year—founding schools and charitable organizations, traveling around the world giving *darshan.*

I'd read this kind of thing before, of course—nearly every saint's life was marked by some kind of spontaneous initiation, such as Ammachi's, where the ripe soul seemed to drop in one clean gesture from the tree of ordinary consciousness into an ongoing state of bliss. Thereafter, if the awakening was real, their personal lives stopped and a selfless life of service began, characterized by superhuman endurance and unbounded energy. I read that Ammachi had been known to give *darshan* to thousands of people in one stretch, not moving from her chair for seventy-two hours straight, with no visible sign of fatigue.

Many miracles had been witnessed around her. One in particular struck me as wonderful: One day at her ashram, Ammachi was sitting on the ground with a circle of her close disciples when she caught sight of a man standing alone at the far end of the yard, watching her. The man was a leper in the later stages of his disease, covered with sores, too ashamed of his smell and appearance to come any closer.

Those present report that, upon seeing the man, Ammachi stood up and ran toward him with her arms outstretched. The man turned away. "No, Ma!" he called out, covering his rotting face. "Not too close. I'm unclean!" But Ammachi, ignoring his words, took the man against her breast and kissed his sores, holding him close for many minutes. She stroked his head and told him that he must visit her three times a week without fail. Every few days, the leper would appear as he'd been instructed, and Ammachi would keep him close by, touching him often, cooing like a protective mother. At the end of a month, observers reported that the leper's sores had closed and that his stumpy fingers were regenerating. At the end of six months, the man was completely cured, without so much as a scar on his body to show where the leprosy had been.

I closed the pamphlet and looked at the smiling photograph of Ammachi at the center of the stage. This was the power of holy love, I thought—not the love we talk about in romantic songs or even the love between close friends—but the love that can come only from a liberated being, a love without bounds or conditions. That kind of love could indeed create miracles, healings of body and mind and spirit. I turned from Ammachi's picture to Carole, who was lying on her back with her eyes closed—exhausted from the ten-block walk—her rosary in her hands folded across her chest. I thought of the Christian word for that kind of holy love—*agape*—

and Ammachi putting her arms around my sick friend. For a second, I hoped.

A hush came over the hall as Ammachi entered from the back of the church. The crowd rose to its feet as the woman in the white sari bustled, smiling, toward the stage, touching bowed heads as she passed. She was small and chubby and very dark, barefoot, with a round childlike face, a large jewel in her left nostril, a white circle of powder across her forehead, and two strands of thick wooden beads around her wrists. She climbed the stairs to the stage and turned to face the crowd, flashed her wide smile, then gestured for everyone to be seated.

With closed eyes, rocking from side to side with her face upturned, Ammachi began to sing, the group repeating with her. *"Jaya shiva om—ma ma—jaya shiva om—ma ma,"* came the chant, quietly at first, then more animatedly, until she seemed possessed by the music, drunk on the divine names she was singing. Now her hands were folded across her chest; now she was flinging them up toward the sky. Now her hands were folded under her cheek, shoulders raised, as if speaking to a lover on the pillow; now she was breaking the tune to whisper, "Shiva, Shiva, Shiva," into the microphone, or crying out for Krishna, then giggling to herself, as if the god had answered her.

Soon after the singing ended, *darshan* began. Ammachi sat in a chair taking people into her arms and hugging them, rocking them, stroking their heads and whispering into their ears. Touched as I was by her holy appearance, I was, as always, on the lookout for any glitch of behavior that might betray her. But she was exactly as one would imagine the mother of the world might be, opening her arms, taking each visitor to her breast. Carole and I watched her embrace Upper West Siders in yarmulkes, teenage girls with Walkmans, muscled gay men and toddlers, old people in wheelchairs, a girl who looked like Donna Summer in spandex knickers and a push-up bra.

When we reached the head of the line, Carole went first, shyly, laying her head on Ammachi's shoulder. I watched the small dark hands circle Carole's body, then pull her close and rock her back and forth, as if greeting a beloved child. When she finally let Carole go, I approached, feeling nervous.

The fear dissolved as soon as she grabbed me and nestled my head against her soft belly. I closed my eyes and smelled the faint sandalwood scent of her white cotton sari as she rocked me. My mind relaxed, and in that moment of surrender, a feeling of great relief passed through me. She lifted my head and brought it next to hers, then hissed into my ear, "Shiva, Shiva, Shiva," holding my face between her hands. Then she reached out and stuck a finger into a pot of sandalwood paste, pinned the gooey finger in the center of my forehead, and pushed my head straight back.

My mind went white. My eyes were open, looking into Ammachi's face as she stared at me with her brilliant smile, the light nearly outshining her face as she pushed my head farther and farther back until I thought I would faint. The room behind her head disappeared. I saw nothing but an enormous, fluorescent white moon with the outline of her face inside it. Then she let out a giggle, popped a Hershey's kiss into my mouth, and scattered a handful of flower petals over my head.

Ammachi's holy touch stayed with me. In the days after her *darshan,* I wandered around in a sort of afterglow; everyone on the street looked like a lover, a brother, a sister, a friend; the city itself seemed friendlier. I felt unnaturally peaceful and at ease, my jittery pace slowing down to a stroll. Carole felt the same way—"like I'm carrying her inside of me," is how she put it. It was true; it was almost as if the bliss streaming out of Ammachi's face had entered and uplifted me.

I began to notice something else, as well: a kind of brightening, as if my eyes had been pried open a couple of extra degrees, rendering the mundane surface of things completely magical—events, people, objects swirling and undoing themselves like flecks in a kaleidoscope before my eyes. At times, I became inadvertently psychic--or simply hypersensitive—to the world around me. I suddenly "knew" things in unexpected flashes. One day, I was walking down Fifth Avenue during rush hour, and the face of a man coming toward me seemed to stand out from the crowd, magnified, like a cutout pasted to a background where it didn't belong. The next night, a friend brought this man to dinner at my house. At other times, I would think of someone whom I hadn't seen in months, walk out the door, and run straight into him. Once or twice, the thought occurred to me to call a particular person—I picked up the phone and found him on the other end, before the phone rang. In these uncanny moments, too frequent for my skeptical mind to deny, I realized that my view had indeed changed; there was a design in the world I once believed chaotic, a force moving me and everything else in ways I could not control or understand. Perceived gently, reality did cohere; it was the difference between seeing a piece of paper as a blank white collection of molecules or as an emanation of the cloud that rained to feed the tree from which it was harvested. This sacramental vision changed *everything,* breathing poetry back into the prosaic world, turning the flat material world into a hologram of wonder.

Still, there was the everyday business of coping with Carole's illness and my own T-cell paranoia. When Carole got out of the hospital after two excruciating days on a gurney in the NYU emergency room (the hospital had no beds), passing a kidney stone caused by sulfa drugs, Robert suggested that we go with him to the Healing Circle, a group inspired by the work of Louise Hay that met every Wednesday night at a church in Chelsea. I was wary, but Robert convinced me that it was time for me to learn to "separate the message from the messenger."

Hay, a science-of-mind minister turned New Age Doris Day, had become rich and famous by telling people to heal their lives through self-love. While this message had its good points, however, the dark side of Hay's delivery was not unknown to me. Shortly before he died, another friend, John, had come back from one of her weekend workshops in a deep depression.

"She told us that we were responsible for being sick," I remembered him saying. "She told us we had to find out why we wanted to get sick in the first place and that if we changed our thoughts, we could heal ourselves." John had gone to the workshop needing support and had come back with a guilty conscience. There was nothing new in the axiom that thoughts affect physical health, of course; what *was* offensive was the implication of blame that Hay's message may have carried, a kind of New Age feel-good, get-positive-and-live-forever fascism that caused many sincere but confused people to believe that healing was as easy as looking into a mirror—one of Hay's tricks—and affirming, "I love and respect myself exactly as I am."

Carole was feeling blue but willing to give it a try. She'd finally come to the conclusion that even if she was dying, she wasn't dead yet and would have to find some way of confronting her despair on a day-to-day basis.

"As long as they don't get all woo-woo," she said when I helped her from the cab on Sixteenth Street. "One word about pink lights and I'm out of there."

At the door of the church, a middle-aged man was handing people teddy bears. "Can I give you a hug?" he asked us.

Carole shot me a look that said, "I told you so," and let him embrace her. Then he wrapped his arms around me as if he'd known me since kindergarten and murmured *Mmmmmm* into my ear.

"I'm so glad you came."

"Thanks," I said, pulling away.

"First time?" Carole and I both nodded. He handed us each a bear and a tiny hand mirror. "Just remember something. No matter what comes up for you in there, you are perfect exactly as you are."

"Oh, my God," whispered Carole, moving past him into the church.

Inside the darkened auditorium two hundred people were standing around, hugging, laughing. Gloria Gaynor's *I Will Survive* blared from the speakers, and here and there, someone was dancing disco style, twirling his arm like a rodeo rider with a lasso. In the center of the room, a man who looked Native American was constructing an altar of candles, feathers, stones, and religious paraphernalia, lighting sage and holding it up to the four directions. There were many faces that I knew from years past; only now the men I'd seen lounging in steam rooms or ordering beers at Uncle Charlie's were milling around with crystals hanging from their necks, hugging one another like nuns. How brilliant of gay men, I thought, to have found a new way to cruise in the midst of this virus.

We formed an enormous circle, joined hands, and were led in an affirmation prayer by an Israeli with a hypnotic voice, who guided us through inner space toward the golden light at the center of our foreheads. When we opened our eyes, the group was peaceful, and people started telling their stories. The theme was transformation: Again and again, men and women, ranging from healthy to extremely ill, revealed how AIDS had activated positive changes in their lives, giving them "permission" to leave jobs, cities, and lovers; to discover in the quest for healing (if not a cure) who they were, what they wanted, and how they intended to spend the rest of their lives.

I was moved by these stories, proud of how our community had bonded together in crisis. But I detected something not quite honest in the tone of the meeting, a hint of false cheer, a reluctance to talk about the pain. Just as this thought crossed my mind, an emaciated man stood up and started screaming.

"I'm getting sick and tired of listening to this bullshit every week," he shouted, scaring the people around him.

"Do you have something to share?" asked the Israeli moderator.

"No, I don't have anything to *share*," said the man sarcastically. "I have something to say."

"Please say it then. Without judgment."

The sick man glared. "Have you ever been sick?" he asked the man with the mellifluous voice.

"No," he answered.

"Do you know what it's like to be in a hospital for six weeks with a hundred-and-four fever, puking all over yourself, with a catheter up your prick?"

The moderator shook his head.

"No, you don't. And yet you sit here talking to *me* about positive thinking and finding my spirit. When I'm depressed, you tell me it's just the dimming of light. When I'm in pain, you tell me it's there to teach me something. When I tell you I'm scared to die, you tell me it's just a passing thought. You've got a fucking platitude for every complaint in the book because you're afraid of what it feels like to just hurt, plain simple hurt—not noble, not righteous, just stinking pain."

The room fell silent. The man started to weep. "I came here to be with people like me, but now I find out you don't want to tell the truth, either. There's no place for me now, 'cause I can't think positive. I'm scared. I'm not a hero. I'm just dying." The man broke down sobbing, and the woman next to him put her arms around his shoulder. I heard whimpering and saw that Carole was quietly crying, too. This guy was telling the truth, I realized. These well-meaning people were covering up plain old death, in an effort to cope, dressing it up in the banner of enlightenment, making it heroic, not allowing it simply to be what it is, without cosmetics.

More than ever, I realized that if dying was to become my teacher, I needed to look it straight in the face and see what was really there, beyond philosophy. I needed to move to the front lines.

17. ALEC HOLLAND

Alec Holland is the pseudonym of a San Francisco writer who isn't ready to come out as HIV-positive. His dilemma about whether or not to disclose his status, especially now that protease inhibitors have brightened his prospects for the future, fuels this thought-provoking self-examination.

Heaven Can Wait

UNLESS MY FRIENDS ARE BIG MOUTHS, AS FAR AS I CAN TELL, ONLY five people know that I am HIV-positive, including my doctor. I have kept it a closely guarded secret for any number of reasons, perhaps the biggest one being that I didn't want to be treated differently. Oh yeah, and there's also denial.

But I've always thought that any shrewd individual could guess. My partner died a few years ago from HIV. I cashed in my 401(k), I take expensive trips, buy expensive toys. There's nothing in my savings account. Identifying myself as a high-risk guy, I am compelled to do high-risk things. In a remote corner of Alaska last year, some people offered me a chance to bungee-jump off a bridge into a deep chasm for five dollars. Why the hell not? The actual falling part was not so sickeningly rife with vertigo as the moment ten minutes before when I thought through to the decision: "What, are you afraid you'll be ending your life too soon?" Nothing I could do could endanger my life more than what I'd already done in the past. You can't fire me, I quit.

HIV is my alter ego, my Swamp Thing secret, Hyde to my Jekyll. I've gone to great lengths to conceal it. Once I ate a plateful of raw oysters, in order to "pass" with some friends as negative. For the immunologically compromised, oysters can be more dangerous than bungee-jumping.

You wouldn't know I was a risky guy to look at me. I dress conservatively, keep regular hours, and buy season tickets to the symphony. If I thought it would do me any good, I would have a 401(k). I take care of my health, keep the drinking down, get enough rest, meditate privately to lower stress.

And for the last two years, I have participated in a study for one of the new drugs that are changing the face of AIDS here at the end of the century, a protease inhibitor.

For those of you out of the loop, protease inhibitors are the new generation of drugs many people with HIV are looking to with a lot of hope. The way protease inhibitors work is like this: The drug goes into the virus and inhibits one of the enzymes HIV uses to replicate itself. This makes for defective viruses, duds that can't infect you. Kind of like those roach killers that sterilize the male so they can't reproduce.

Well, for me, it's working. There are two ways to know how healthy you are if you're HIV-positive. The old-fashioned method is through a CD4 or T-cell count: Most uninfected folks have over a thousand T-cells per cubic millimeter of blood. If an HIV-positive person has fewer than 500 T-cells, then it's time to think about getting some preventative drugs. But more attention is paid by my doctors to the newer, improved way to measure HIV's attack on the body, through viral load testing. This is a measure of how many "copies" of the virus are present in a milliliter of blood. If you have a viral load of more than 10,000, it's time to get on the stick.

When I first started the study thirteen months ago, I had a T-cell count of 289 and a viral load of 22,000. Within a week of taking a protease inhibitor, my viral load went down below the measuring point and has stayed below 2,000 for over two years, while my T-cells have made a slow but steady climb above 600 (at the time I write this, my viral load is undetectable).

What's also pleasing to me is that the drug has had virtually no side effects. I've had my flirtations with AZT, and remember barfing in the middle of a very expensive French restaurant. HIV-positive people tell me of bad reactions they've had to all the prophylactics, like rashes, diarrhea, lowered sex drive (yikes!), liver damage, you name it. With my particular protease inhibitor, I haven't felt a thing.

I'm happy with the results. So's my doctor. There's more in the pipeline, and during the 11th International AIDS Conference held in Vancouver in July 1996, Dr. David Ho of the Aaron Diamond AIDS Research Institute theorized that if viral reproduction could be shut down for three years, it might be possible to clear the virus completely from infected individuals.

Well, that's a big if, and so are a lot of other things—who knows how long the drug will work in my system? Who knows if I'm not destroying some other part of my body in the process? Viral load measures count HIV copies in the bloodstream, not in the lymph nodes, where trouble is often hiding. And who knows, maybe I'll get hit by a bus next week.

Nevertheless, I have been in a much better mood lately. I even thought to myself, "Damn, maybe I shouldn't've cashed in my 401(k) after all." Maybe I should stop bungee-jumping.

Companies that make a living off of AIDS are also having second thoughts. Perhaps you have heard of the viatical settlement industry, companies like San Francisco's Dignity Partners, Life Partners Inc., of Waco, Texas, and Viaticare Financial Services of Minneapolis. These businesses sprang up over the past decade as people dying of AIDS (and now cancer and Alzheimer's) needed the kind of money an out-of-work sick person requires. The way viatical settlements works is this: A person with a terminal illness wants to sell a life insurance policy to get money on which to live. The policy is worth $100,000. Dignity Partners acts as a broker, and finds an investor willing to buy the policy for, say, $65,000. Dignity Partners would get $15,000 as a percentage and the investor who bought the policy would get $20,000 of that $100,000, provided that the dying person actually dies. Everybody wins!

Well, now there's this problem. The investor gets more money if the person dying dies faster. If a dying person doesn't die, well, obviously, the life insurance policies of AIDS patients are not good investments.

Say what you will about what seems a ghoulish industry, viatical insurance has helped a lot of sick people make ends meet. But at the Vancouver AIDS conference, after the Great Hopeful Pronouncements, Dignity Partners Inc. officially announced that they are temporarily refusing new applications for life insurance sales from AIDS patients (Oh no, there goes *that* source of income!). And while the company has probably been losing money for a while because people with HIV have been living longer than predicted, Dignity Partners's announcement did tie in nicely with the hope many are feeling.

The AIDS epidemic has gone on for so long a time that an economy has sprung up around it. Hospices, food banks, viatical insurance, research, publishing. It's no wonder that people who have made a career of AIDS care and prevention are slow to embrace a possible shift toward hope. Business is down at the viatical insurance brokerages, and it's also down at the buyers' clubs (groups who purchase large quantities of nonstandard therapies, including herbs), acupuncturists, and other alternative healing outlets. My guess is that business will pick up again—before HIV I never would have considered acupuncture; now I wouldn't live without it. The distrust of so much euphoria is real, but also reactionary. What needs to happen next is a foregoing of reaction, and a careful consideration of what the future has to offer.

Back to Work

In an old Jerry Lewis movie called *Hook, Line, and Sinker,* Lewis plays a traveling salesman who learns he is dying and goes on a spending spree around the world, only to discover that his doctors have made a terrible mistake: He isn't dying at all. Then Jerry has to go underground, in order to hide from all the people he owes money.

Could it be that my life is imitating a Jerry Lewis movie? My friend Paul found out he was positive back in 1987, although he assumes he's been positive since the early eighties. With so few T-cells that he had names for them (Huey, Luey, Duey, Chewy) in 1991, Paul went on permanent disability—if you have fewer than 200 T-cells, you are considered to have full-blown AIDS—and planned to live out the rest of his foreshortened life with the savings he'd pulled together, as well as a credit card or two. "Your credit-card balance should rise in direct correlation to the drop in your T-cell count," goes the old chestnut. Paul went to Europe, Paul took up some quiet hobbies, Paul became a café fly. He takes good care of himself and, with the exception of a bout with shingles and a few skin rashes, he's been well. Then Paul started taking one of the new protease inhibitors. Paul's T-cell count has been rising steadily into the hundreds, and his viral load has disappeared. Paul is going to have to go back to work.

Paul's savings are almost gone, and pretty soon his T-cell count is going to rise above the range considered to be full-blown AIDS, making him no longer qualified to receive certain benefits. Oh no, Paul's gonna live, at least for a good deal longer than he'd planned!

There's another big issue: Who gets the new drugs? If you are unemployed and on Medicare, will the system pay for the cost of living longer?

I know what's on the tip of your tongue: "Go back to work." But many of these people did have insurance—it just ran out at some point, and, unable to pay the premiums of health-care plans designed not for prevention but for profit, they turned to Medicare and California's ADAF (AIDS Drug Assistance Fund). Now many are debilitated by the disease, and protease inhibitors may give them five T-cells where they had none, but their immune system has been so trashed out that it may be a little too late to hope for a complete comeback—just a further lengthening of life. And even if they did go back to work and get a new health-care package, AIDS will hereinafter be referred to as a "pre-existing condition," meaning that their insurance might not pay to treat it.

Then there's Jaimie who maxed out his credit card buying all-leather furniture. He sold his life insurance policy for $35,000 when he had 300 T-cells, and a week later his T-cells plummeted to 30. Another old chestnut: The fewer T-cells you have, the more money you get from a viatical insurance broker. "Damn," he lamented, "I could've gotten $10,000 more if I'd just waited a week."

Well, now Jaimie needs a lymph-gland transplant and he can't seem to unload all that leather furniture. Will Medicare pay for the luxury of a new lymph gland?

Out of the Closet

My own situation doesn't seem quite settled to me. I do have health care, have paid faithfully on it for many years and, since I'm asymptomatic and keep well, they've made a tidy profit off me. The protease inhibitor I receive is part of a study. My doctor has helped me keep my HIV status away from my insurance. Now I'm being pressured to take other drugs in combination with the protease, drugs that cost lots and lots of money. This will require that I reveal my secret to my health-care company, and they will know just what sort of Swamp Thing I am. I am not thrilled with divulging my status to anybody, especially to my caretakers.

Nothing in my experience of telling people has encouraged me to come further out of the closet with my status. With the recent good news, I decided to tell a close friend about being positive, because I wanted her to share my hope. Now she thinks I'm going to die any day now. Now I have to hold her hand and assure her that, on the contrary, I'm further away from death than I have been for years.

It's even difficult for me to tell my fellow HIV-positive friends. People who are out with their status are very impatient with guys like me: They see me as a guy reaping all the benefits of a screamy band of ACT UP members. My silence, they say, equals death. For the record, I've been screamy myself, I'm diligent with my advocacy, send a lot of my money out into the world, and have even sat in now and then, but always in the third person, for my brothers and sisters with HIV, not for myself. In a time when Larry Kramer presses the need for us to band together, get with group, I've never felt more protective of my individuality.

Another positive—but asymptomatic—friend is supposed to meet me for dinner. I sit at the bar and shrug to the hostess: Sorry, you'll have to hold my reservation another fifteen minutes, my friend hasn't shown yet. Half an hour goes by, forty-five minutes. I'm a busy man, I've got a lot to do before I die, better things than swilling beers waiting for a slugabed friend. When he does finally show up, I screw up my eyes in irritation and he cuts me off: "Don't you yell at me. I'm *sick*. And *dying*." I smile, it's supposed to be a joke, but I remember why it is we don't get together more often. What excuse will he have, I wonder, if he too responds well to the life-prolonging drugs? Many of my fellow positivists have lived so long with this death sentence that they've come to think of it as something precious, something noble. What would happen if it became ordinary, treatable, like diabetes or dry rot?

Certainly HIV has changed my life, in some small ways for the better. Maybe even ennobled my behavior now and then. Yes, I bungee-jumped, but I've also done all the other things I was setting aside for the future: riding horseback, singing to a karaoke machine, learning to play the violin. It's put the fire under my butt. I've learned not to be ashamed of my status, but I've also decided that there's nothing particularly heroic about it, either. Sometimes I do have this image of myself as Indiana Jones being chased by a giant boulder, always a few feet ahead of it: Will he make it? Will he make it? But that's Indiana Jones fleeing danger, not facing it head on. And Swamp Thing, Mr. Hyde—weren't they searching madly for the antidote to counteract their super powers?

Would my coming out be a noble deed?

Well, sooner or later I'm going to have to come out, if I'm going to get what I need to go on living. First to my health care company, already deluged with once-secretive positive people like me. They—and you—will be surprised at how many of us there are, all living on the edge, high risk, the Incredible Hulk disguised as Dr. Bruce Banner.

I've never been good at planning ahead, with or without HIV. I've solved problems when they arise, I've made all my gains, as well as losses, through risk. But I am a San Franciscan, and the typical San Franciscan lives an unplanned lifestyle, positive, negative, male, or female. We live in this beautiful city with many pleasures. But the cost is incredible—most of us can't afford to buy real estate around here, and rents are so high, it's tough to save money. Many of my friends—intelligent, hard-working, well-paid—still live hand-to-mouth.

Relationships are hand-to-mouth in San Francisco, too. If you're gay, you've probably lost friends to AIDS, and have to go out and meet new ones. If you're not gay, you know this is a city of transients—people move to and from the city so fast your head spins. I'm constantly constructing new friendships and saying good-bye (geographically or mortally) to not-very-old ones.

We never have to prepare for winter. We are often single and don't have to provide for the family. The way we live now in San Francisco seems less proactive and more reactive, and that can't help but affect the way we look at the value of life.

If you have HIV, San Francisco, as well as any major urban center, has become a place where the latest treatments, the best care, and the most supportive community make it a great place to come and die. And now, with the new treatments, it's becoming more and more like a great hothouse, where we delicate orchids can flourish. Or maybe a better metaphor is a huge walk-in freezer, where we cool snowmen can keep from melting until the weather improves.

And yet, with the advent of the new drugs, I'm getting restless, itching to come out of the deep freeze, or the hot house, move someplace where the land is cheap and I can think about something else besides staying alive. But the other thing about the existing protease inhibitors is that once you've started taking them, you can't stop. HIV is a tricky little bastard, and the moment it isn't being bombarded with the drug, it figures out what's been screwing with it and mutates around it. One of my fellow study members was on a trip through Europe and had his luggage stolen. It was eight days before he got back and was able to get more of the protease inhibitor. By then it was too late—HIV wised up. And so I am stuck again, an orchid, or a snowman, in this inert, trapped situation, ever-vigilant, beholden to a drug company and the kindness of strangers. How can a guy take charge of the rest of his life when so much depends on outside circumstances?

Here in the late nineties, there is a trend for gays to move back into the suburbs. Even into rural places. Does that trend represent a kind of weariness on the part of gays of being trapped in the city for so long?

If I'm not good at planning ahead for living, I'm also not very good at dying. When my partner lay on his deathbed, I'd ask him if he wanted to go someplace—to the movies, for a ride, anything. When he could hardly keep down soup, I'd open a bottle of champagne. The day before he died, I handed him a bowl of potatoes and a paring knife, and asked him to peel the bunch.

I am not interested in a half-life. Nor was my partner. In the evening, after the potato peeling, I remorsefully dropped my head on his bed and told him how sorry I was to make him peel potatoes. He told me it made him feel better just to do something.

Now I want to do something, too. Not necessarily bungee-jumping, not necessarily end-of-the-world. I want to do something that I haven't been able to conceive of in several years: plan for the future. That my desire coincides with the turn of the century, when the whole world is thinking about the future, seems a hopeful thing to me.

One of America's most widely respected poets, Mark Doty turned to prose to document the experience of losing his lover Wally to AIDS. In this powerful excerpt from the epilogue of the resulting memoir, *Heaven's Coast,* Doty writes radiantly of finding the will to go on.

Consolations

OF COURSE THERE IS NO CONSOLATION, FOR THE DREADFUL FACT OF a death. Nothing makes it right. Nothing can remedy that absence, that break in the continuity of things. Nothing can fill the space Wally occupied in my life; nothing takes his place.

On an absolute level he is gone, utterly, and that absence rings at the core of every one of my days, the aftermath of a struck bell.

And yet. And yet.

There are these gifts, these perceptions or moments or aspects of experience which make it possible, desirable, to continue. Any consolation can and does dissolve, any day, into the lake of grief, that liquid realm where all bright or solid things darken and disappear. One does not lose—one does not *want* to lose, entirely—grief.

We live, instead, into, toward a different relation to loss, a shifting perspective: the grief not as large and overwhelming, not every day, not erasing, not entirely, what there is to praise.

And what is left, when you've lost what you loved most, to praise?

Bitterness

Gridlock in New York; the President's in town and his cordon of vehicles has Fifth Avenue closed, so there's some kind of chain reaction all the way to La Guardia. The taxi driver wants to take an alternate route, so after I agree we wind up on some side street in a particularly beat part of Queens. This would probably help matters except that it seems every other taxi driver in the universe has had the same idea, so that this sad little retail neighborhood with its on-the-skids businesses and wildly graffitied walls is totally choked with yellow taxis, all of them idling and cursing and champing at the bit. Nobody's moving.

Which allows me a really good look at the guy on the corner, a middle-aged black man in shabby clothes, too many layers of them for the weather. He's standing right on the curb, rocking back and forth a little, surveying the air above the cabs, the gridlock, me, and when he speaks, loud as a street preacher, his judgment seems to take in us all.

"The world," he says, "is shit."

It makes me laugh, as well as scaring me a little—he's right outside my window. But all he wants to do is pronounce.

And in fact I know how he feels. Because grief has taught me that bitterness is itself a strange kind of consolation, that clear-eyed, sober bleakness that sees right through the sentiments of consolation, that knows better than all the things that *fail* to console. Time, for instance; my friend Renate, her husband dead three years, saw the wind rocking the chair on the deck where her husband used to like to sit, and the movement of the empty chair tore her apart; she felt, in fact, that her grief had gotten *worse* with the passage of time. Is the way that time "heals" us simply that it encourages us to turn away?

Or memory. People love to say, "Your pain will fade and you will be left with beautiful memories." But my memories are also a narrative of pain and of diminishment, and that history's vivid to me, too.

Sometimes all that would help would be to allow myself to feel ferocious, to feel like a raging fire burning up the false offerings of consolation, burning right at the dark heart of things. We need, sometimes, to consign it all to darkness. We need to look at the world and proclaim it shit.

Whose ignorant words, says the voice in the whirlwind in Job, smear my design with darkness?

Ours. Because everything around us races toward disappearance. Our brief moment's a flash, an arcing flare which itself serves to illuminate the face of death.

Aren't we always on the verge of vanishing? Isn't the whole world nowhere's coast?

Sometimes all that helps is a deep, bracing breath of emptiness.

The Present

I'm writing in the wild glamour of an early Italian spring, smoke of olive wood drifting up the hill from the grove. This is a world of fragrance: Parma violets, in the shade of the woods, and on days it rains something like eucalyptus, a camphory, resinous scent floating among the trees. Small-cupped yellow narcissus, on the sunny banks. The armoire in my room gives out a deep, contained smell, decade after decade of wools and silks, ancient sachets, long quiet hours when the sun's poured in through the tall windows and heated the redolent wood till it releases something of itself into the atmosphere.

Today is the first of March; I've come here for a month to work in a grand old villa hundreds of steep cobbled steps up the hill from the village of Bellagio. My room is a buttery Naples yellow, thick walls pierced by two windows and French doors opening on to a balcony. My first day, my first moment alone in the room, I opened the doors and stepped out onto the stone shelf suspended above the steep switchback paths of rosemary and lavender, above the green-black cypresses flinging themselves vertically toward heaven, above the jigsawed rose-tiled roofs of the village, above the softly luminous hazed expanse of the lake and its distant mountains, behind their smoky blue veils—a landscape like the background in a Leonardo.

How could one not, in that moment, be completely absorbed in the present? What possesses us like the present does, when we give ourselves to it completely?

And then I realized, on that steep little ledge with its lace of iron railing, that this time I didn't imagine myself falling, had no desire, now, to jump. There was too much in the world to see, too much I wanted to pour myself into, to encounter and absorb, too much I wanted to do.

The present begins to hold a possibility, in its thin, luminous edge. It suggests and supports a future.

I want to know how the story of my life will turn out.

Dogs

Dogs, in a way, *are* the present. Animals are infinitely attentive to now, wholly present with what's in front of them. Entirely themselves, without compromise or dissembling. Pure directness of being, the soul right in the eyes, brimming to the edges.

Arden and Beau: heart's companions, good boys, eager, steady, always exactly where they are.

And what is right in the present, at this moment's fresh edge, also seems to lead right into the next moment. Last month, with Michael at the animal shelter, I sat in a pen while a dozen puppies climbed over and around us, all eagerness to be just where they were, these dozen new beings come into the world of time, to follow each moment into the next, along the arc that passing through time makes. In those almost identical faces, eyes becoming equal to the light, I couldn't miss it: desire for the next moment, and the next, one at a time, each entirely attended to.

Heaven

Ongoingness, vanishing: the world's twin poles.
Each thing disappears; everything goes on.
The parts pour into nowhere, the whole continues.
And to be nowhere is to be in heaven, isn't it, in the boundless, loose from the limits of time and space?
Isn't the whole world heaven's coast?

19. TONY KUSHNER

Pulitzer Prize– and Tony Award–winning playwright Tony Kushner, whose sweeping AIDS epic *Angels in America* stunned audiences with its dramatic scope, is one of the nation's most effective lay preachers. He composed this stirring text for the Episcopalian National Day of Prayer for AIDS.

A Prayer

DEARLY BELOVED: TODAY IS A NATIONAL DAY OF PRAYER FOR AIDS. Let us pray.

God:

A cure would be nice. Rid those infected by this insatiable unappeasable murderer of its lethal presence. Reconstitute the shattered, restore to health all those whose bodies, beleaguered, have betrayed them, whose defenses have permitted entrance to illnesses formerly at home only in cattle, in swine, and in birds. Return to the cattle, the swine, and the birds the intestinal parasite, the invader of lungs, the eye-blinder, the brain-devourer, the detacher of retinas. Rid even the cattle and birds of these terrors; heal the whole world. Now. Now. Now. Now.

Grant us an end that is not fatal. Protect: the injection-drug user, the baby with AIDS, the sex worker, the woman whose lover was infected, the gay man whose lover was infected; protect the infected lover, protect the casual contact, the one-night stand, the pickup, the put-down, protect the fools who don't protect themselves, who don't protect others: *YOU* protect them. The misguided, too, and the misinformed, the ambivalent about living, show them life, not death; the kid who thinks that immortality is part of the numinous glory of sex. Who didn't believe this, once, discovering sex? Everyone did. Protect this kid, let this kid learn otherwise, and live past the learning; protect all kids, make them wiser but, until wise, make them immortal.

Enlighten the unenlightened: The pope, the cardinals, archbishops, and priests, even John O'Connor, teach him how Christ's kindness worked: Remind him, he's forgotten, make them all remember, replace the ice water in their veins with the blood of Christ, let it pound in their temples: The insurance executive as well as the priest, the congressional representative, the Justice and the judge, the pharmaceutical profiteer, the doctor, the cop, the anchorwoman and the televangelist, make their heads throb with memory, make them see with new eyes Christ's wounds as KS lesions, Christ's thin body AIDS-thin, his shrunken chest pneumonia-deflated, his broken limbs, his pierced hands: stigmata of this unholy plague. Let the spilled blood which angels gathered, Christ's blood be understood: It is shared and infected blood.

Even John O'Connor, even Bob Dole, Giuliani and Gingrich, Jesse Helms and Pat Robertson—tear open their hearts, let them burn with compassion, stun them with understanding, ravish their violent, politick, cynical souls, make them wiser, better, braver people. You can. You, after all, are God. This is not too much to ask.

Grant us an end to this pandemic: Why, after all, a pandemic? Why now? Give aid to the needy, not AIDS, give assistance to those seeking justice, not further impediment. Find some other way to teach us your lessons; we're eager to learn, we are only reluctant to die.

Bring back our dead, all our dead, give us certain knowledge of the future recovery of all those we've lost, restitution of all those we've lost, in Paradise if not on earth, but guarantee it. Don't ask faith of people who have lost so much. Don't *dare*.

Manifest yourself now. With a cure, now. With a treatment, now. With a treatment that isn't more snakebite venom, more spiderbite poison, which is all that fourteen years of prayers and waiting and searching have given us. Reveal yourself with an imminent medical miracle. Announce it on the evening news: something, finally, that doesn't fail to live up to its promise by morning of the following day. Reagan is gone, more or less, and Bush is gone, and Nixon and the Cold War are finally gone, and apartheid is gone, but AIDS is still here. And we are waiting. For the end of it.

Hear our prayer.

Must grace fall so unevenly on the earth? Must goodness precipitate so lightly, so infrequently from sky to parched ground? We are your crop, your sprouted seed, the harvest perishes in its faith for you for lack of lively rain.

Your silence, I must tell you, so steadfastly maintained, even in the face of our appalling need, is outrageous.

I speak now not for those assembled here but for myself, from the considerable rage that vexes my heart. So many have died this year alone: In case you were absent, God, or absentminded, may I mention a few of them, commend their ends to your accounting?

Randy Shilts, Jeff Schmalz, Paul Walker, Mary Darling, Harry Kondoleon, Bill Anderson, Ron Vawter, Tim Melester, Paul Monette.

· · ·

Let each name stand for ten thousand more, and a hundred thousand others will remain unnoted. And many more are sick and have worsened; they take flight in number, I've noticed, they travel multiply, in flocks, like birds, these critically ill: Having heard the call of a general departing, they test their wings, the thermal currents, fighting for updrafts to carry them to, or carry them from, life. Here is courage and will and imagination and tenacity. Where, God, are you?

Your silence, again, is outrageous to me, it places you impossibly among the ranks of the monstrously indifferent, no better than a Washington politician, no better than an Albany Republican, Alfonse D'Amato, something that meager, that immured against Justice.

Where you must not be placed. Must grace fall so unevenly on the earth? Must goodness precipitate from sky to ground so infrequently? We are parched for goodness, we perish for lack of lively rain; there's a drought for want of grace, everywhere. Surely this has not escaped your notice? All life hesitates now, wondering: in the night which has descended, in the dry endless night that's fallen instead of the expected rain: Where are you?

One of the Hasidim, Menachem Mendl of Kotsk, sealed himself up in a hermitage, and for an entire year refused to answer the pleas of his disciples; would not respond when they knocked at his door, would not answer no matter how hard they knocked; their repeated inquiries after his health did not elicit a single response, their concern produced only silence, their bewilderment, their grief, their fears that he had died behind the door of his cell—for a year they heard nothing from Menachem Mendl of Kotsk.

And then one day he emerged from his cell. His door stood open, and there he was. His disciples demanded an explanation. He told them: "Now perhaps you understand my relationship with the Almighty, who will not reveal Himself no matter how hard I beg, who hides His face from me."

Except one must mention: They had only a year to wait, those tormented, aggrieved disciples, and then they had answers, and explanations. The analogy fails. We've waited a decade and a half for your help. We have ashes, and graves, and grief so overtopping it can no longer be recognized as grief, but has become a kind of dark amazement that so much can be endured; you hide your face from us.

I've been to the Wailing Wall, and I watched men and women daven, as they'd been davening for centuries, Jews before the impassive wall of history, believing their rocking could melt or move those great stones, believing that the messages they stick in the cracks could travel somehow to the other side. The anchorites, too, in the Syrian Desert, would weep over rocks, committed to dissolving the stones with their tears. Is prayer mere attrition, a kind of endurance?

If prayer is a beseeching, a seeking after the hidden heart and face of God, then this peremptory, querulous, insistent demanding, this pounding at your door cannot be called a prayer, this importunate sleeve-tugging while you are distracted—concerned, perhaps, with something more important, holding the earth to its orbit, perhaps, keeping it from careening into the sun; or perhaps you tend another world other than ours, and do a better job with that one, where there is nothing like AIDS, and your tutelage is gentler, and the lessons are easier to learn.

Four years ago a thirty-one-year-old woman named Milagros Martinez drowned herself off the shore of upper Manhattan Island. Infected with the virus, she went to the river and threw her body, which had become a fearful thing to her, her enemy now, she threw her body and the soul it housed into the Hudson, ending her life. Before she drowned, from the edge of drowning, she called to her son, seven years old: She'd left him standing on the riverbank. According to police, and the sixty-seven-word newspaper article that is, as far as I know, her only memorial, Milagros Martinez begged her son to join her in the water, but the child refused, watching instead as his mother was taken, by tributary currents, to some dark, unknowable bed.

• • •

What's become of the child of Milagros Martinez? Where is he now? What dreams does he have, what river courses through his dreams at night? What bodies does it bear? From what raging sea is that river flowing, and toward what conceivable future?

I am in the habit of hoping. But it's become wrong to draw hope from this conflagration. If holocaust alone is the only lesson we attend to, then what bat-winged butcher angel is our teacher, and toward what conceivable future, along the banks of what river of the dead, do we make our way?

I am in the habit of asking small things of you: one of the guilty who hasn't done enough, one of the lucky, the survivors by accident. When I was ten an uncle told me you didn't exist: "We descend from apes," he said, "the universe will end, and there is no God." I believed the ape part—my uncle had thick black hair on his arms and knuckles, so apes was easy—and the universe become a nulliverse, that, too, was scary fun. And since his well-meaning instruction I have not *known* your existence, as some friends of mine do; but you have left bread-crumb traces inside of me. Rapacious birds swoop down and the traces are obscured, but the path is recoverable. It can be discovered again.

So a cure for AIDS. For racism too. For homophobia and sexism, and an end to war, to nationalism and capitalism, to work as such and to hatred of the flesh. Restore the despoiled world, end the pandemic of breast cancer, too, bring back Danitra Vance, and Audre Lorde, and Sigrid Wurschmidt, dead at thirty-six, and my mother, dead at sixty-five. Or at least guarantee that loss is not irrecoverable, so that life can be endured. But above all, since this is my job today, a cure.

If you cannot do these things for us, we will do them for ourselves, but slowly, because we can't see far ahead. At least give us the time to accomplish the future. We had a pact; you engendered us. Don't expect that we will forgive you if you allow us to be endangered. Forgiveness, too, is a lesson loss doesn't teach.

I almost know you are there. I think you are our home. At present we are homeless, or imagine ourselves to be. Bleeding life in the universe of wounds. Be thou more sheltering, God. Pay more attention.

PART THREE

Community

Thirty years ago, the notion of a "gay community" was unworkable—if not unimaginable—because there weren't enough openly gay individuals to form the necessary critical mass. Today, the notion of a single "gay community" may be unworkable because there are too many.

Consider the evolution of what we call ourselves for the purposes of our annual pride parades. We were originally the gay community; then the gay and lesbian community; then the gay, lesbian, and bisexual community; and most recently, the gay, lesbian, and bisexual and transgender community. I imagine, in decades to come, the moniker accumulating more and more categories until the pride parade banner stretches as long as the parade itself.

And why not? "We Are Everywhere" proclaims the gay rights slogan, and the gay movement's hallmark has been its open-door policy, emphasizing each individual's right to identify himself however he sees fit. At a certain point, however, such a notion threatens to deconstruct itself.

The last time I attended a gay pride parade, I noted, among other contingents: gay police officers, gay Brazilian drag queens, gay bankers, gay two-step dancers, the "Girth and Mirth" club for chubby queers, gay men who love cats, boy-lovers, gay men with AIDS, gay Republicans, queer science-fiction aficionados, gay social workers—and all manner of other folks who seemed likely clients of the latter group.

What, one is forced to ask, binds such a disparate mishmash of humanity? Is it enough that we share a predisposition for sex with people of our own gender (overlooking, for the moment, the vast variety of ways in which that predisposition is manifested)?

In the era after Stonewall, being gay was as much a *political* stance as a sexual orientation. Gayness represented a revolutionary commitment, in solidarity with other countercultural movements, to change the fundamental assumptions of society. The "gay community" was indeed a community of people—who had come out of the closet, who chose to see the world primarily through the lens of their sexuality, who worked together for a common goal. It was not really possible, then, to be a "gay banker" (unless you were infiltrating Chase Manhattan to plot an overthrow). A "gay Republican" was truly an oxymoron.

But, as is almost always the case with revolutionary movements, the gay liberationists' growing success sowed the seeds of their own undoing. The easier it is for people to come out as gay, the less they feel the need for revolution. The radical cutting edge cleaves a cultural space in which it's not essential to be radical. And thus, while an organized contingent of "gay Republicans"—such as now lobbies prominently in Washington—may be anathema to a gay liberationist, in one sense such a phenomenon represents the ultimate triumph of gay liberation.

But when the gay community is no longer (or no longer has the appearance of) a group of like-minded individuals, it remains to be seen what, if any, meaning inheres in such a notion. At the end of the millennium, the "gay community" runs the risk of being nothing more than a convenient marketing niche.

The profit-minded are already cashing in on that assumption. The latest survey by Simmons Market Research Bureau—intended to promote gays as upscale consumers—claims that 21 percent of gay men and lesbians have incomes over $100,000; that 48 percent have college degrees; that 50 percent drink vodka; and that 72 percent attended a live theater performance during the past year. In an interesting twist on the notion of antigay discrimination, the Gay and Lesbian Alliance Against

Defamation issued a statement warning that the survey results are misleading, representative only of a self-selecting elite. This kind of image could harm the gay rights cause, GLAAD pointed out, by feeding into the right wing's claim that gay men are not oppressed but in fact *better off* than the average citizen. On the other hand, GLAAD conceded an upside to the survey: it might inspire more gay ads, which would "give us greater visibility."

But GLAAD's response begs the question: Who is "us"?

When I'm driving along the highway and pass a car with a rainbow-flag bumper sticker, I'm swamped by an ambivalent mixture of emotions, ranging from solidarity to self-consciousness to estrangement. Part of me wants to honk and shout, "Hey, me too!" But then I wonder, "Hey, me too *what?"* What do I really know about that person? In fact, all I know is that he's the kind of gay person who would buy a rainbow-flag bumper sticker as a defining emblem of his identity, which is generally a kind of gay person (if one can make such generalizations) that I don't hang out with. The odds are that I would have more in common with someone who drives a car *devoid* of any gay identifiers.

Gay men do share the crucial experience of being misfits—in our own families, in society. The tension arises because some relish their outcast status, while others want nothing more than to fit in.

But no matter our internal disputes and differing worldviews, the gay community remains a unified front to the extent that our opponents view us as such. Mainstream America does not perceive the many shadings of our rainbow coalition; to them, gay Republicans and gay leathermen and gay nurses are all simply "gay."

As we face the year 2000, the question, then, is how do we respond? Do we strive to see beyond our differences in order to fight effectively for the maximum benefits for all? Or do we splinter into our respective subgroups and fend for ourselves? My mind favors the former approach, but my heart might opt for the latter. Can I struggle for an "us" I don't feel part of?

The writers in the following section contend with a wide range of conflicts—both those within various gay worlds, and those between gays and outside forces—about politics, identity, and the idea of community.

The highest profile gay issue in the late 1990s, which will likely continue as such well into the twenty-first century, is the battle over gay marriage. The debate about the right of same-gender couples to have their relationships sanctioned by the state has thrust the notion of gay love into a national spotlight, from the floor of Congress to the evening news. But amid the legal wranglings and the forceful rhetoric on both sides, startlingly little attention has been paid to the essential meaning of matrimony.

Fenton Johnson's essay "Reinventing Marriage" examines the historical evolution of marriage and some of its inherent imbalances. Rather than simply fight for inclusion in an institution deeply rooted in sexism and sexual control, Johnson suggests that gay people instead take this opportunity to reimagine what marriage might be. Our creative and perhaps more egalitarian forms of coupling—devised of necessity in the face of societal condemnation—might serve as models, he proposes, by which gay men could in fact resuscitate the sanctity of marriage for everyone.

The most strident opponents of gay marriage are the members of the religious right, who have made the issue a central rallying point in their rhetorical holy war against the gay rights movement. Gay activists and religious fundamentalists face off across a seemingly unbridgeable gulf of conflicting morality, adversaries in perhaps the most incendiary political struggle at century's end. But in "From Arms to Armistice," journalists Chris Bull and John Gallagher point out striking similarities between the two groups—both originally marginalized but rapidly gaining clout; both dependent on grassroots organizing—and seek ways of restoring civility to the debate. While most critical of religious conservatives, Bull and Gallagher also call to task gay activists, whom they charge have undercut their moral authority by demonizing the other side. They express the hope that both groups—by listening to and acknowledging each other—might bring the battle to a truce.

As Keith Boykin points out in "Are Blacks and Gays the Same?", one of the religious right's most successful tactics has been to pit other minority groups—particularly African-Americans—against homosexuals by claiming that granting lesbians and gay men "special rights" will damage black people's struggle for "legitimate" civil rights. When gay activists position themselves as heirs to Martin Luther King's legacy, many black religious leaders dispute the validity of the comparison. But Boykin argues forcefully that the two groups are—and must be—joined in their fight against oppression. Examining the links between racism and homophobia, he envisions commonalities overcoming differences as black and gay people build a powerful coalition.

One issue Boykin singles out as critical for both blacks and gays is the longstanding question of assimilation. Every minority group contends with this conundrum: whether to seek acceptance for individuals who fit in more easily with the mainstream, and hope that the acceptance "trickles down" to other less "presentable" group members; or to demand inclusion for everyone on their own terms. As we approach the millennium, the conflict among gay men becomes ever more acute, because with each step forward—openly gay men in the movies and television, in Congress and corporate boardrooms—those who don't fit into current definitions of "acceptable" feel left farther behind. Do drag queens and leathermen hinder the push to liberation; or is liberation impossible—or meaningless—without these elements of the community?

In "A Place for the Rest of Us," David Bergman is a strong voice for the latter position. The essay originally appeared in the *Harvard Gay and Lesbian Review* as "An Open Letter to Bruce Bawer," whose book *A Place at the Table* garnered widespread mainstream praise but was controversial within gay circles for its critique of the radical gay subculture. In the journal's next issue, Bawer published an angry response to Bergman's essay, calling it "the most systematically dishonest and unfair account" of his book. I include the piece here not as an attack on Bawer or his book, per se, but for its broader critique of the assimilationist perspective, of which Bawer's book is only one example. Those interested in the debate should certainly read *A Place at the Table* and form their own opinions based on Bawer's complete argument.

Whether they favor an assimilationist or a more radical approach, gay rights proponents share the common vision of a day when all gay people have a safe space in which to thrive. But as that day draws nearer than it's ever been, some gay men are beginning to realize that there may be drawbacks to their long-sought goal. Daniel Mendelsohn's "Decline and Fall: How Gay Culture Lost Its Edge" addresses a problem that could arise only in a time such as ours: What happens when we become *too* acceptable, too normal, too mainstream? The gay movement may be one of those paradoxical entities whose object is its own obsolescence. But once it's gone, Mendelsohn asks, what else may go with it? There is an excitement inherent in being an outcast and a transgressor. There is an energy released in grappling with opposition. For gay men who have staked their identity on living at the edge, being welcomed into the center, he suggests, may be a mixed blessing.

John Weir is another writer unhappy with the current direction of the gay movement. In his blistering manifesto, "Going In," Weir declares himself no longer "gay"—if being gay means shopping at Ikea and working out at the Chelsea Gym. He is angered by a gay community he perceives as banal, eager to sell out, and obsessed with an elite group of affluent, urban, white men. Further, Weir questions the continuing relevance of the category "gay," or the notion that sexual orientation should be the defining characteristic of one's life. He's "postgay," he says. He's over it. Weir's critique, of course, is only possible because of the freedoms that have been gained by the gay movement thus far; nonetheless, his frustration forces the question: Has identity politics outlived its usefulness?

James Earl Hardy, too, finds fault in a gay community that he charges has defined itself as much by whom it excludes as whom it includes. Examining the code words with which even self-professed liberals discuss racial issues, he argues that whites are in deep denial about their latent (and sometimes blatant) racism. Gay people and organizations are no exception, he insists. If anything, Hardy finds it even more painful when a gay group marginalizes or belittles African-Americans. "The River of De-Nile" is a painful reminder that the status quo still depends on some people having less status than others.

Andrew Holleran's "Survivors" is about a different kind of second-class status. Holleran reflects on what it means to grow old in a subculture so worshipful of youth. Gay life, in his view, has always been about coming out, the moment, cruising, being cruised; no one gave much thought to what might happen down the road. But as the contemporary gay rights movement nears its thirtieth birthday, for the first time there is a population of openly gay men moving into midlife and maturity. Holleran, for one, feels barred from the very house he helped to build. And for gay men "of a certain age," he posits, the usual difficulties of aging are exacerbated by the fact that so many of their peers have died. AIDS has left them not only grieving for lost friends and lovers but isolated in their struggle to come to terms with the loss of youth.

There are clearly many contentious issues—from within and without—that threaten to divide the gay community, but there remains much that unites us. Our individual and collective choices about how to define ourselves share a courageous creativity, an inventive questioning of established norms. If it is particularly confusing to be a gay man at the dawn of the new millennium, it is also thoroughly exhilarating. Never before have there been so many options.

Rafael Campo is someone who has difficulty knowing which community is most his: He is a poet, but also a doctor; an expatriate Cuban, but a politically liberal American; a gay man. And yet, despite his confusing conglomeration of identities—or, more likely, *because* of it—he is able to pinpoint the core of what community can mean. "Giving It Back" is about the ways in which simple acts of generosity can bridge the seeming gaps between disparate individuals. Campo describes how in his clinical work with patients, he confronts the democratic vulnerability of naked human bodies and is thus reminded daily that while we are all part of distinct subgroups, we also share a place in a single, transcendent community. "In illness," he writes, "as in desire, all people are indeed created equal."

20. FENTON JOHNSON

Appearing as a *Harper's* cover story just before the 1996 presidential elections, Fenton Johnson's insightful view of marriage—and how gay people might revamp the institution—galvanized nationwide discussion. Johnson is the author of two novels and a recent memoir about his own gay marriage, *Geography of the Heart.*

Reinventing Marriage

IT IS A TRUTH UNIVERSALLY ACKNOWLEDGED, THAT A QUEER IN POS-session of a good fortune must be in want of a mate.

Or so it seems these days in the gay and lesbian communities of America. What is this craze for coupling that has swept Castro and Christopher Streets, New Town and West Hollywood, Dupont Circle and South Beach and every other gay ghetto? Even as gays and lesbians are smarting from defeat over the issue of gays in the military, the national leadership launches a fight over access to an institution I eliminated from my personal cosmology sometime in my early twenties, around the time I understood that life had presented me with a choice between love and propriety.

And so we have come to this: Congress overwhelmingly passing the "Defense of Marriage Act," sponsored in the House by Representative Bob Barr (three marriages to defend) and endorsed by 1996 Republican presidential candidate Bob Dole (defending two). The White House press office called the bill "gay-baiting"; President Clinton (he of the colorful personal life) denounced it as "unnecessary," then proceeded to sign it.

Marriage. What can it mean these days? Peau de soie, illusion veil, old, new, borrowed, blue? Can it mean the same thing to a young lesbian—out since her teens, occasionally bisexual, wanting a child, planning a career— as to me, a forty-plus shell-shocked AIDS widower? Can it mean the same thing to a heterosexual couple, raised to consider it the pinnacle of emotional fulfillment, as to a same-gender couple, the most conventional of whom must find the label awkward? And in an era of no-fault divorce, can it mean to any of us what it meant to our parents?

In the 1996 presidential election, both major political parties attempted to make political opportunities from the battle over gay marriage, but the issue has been on the legal agenda for as long as twenty-five years— Minnesota (1971), Kentucky (1973), and Washington State (1974) each witnessed unsuccessful lawsuits seeking legal sanction of same-gender couples. Then in 1991 three Hawaiian couples—two lesbian, one gay male—sued the state over the denial of their applications for marriage licenses; on principle, a heterosexual ACLU attorney took the case. Two years later, to everyone's amazement, the Hawaii Supreme Court ruled in *Baehr v. Lewin* that the state's denial of licenses violated the Hawaii constitution's equal-rights protections. The court took care to note that the sexual orientation of the plaintiffs is irrelevant. Instead, at issue is discrimination based on gender: The state discriminates by offering benefits to married men and women that it denies to exclusively male or female couples.

This is no minor point. What the court ruled on in Hawaii is *not* "gay marriage" but simply *marriage*—whether the union of two people of the same gender qualifies for the benefits the state offers to mixed-gender couples, no matter if the spouses' reason for marrying is love or raising children or better Social Security benefits, no matter if they are gay or straight or celibate—in other words, all those reasons, good and bad, for which men and women currently marry.

The Hawaii justices remanded the case to the lower Circuit Court, presenting the attorney general with the challenge of justifying gender discrimination in marriage benefits. As expected, late in 1996 the Circuit Court found the denial of licenses to same-gender couples unconstitutional but immediately stayed its decision pending appeal to the state Supreme Court. As of this writing, attorneys for the plaintiffs expect that sometime in 1997 the Hawaii Supreme Court will reaffirm its initial decision, though given the determination and financing of the opposition, more litigation seems at least as likely.

If in fact the state court orders issuance of same-gender marriage licenses, the matter will surely be taken to the federal level. The issuance of marriage licenses is a matter of individual state policy, outside federal jurisdiction, but the recognition of those marriages across state lines is another matter. Politicians' rhetoric to the contrary, the "full faith and credit" clause of the U.S. Constitution does not necessarily require states to recognize marriages performed in other states; interstate recognition of marriage remains largely unexplored legal territory. If a couple marries in Hawaii, then moves to New York or Georgia, can those states refuse to recognize their marriage? The "Defense of Marriage Act" restricts federal benefits and rights to mixed-gender couples and permits states not to recognize marriages performed in other states.[1] Many legal experts doubt the act will survive a constitutional challenge, but in any case it invokes a resonant precedent: As recently as 1967, sixteen states refused to recognize mixed-race marriages legally performed elsewhere. Those anti-miscegenation laws were struck down that year by the U.S. Supreme Court in *Loving v. Virginia,* a landmark case which the Hawaii court cited at length in *Baehr v. Lewin.*

At stake first and foremost are the rights of gays and lesbians to assume the state-conferred benefits of marriage. The assumption of these rights is controversial enough, but *Baehr* invokes still larger considerations for an institution that has historically served as the foundation of a male-dominated society.

It's instructive to recall that in the late 1970s Phyllis Schlafly and her anti-Equal Rights Amendment (ERA) allies predicted that the codification of the equality of women and men, as embodied in a federal ERA, would lead to gay marriage, presumably because they felt that to codify the equality of women and men would be to undermine the social foundation on which traditional marriage rests. The federal amendment failed, but Hawaii (along with several other states) adopted its own ERA—and here we are, just as Ms. Schlafly predicted; right in the place, I argue, where we ought to be. For this is the profound and scary and exhilarating fact: To assume the equality of women and men is to demand rethinking of the institution that more than any defines how men and women relate.

Marriage has always been an evolving institution, bent and shaped by the historical moment and the needs and demands of its participants. The ancient Romans recognized the phenomenon we call "falling in love," but they considered it a hindrance to the establishment of stable households. Marriages certified by the state had their foundations not in religion or romance but in pragmatics—e.g., the joining of socially prominent households. Divorce was acceptable, and women generally powerless to influence its outcome; the early Catholic Church restricted it partly as a means of protecting women and children from easy abandonment.

At the beginning of the thirteenth century, faced with schisms and heresies and seeking to consolidate its power, the Catholic Church institutionalized marriage, officially declaring it a sacrament and requiring for the first time that a priest officiate—a crucial step in the intrusion of organized religion into what had previously been a private transaction. Several centuries later, the conception of "family" began transforming itself from an extended feudal unit, that often included cousins, servants, and even unrelated neighbors, to a tightly knit nuclear unit composed of parents and children and headed by a man. With marriage as its cornerstone, that idealized unit forms the foundation for virtually all legislation and litigation in American family law.

Throughout these developments, one aspect of marriage remained largely consistent: Even as they were idealized, women were widely regarded as chattel—part of the husband's personal property; marriage was state certification of that ownership. Then came the women's suffrage movement and a growing acceptance of the equality of women and men, along with the principle that the individual's happiness is of equal or greater importance than the honoring of social norms, including the marriage contract. Divorce became both common and accepted, to the point where even the woman who marries into wealth gains little economic security (absent a good lawyer or a prenuptial agreement).

Women have arguably gotten the worst of both worlds: Men may more easily leave their wives, but women are nowhere near achieving earning parity, so that now they get to cope with economic insecurity *and* the fear of being dumped. For every woman who revels in freedom and income from a fulfilling career, many more face supporting themselves and often their children on welfare or at a low-income salary with few benefits and no job security, dependent on child support or alimony often in arrears. No wonder that almost a third of babies are now born out of wedlock, a figure that has risen consistently since the 1950s. Some of those mothers (some of them lesbians) are choosing to build matriarchal families, but many more are giving birth to unplanned and probably unwanted children. Whether by design or happenstance, these unmarried women are the primary force in changing the profile of the family; any discussion about contemporary marriage that excludes them is pointless.

Given these dramatic changes in the practice and place of marriage as a cultural cornerstone, the time seems ripe for some new thinking, informed by the understanding that what's at stake is the evolution of our perception of the marriage contract and women's role in defining it. Understandably, advocates of same-gender marriage have shied away from territory so daunting, focusing on the narrower civil-rights issues—the need to extend, as required by our American commitment to equal treatment before the law, the invitation to another class of people to participate in the same troubled ritual, with one likely tangible result being a bonanza for attorneys specializing in gay divorce.

That fight is important, but in the long run the exclusive focus on civil rights minimizes the positive implications of the social transformation lesbians and gays are helping to bring about. For centuries, gay and lesbian couples, along with a significant number of nonmarried heterosexuals, have formed and maintained relationships outside of legislative and social approval that have endured persecution and duress for this simple reason: love. This is not to downplay the importance of the marriage license, which comes with rights and responsibilities without which gays and lesbians will never be considered full signatories to the social contract; nor is it to imply that these relationships are perfect. It is rather to point out the nature of gay couples' particular gift, the reward of those lucky enough to be given the wits to survive and courageous enough to use them: Many of us know as much or more about partnering than those who have fallen into it as a given, who may live unaware of the measure in which their partnerships depend on the support of conventions—including the woman's acceptance of the man's primacy.

Baehr v. Lewin represents the logical culmination of generations of challenge, by feminists joined later by gay and lesbian activists, to an institution once almost exclusively shaped by gender roles and organized religion. As such, it presents a historic opportunity to reexamine the performance and practice of the institution on which so many of our hopes, rituals, and assumptions are based; to reconsider what we are institutionalizing and why.

The Hawaii attorney general's years of intensive legal research have only confirmed that if one subscribes to the principles that government should not serve specific religious agendas and that it should not discriminate on the basis of gender, there is no logical reason to limit marriage benefits to mixed-gender couples. Opponents argue that same-gender marriage contradicts the essential purpose of the institution, which is procreation; but the state does not ask prospective mixed-gender spouses if they intend to have children, and the law grants a childless married couple the same rights and benefits as their most prolific married neighbors. Invoking the nation's Judeo-Christian heritage is no help—even if one believes that Christians and Jews should dictate government policy, a few of the most liberal denominations have already endorsed same-gender marriage, and the issue is under serious debate among mainstream sects.[2] How may the state take sides in a theological debate—especially when the parties to the debate are so internally divided? In 1978, the Supreme Court established in *Zablocki v. Redhail* that a citizen's right to marry is so fundamental that it cannot be denied even to individuals who have demonstrated they are inadequate to the task. Given that the law guarantees the right of deadbeat dads and most prison inmates to marry, what could be its logic for denying that right to two men or two women who are maintaining a stable, responsible household?

The strongest argument against same-gender marriage is not logical but arbitrary: Society must have unambiguous definitions to which it turns when faced with exactly these kinds of conflicts between the desires of its citizens and the interests of its larger community. In this case, marriage consists of a union between a man and a woman because that is how the majority defines the word, however unjust that may be for same-gender couples who wish to avail themselves of its rights.

Advocates of same-gender marriage respond that "larger community interests" is an evolving concept. Because an institution embodies social norms does not render it right or immune from change—slavery was once a socially accepted norm, just as mixed-race marriages were widely forbidden and divorce an irreparable stigma.

The rebuttal is accurate, but it evades the question of where the state draws the line in balancing individual needs and desires against the maintenance of community norms. In the case of marriage, why should it endorse same-gender couples but not (as communitarians argue will result) polygamists or child spouses? The question is more pressing because of the prevailing sense of cultural breakdown, wherein nothing seems secure, not even the definition of . . . well, marriage.

Surely the triumph of Reaganomics and corporate bottom-line thinking is more responsible for this accelerated breakdown of the social contract than the efforts of an ostracized minority to stabilize its communities; and in any case marriage and the family began their transformation long before the gay civil rights movement—by 1975, only six years after the Stonewall rebellion that marked the first widespread public emergence of lesbians and gays, fully 50 percent of marriages ended in divorce. But in uncertain times people search for scapegoats, and unless gays and lesbians can make a convincing case for the positive impact of our relationships, we are not likely to persuade any but the already converted.

Tellingly enough, male writers (gay and straight) have been more passionate than women in their attachment to traditional marriage forms. Among gay male writers, Andrew Sullivan *(Virtually Normal)* and William Eskridge *(The Case for Same-Sex Marriage)* have written lengthy supporting arguments. (In contrast, *Virtual Equality,* lesbian activist Urvashi Vaid's 400-page treatment of gay and lesbian civil rights, mentions same-gender marriage only glancingly, by way of offering a generalized endorsement.) Both Sullivan and Eskridge consider the legalization of same-gender marriage as a means toward encouraging same-gender couples to form stable, coupled units modeled after heterosexual marriage.

Sullivan makes an eloquent argument for gay marriage but gives only a nod to the high failure rate of heterosexual marriages. Eskridge is sensitive to the women's issues inherent in marriage, but like Sullivan he endorses the institution as it exists, albeit together with other options for partnering. Along the way he implicitly endorses the myth that marriage conveys the means to control sexual behavior to men (or women) otherwise unlikely to achieve such control, as well as the myth that gay men are more promiscuous than their straight counterparts.

Since great numbers of gay men remain partly or wholly in the closet, there's no accurate way to measure or compare gay and straight male experiences. But generalizations about gay male life based on behavior in bars and sex clubs are surely no more accurate than generalizations about heterosexual male behavior drawn from visiting America's red-light districts, where straight men guard their power by paying for a transaction they have previously outlawed, thereby rendering it dangerous for the women—the same transaction, it's relevant to note, which gay men (and, in very different ways, lesbians) accomplish for free between mutually consenting partners.

More discouraging is Eskridge's acceptance of the assumption that sexual desire is the beast lurking in our social jungle, whose containment is a prerequisite for a moral civilization (he subtitles his book *From Sexual Liberty to Civilized Commitment,* epitomizing in a phrase the puritanical equivalency of bachelorhood with moral lassitude, where single persons are morally suspect and sexual expression outside wedlock morally tainted). That sexuality and morality are intimately connected I take as a given; one loses sight of that connection at peril of one's self-respect, and by extension one's ability to love oneself and others. We are surrounded by evidence of that loss of respect, particularly in television and advertising, whose relentless promotion of amoral heterosexual sex is surely the greatest factor in breaking down public and private morality. But to presume that morality follows on marriage is to ignore centuries of evidence that each is very much possible without the other.

Among heterosexual male writers, even the most intelligent dwell in fantasy logic, where when they arrive at a difficult point they invoke God (an unanswering and unanswerable authority), or homophobic bombast, or both. James Q. Wilson, management and public policy professor at UCLA, is among the more reasonable, but even he attacks (with no apparent irony) the "overeducated," whom he accuses of "mounting a utilitarian assault on the family." As the ninth of nine children of a rural, blue-collar family whose parents (married forty-seven years) sacrificed a great deal to educate their children, I note that the only "overeducated" people I have met are those who take as gospel the rules they have been taught rather than open their eyes to the reality in which they live; who witness love and yet deny its full expression.

Not all men and women fall into marriage unconscious of role models, of course. But it's hard work to avoid a form shouted at us daily in a million ways; whereas for same-gender partnerships to fall into that form requires some deliberate denial. For same-gender relationships to endure, the partners have to figure out that we're required to make them up as we go along.

To point out as much is not to contend that we're always adequate to the task. In discussing modern marriage, real or potential, it's never a bad idea to consult a lawyer; and so I talked with my friend Frederick Hertz, an Oakland attorney specializing in same-gender partnerships.

Hertz originally entered the field opposed to same-gender marriage. "Marriage as it exists imposes a legal partnership on people that is seldom in sync with how they think about their relationship," he tells me. "Marriage is designed to take care of dependent spouses, people who stay home to take care of the children, as well as to compensate for economic inequalities between genders. The idea of supporting a spouse for the rest of his or her life is totally contrary to the way most people nowadays think." Hertz (a partner in a fourteen-year relationship) resists the "couple-ism" that he perceives arising among gays and lesbians because he believes it imitates a heterosexual world in which women whose partners die or abandon them are left with almost no social support. "I talk to straight divorced women in their forties and fifties," he says. "They have a lack of self-worth that's devastating. My single gay friends have a hard enough time—imagine what things would be like for them if marriage were the norm."

Then the realities of years of working with same-gender couples changed his opinion. "The problem is, wanting people to make their own, different, creative arrangements doesn't mean they'll do that," he says. "I think people should find their own ways to such agreements, but the fact is that they usually don't."

Enough experience with couples struggling without social approval brought Hertz to an uneasy support of the battle for same-gender marriage rights. Unlike most advocates, however, he qualifies his endorsement by adding that "while we're working for gay marriage rights we should also be talking about issues of economic and emotional dependency among couples. . . . a partner can contribute emotional support to a relationship that is as valuable to its sustenance as an economic contribution. We need to find legal ways to protect those dependent spouses."

To that end he argues for a variety of state-endorsed domestic partnership arrangements in addition to marriage, noting that though such categories may create a kind of second-class partnership, they're a step toward the state offering options that reflect contemporary life. "I want to go to the marriage bureau and have options among ways of getting married," he says. "I want the social acceptance of marriage but with options that are more appropriate for the range of couples' experiences—including childless couples."

In other words, rather than attempt to conform same-gender couplings to an institution so deeply rooted in sexism, why not consider ways of incorporating stability and egalitarianism into new models of marriage? Rather than consider the control of sexual behavior as a primary goal of marriage, why not leave issues of monogamy to the individuals, and focus instead on marriage as the primary (though not only) means whereby two people help each other and their dependents through life?

Invoking the feminist writer Martha Fineman, American University law professor Nancy Polikoff argues that organizing society around sexually connected people is wrong; the more central units are dependents and their caretakers. Extrapolating from this thinking, one can imagine the state requiring that couples regardless of gender accomplish steps toward attaining the benefits currently attached to marriage. Under this model, the state might restrict the most significant benefits currently reserved to marriage to those couples who demonstrate stability. The government might get out of the marriage certification business altogether—among others, Hawaii Governor Ben Cayetano has suggested as much. Government-conferred benefits currently reserved to married couples would instead be allocated as rewards for behavior that contributes to social stability. Tax breaks would be awarded regardless of marriage status to stable lower- to middle-income households financially responsible for children or the elderly or handicapped. Other state- or federally conferred privileges—such as residency for foreign spouses, veteran's benefits, tax-free transfer of property, and the right to joint adoption—would be reserved for couples who had demonstrated their ability to sustain a household over two or five years. The decision to assume the label "marriage" would be left to the individuals involved, who might or might not seek ratification of their decision by a priest or minister or rabbi. The motivation behind such changes would be not to eliminate marriage but to encourage and sustain stable households, while leaving the definition and sustenance of marriage to the partners involved, along with their community of relatives, friends, and—if they so chose—churches.

• • •

In the most profound relationship I have known, my partner and I followed a pattern typical of an enduring gay male relationship. We wrangled over monogamy, ultimately deciding to permit safe sex outside the relationship. In fact, he never acted on that permission; I acted on it exactly once, in an incident we discussed the next day. We were bound not by sexual exclusivity but by trust, mutual support, and fidelity—in a word, love, only one manifestation of which is monogamy.[3]

Polikoff tells the story of another model, unconventional by the standards of the larger culture but common among gay and lesbian communities: A friend died of breast cancer; her blood family arrived for the funeral. "They were astounded to discover that their daughter had a group of people who were a family, who'd been providing support—somebody had organized a schedule, somebody brought food every night," she says. "In some ways it was the absence of marriage as a dominant institution that created space for the development of a family defined in much broader ways." I find it difficult to imagine either of these relationships developing in the presence of marriage as practiced by most of our forebears; easier to imagine our experiences influencing in beneficial ways the evolution of marriage to a more encompassing, compassionate place.

Early in this journey I called myself an "AIDS widower," but I was playing fast and loose with words—I can't be a widower, since my partner and I were never married. He was the only child of Holocaust survivors, who taught me, an HIV-negative man preoccupied with the future, the lessons his parents had taught him: the value of living fully in the present and the power of love in bringing us to this place.

He fell ill while we were traveling in France, during what we knew would be our last vacation. After checking him into a Paris hospital, I had to sneak past the staff to be at his side; each time they ordered me out, until finally they told me they would call the police. Faced with the threat of violence, I left the room. He died alone as I paced the hall outside his door, frantic to be at his side but with no recourse—I was, after all, only his friend.

At a dinner party I asked a mix of gay and heterosexual guests to name ways society might better support the survival of gay and lesbian relationships. There followed a beat of silence, then someone piped up: "You mean, the survival of *any* relationships." Everyone agreed that all relationships are under stress; that their dissolution had become an accepted, maybe assumed part of the status quo.

The question is not, as opponents would have us believe: Will marriage survive the legalization of same-gender partnerships? Instead the questions are: How do society and the state support stable households in a world where the composition of families is changing, and how might same-gender relationships contribute to that end?

Denied access to marriage, lesbians and gays inevitably idealize it, but given the abuse the dominant culture has heaped on the institution, maybe it could use a little glamour. In my more hopeful moments, I think gays and lesbians might help revitalize and reconceptualize marriage by popularizing the concept of rich, whole, productive couplings based less on the regulation of sexual behavior and the maintenance of gender roles than on the formation of mutually respectful partnerships. *Baehr v. Lewin* presents us with a chance to conceive of a different way of coupling, but only if we recognize and act on its implications. Otherwise, the extension (if achieved) to same-gender couples of the marital status quo will represent a landmark civil rights victory but a subcultural defeat, in its failure to incorporate into the culture at large lessons learned by generations of women and men—lesbian or gay or straight—who built and sustained and fought for the integrity of partnerships outside the bounds of conventional gender roles.

In *Word Is Out,* the landmark 1977 documentary portraying lesbian and gay lives, comedienne Pat Bond described butch and femme role-playing among lesbians in the 1950s—roles as assigned and unvarying as those of Ozzie and Harriet. "Relationships that lasted twenty or thirty years were role-playing," she says. "At least in that role-playing you knew the rules, you at least knew your mother and father and you knew what they did and you tried to do the same thing. . . . Now you say, 'OK, I'm not butch or femme, I'm just me.' Well, who the hell is *me?* What do I do? How am I to behave?"

To heterosexuals who feel as if the marriage debate is pulling the rug of certainty from beneath them, I say: Welcome to the club. Gays' and lesbians' construction of community—which is to say identity—is the logical culmination of the American democratic experiment, which provides its citizens with an open playing field on which each of us has a responsibility to define and then respect her or his boundaries and rules. Human nature being what it is, the American scene abounds with stories of people unable, unwilling, or uninterested in meeting that challenge—people who fare better within a package of predetermined rules and boundaries. For those people (so long as they're straight), traditional marriage and roles remain. But for the questioning mind and heart, the debate surrounding marriage is only the latest intrusion of ambiguity into the artificially ordered world of Western political, social, and religious thinking.

And Western culture has never tolerated ambiguity. The Romans placed their faith in the state, the Christians in God, the rationalists in reason and science, but (in marked contrast to Eastern religions and philosophy) all have in common their search for a constant governing structure, a kind of unified field theory for the workings of the heart. The emergence of gays and lesbians from the closet (a movement born of Western religious and rationalist thinking) is only one among many cultural developments which reveal the futility of that search—how it inevitably arrives at the mystery that lies at the heart of being.

But the rules are so comforting and comfortable! And so it is easier to oppress some so that others might live in certainty, ignoring the reality that the mystery of love and life and death is really grander and more glorious than human beings can grasp, much less legislate.

Notes

1. States have always established their own standards for the recognition of marriage; no consistent, nationwide definition of marriage has ever existed. Currently, a few states (e.g., Pennsylvania) still recognize common-law marriages, though for such a marriage to be recognized in a non-common-law state, participants must usually submit to some official procedure. Some states allow first cousins to marry, some do not, and the minimum age for legal marriage varies from state to state, as does the actual recognition of such a contract across state lines.

2. Many gay Protestant congregations, Reform Jews, Unitarians, and a number of Quaker congregations have endorsed and/or performed same-gender marriage. Presbyterians recently passed a resolution urging the national office to explore the feasibility of filing friend-of-the-court briefs "in favor of giving civil rights to same-sex partners," and the Episcopalian church is studying the issue of blessing same-gender unions. In addition, Hawaii's Buddhist bishops have announced their support of same-gender marriage.

3. This is not to say that I find monogamy old-fashioned or useless. On the contrary, I learned from my partner its significance and necessity as one means to the end of unqualified trust and intimacy.

21. CHRIS BULL & JOHN GALLAGHER

As seasoned political correspondents for *The Advocate,* Chris Bull and John Gallagher were well positioned to pen *Perfect Enemies: The Religious Right, the Gay Movement, and the Politics of the 1990s.* The book's conclusion maps the possibility of a more peaceful coexistence between these warring grassroots factions.

From Arms to Armistice

THE RELIGIOUS RIGHT'S INTENTIONAL MISREADING OF HOMOSEXU-
ality deprives the public of accurate information about the lives of gays and
lesbians. If Americans were to take the religious right's depiction of homosexuals at face value, they would assume that gay life consists entirely of
NAMBLA conventions, S/M orgies, and Queer Nation demonstrations. In
reality, the gay community is at least as diverse as the evangelical community, and its "gay agenda" encompasses every imaginable ideology. Homosexuality and left-wing politics are not necessarily any more analogous than
evangelism and political conservatism. Indeed, the genius of the modern
gay rights movement is that it has translated homosexuality into gay iden-

tity, which has spawned a rich plethora of churches, businesses, political groups, sports associations, and publications across the country. Instead of furtive sex and clandestine relationships, gay identity offered a way for gays and lesbians to contribute to each other and to the larger community. The communal spirit of gays and lesbians, born to protect one another from the slings and arrows of a prejudiced society, has been exemplified by their response to AIDS. While the government dragged its feet in the early days of the epidemic, the gay community set up organizations to care for its sick and dying, launched massive HIV-prevention campaigns, and sounded the alarm for other communities at risk. But because the gay cause has often been framed by left-wing activists in terms of individual freedom and sexual liberty, the familial and communal aspects of gay life in America—and its contribution to and integration within the larger society—have largely been lost on the general public.

The religious right's limited understanding and mischaracterization of gays and lesbians represents the ultimate victory of fear over fact. By its obsessive focus on sexual behavior, it overlooks the depth and complexity of gay lives. To some evangelical activists, gays and lesbians can never compensate for the intrinsic "immorality" of their sexual orientation. As a "sin," it negates every other virtue, no matter how considerable. In a 1992 interview with *The Advocate*, Jay Grimstead, who as a dominion theologian contends that Christians are entitled to complete rule over all political institutions, explained that even a monogamous lesbian couple who contributed mightily to the larger community by caring for the homeless should be imprisoned or possibly even executed for their sexual sins. Heterosexual Americans, Grimstead explained, could simply be recruited to fill their vacant charitable role.

The evangelical drumbeat against gays and lesbians takes a heavy toll. The heat of the rhetoric has a dehumanizing effect on individuals, making them and their lives seem worthless both to others and themselves. Gay and lesbian youths, who often lack a community to protect them, are particularly vulnerable, succumbing to suicide at an alarming rate. In this hostile environment, it's not surprising that some people take the antigay rhetoric as license to lash out against gay people physically. Statistics collected by groups that monitor hate-inspired violence are staggering. According to Klan Watch, an organization of the Southern Poverty Law Center, gays and lesbians were the victims in over half the hate-inspired physical attacks in 1994, and gay men are the group most likely to be murdered. For gays and lesbians who do not conceal their identity, the fear of being assaulted on even the most gay-friendly streets in America remains palpable. Leaders of the religious right who are garrulous in their condemnation of homosexuality have skirted the all-too-real problem of violence against gays and lesbians, except to deny that they are responsible for it.

Having witnessed the currency of the victim card in contemporary politics, the religious right has sought to deal itself into the game, sometimes without any standing whatsoever. In an effort to portray her group as tolerant, Carolyn Cosby, head of Concerned Maine Families, a group that promoted an unsuccessful statewide antigay referendum in 1995, launched a campaign against gay- and straight-bashing in local churches that supported her antigay efforts. In doing so, Cosby implied that the two types of attacks are committed with roughly equal intensity and frequency. They are not, in fact, although Cosby maintains that antigay violence statistics are inflated in order to garner sympathy for gays and lesbians. There must be easier ways. While Cosby scrambles to cite even one incident of mistreatment of antigay activists, she pays short shrift to one of the most notorious cases of antigay violence in the country, which occurred in her own backyard. When he was attacked by taunting gay-bashers in Bangor in 1984, Charlie Howard, a twenty-three-year-old gay man, pleaded for his life. Instead, the gang threw him from a bridge into a river, killing him.

More often religious conservatives elevate their experiences with a few crank calls and legitimate, if sometimes raucous, demonstrations against their antigay views with Roman-style Christian-bashing. D. James Kennedy, a leading antigay minister in Florida, has repeatedly insisted that he is the true victim of the gay rights battle because he has been subjected to death threats. In 1994, Scott Lively, an Oregon Citizens Alliance activist, sought to have angry phone calls from opponents of his antigay views classified as a hate crime. Sometimes gay rights supporters do include harassment or the threat of violence, the cowardly action of intolerant individuals. But the threats have almost always remained just that. They are not the same as the epidemic of random physical attacks—some of which culminate in murder—against gays and lesbians. Evangelical Christians are not being attacked in the streets on a daily basis because of who they are. Nor do their institutions regularly face the prospect of vandalism and arson, which have proved all too real for gay bars, bookstores, and churches over the last thirty years.

In responding to charges of intolerance, leaders of the religious right regularly invoke their supposed love and compassion for gays and lesbians, but only by wishing their very identity out of existence. "Christians feel compassion for homosexuals and sincerely desire that they receive Jesus Christ as their Lord and Savior and experience liberation from their lifestyle," wrote religious right leaders Tim and Beverly LaHaye in their 1994 book, *A Nation Without a Conscience.* The strategy of offering to bring gays and lesbians to the Lord in exchange for their renunciation of their sexual identity allows the LaHayes and other antigay activists to portray themselves as compassionate and to deny the deleterious effects of their rhetoric. Responsibility for antigay discrimination and violence, they suggest, must lie with gays and lesbians themselves.

Given the dismal state of political discourse in America, it may be hoping for too much for the gay rights discussion to be polite. But at least it should be fair, reflecting a commitment to accuracy, and civilized. Both sides have joined a battle for the hearts and minds of Americans, which goes beyond votes. With cynicism toward political arguments running high, demonstrations of these qualities will go far in impressing people about the sheer urgency of taking a stand on gay rights and in encouraging them to make their judgments informed. Both sides should keep in mind that not just the futures of the gay rights movement and conservative Christianity in America are at stake, as important as these remain. At issue is the very integrity of the political process itself. The struggle, after all, involves not just the combatants.

The current debate casts into clear relief deep fissures in American culture and politics—between individual freedom, a classically liberal cornerstone of the nation's legal system, and absolute adherence to a strict Christian moral code, whose roots advocates claim date back to the country's founding. The contest between gays and the religious right has come to signify a test not only of the core principles of American democracy but also the basic tenets of Christianity. Underlying the debate are not just conservative and liberal views on sex and religion but competing theories of justice. The way America decides to treat its most unpopular members has a lot to say about what kind of society we live in and which direction American democracy is headed.

Ralph Reed, Jr., the executive director of the Christian Coalition, has spoken eloquently about the need to break away from the stereotype of the poor, easily led, inflexible evangelical. He is right when he says that any public debate requires decency, honesty, and respect for the other side. No matter what one thinks of their positions, evangelicals have long felt outside the political process, and their participation in it should be welcomed. Gay activists should recognize this and give their opponents credit for learning how to make the party system work for them.

But standards cut both ways, and Reed has been silent on the religious right's use of the most vicious stereotypes against gays and lesbians. Many of Reed's most fervent supporters, most notably his boss, Pat Robertson, continue a campaign by canard against gays and lesbians. Rabidly antigay fund-raising letters go out under the Christian Coalition letterhead on a regular basis, raking in millions of dollars for the group. Gays and lesbians, a June 1995 fund-raising letter charged, are "undermining" the bond between parents and their children by teaching that "homosexual love relationships can be as fulfilling as heterosexual relationships." That brand of antigay marketing is precisely the reason Robertson dealt so gingerly with a March 1995 hunger strike by Mel White, a gay onetime ghostwriter for Robertson who demanded that his former employer publicly denounce antigay violence. For Robertson and Reed, the stakes were high. If White had succeeded in raising the issue of the Christian Coalition's verbal gay-bashing to the level of a national issue, and had the press taken sufficient notice, it could have rocked the foundation of the group's thriving fund-raising machine. Perpetuation of antigay intolerance has become such a lucrative business, generating such a following among the groups' membership pool, that they cannot afford to step away from their hostility, lest they alienate their base. (In exchange for White's agreement to end his twenty-two-day hunger strike, which garnered little press attention, Robertson released a tepid statement criticizing antigay violence, which he later read on "The 700 Club," the cable-television talk show he hosts.)

Acknowledging the Jewish community's growing alarm at the ascendancy of the religious right and Robertson's history of anti-Semitism, in April 1995 Reed delivered a conciliatory speech to members of the Anti-Defamation League, claiming that "to be an object of fear rather than an agent of love and healing is contrary to all that we aspire to be as people." The reference made Reed's failure to extend an olive branch to gays and lesbians all the more glaring. Robertson is nothing if not an "object of fear" among gays and lesbians. Reed himself has said little about gays and lesbians. In his 1994 book, *Politically Incorrect: The Emerging Faith Factor in American Politics,* Reed scolded gay activists for taking on Eugene Lumpkin, the minister dismissed from the San Francisco Human Rights Commission. But what Reed doesn't say in his book is that Lumpkin had suggested that gays and lesbians should be stoned for their sins. Were the defamation redirected, and the safety of conservative Christians thus so badly threatened, Reed would have been first in line to demand Lumpkin's ouster.

In his Anti-Defamation League speech, Reed pledged to teach the history of the Holocaust—"however painful it may be"—to the Christian Coalition's membership in order to help "insure that Jews are never again the target of hatred and discrimination." But those sentiments were undercut by Robertson's support for a movement among a small group of religious conservatives to pin blame for the Holocaust on homosexuals. "When lawlessness is abroad in the land, the same thing will happen here that happened in Nazi Germany," Robertson said on the September 14, 1994, "700 Club." "Many of those people involved with Adolf Hitler were satanists. Many of them were homosexuals. The two seem to go together." While among the first brownshirts there was a small cadre of homosexuals (who were violently purged early on), no reputable historian has ever suggested that the Holocaust had any connection to Germany's gay rights movement. Gays did not determine the direction of the Third Reich; in fact, gays were among the groups that Hitler targeted for extermination, sacking the offices of an early gay rights advocacy group; ensnaring, arresting, and imprisoning homosexuals; and instituting the pink-triangle insignia, which latter-day gays would reclaim as a symbol of empowerment. The religious right's use of the Holocaust is an attempt to wrest control of the ultimate symbol of political repression away from gay activists, not legitimate historical inquiry.

Thus, some views promulgated by the religious right have no place in the political debate. The line of legitimacy is crossed when religious conservatives call for the "elimination" of homosexuality, as Reed has, as if gays and lesbians were not people, inextricably connected to every institution vital to the nation's survival, their families, churches, and each other, but simply a scourge. One wing of religious conservatives, with ties to a number of prominent leaders of the religious right, is particularly open in its contempt for constitutional democracy and hearty in its call for a theocratic rule in which gays and lesbians would cease to exist. Dominion theologists, or reconstructionists, seek to replace the American legal system with laws derived from the Old Testament. The father of that movement, the Reverend R. J. Rushdoony, advocates instituting the death penalty for "practicing homosexuals," a term one doubts could ever be applied to heterosexuals, as well as abortionists. Robertson has never gone that far. But he has mused openly about the idea. At a 1980 prayer meeting, he told his audience, "You've got a country filled with homosexuals, people who are living together outside of wedlock, who are engaged in drunkenness, fornication, drug addiction, crime, and violence. Now what are you going to do with these people? Are you going to kill them all? Are you going to put them in jail? How are you going to enforce righteousness on them?"

Not all members of the religious right would subscribe to a militant call for theocracy and an antigay pogrom. But they don't necessarily distance themselves from such proposals, either. Robertson, for example, has close ties to Rushdoony, raising questions about the televangelist's commitment to the fair and nonviolent discussion of politics that he claims to want. For all his claims of moderation, Reed's credibility is undercut by the connection to someone so openly theocratic in his leanings. As much disregard for the political process as gay activists occasionally display, they do not go so far as to advocate the overthrow of the democratic system of government, which includes the separation of church and state, or the elimination of antidiscrimination protections for their opponents, enshrined most notably in the same 1965 Civil Rights Act in which gays still seek inclusion.

Reconstructionism may be the most extreme example of the antidemocratic tendencies of the religious right, but it is not the only one. As much as the religious right trumpets the antigay ballot measures as triumphs of democracy, such initiatives are merely facades. True, the method allows issues to be brought directly before the voters. But the intent to harness majoritarian will is essentially antidemocratic, fencing out one group in particular from the political process forever and casting the durability of every minority's legal standing into doubt. Statewide measures are particularly repressive because they inhibit local political autonomy, where personal relationships between gays and the rest of the community, including evangelical churches, have the most potential for fomenting mutually agreeable resolutions on exactly how to protect gays and lesbians from discrimination, harassment, and violence. At any given point in the country's history, other minorities whose legal protections from discrimination would now never be subjected to such campaigns could just as readily have lost a direct vote aimed at them. This includes evangelicals, who, as Reed himself points out, have long suffered bigotry and discrimination. Evangelical activists would do well to consider how the vehicle they have commandeered against gays and lesbians could be applied against themselves.

Worse than the ballot measures are the arguments employed to promote them. The "special rights" slogan is as effective as it is dishonest. The shorthand term *gay rights* generally refers to ordinances that prohibit discrimination on the basis of sexual orientation in housing, employment, and public accommodations. In other words, you cannot be fired if your boss finds out you are gay (or, for that matter, straight). The laws uniformly provide broad exemptions for religious institutions, so that they do not have to obey a law that may run counter to their faith's traditions or beliefs. *Gay rights,* although a handy phrase, makes the legislation look far more sweeping than it actually is, and the religious right plays up that misapprehension. Because voters know little about the dry intricacies of the ordinances, the religious right can get away with raising the specter of quotas and conflating them with affirmative-action policies and far more sweeping civil rights legislation. In fact, no reputable gay leader has ever advocated that affirmative-action laws be extended to gays and lesbians. But gay groups have contributed to the problem. Every time an ordinance passes, gay leaders describe it as a huge victory for gay rights, when in fact it should be just one more step in the ongoing education of the public.

The media has failed in its responsibility to clear up these misunderstandings, much less elucidate the complexity of the debate and the possibility of common ground between the opposing forces. Newspapers from the *Colorado Springs Gazette-Telegraph* to the *New York Times* have failed to explain the elementary distinction between antidiscrimination protections and gay rights or special rights. Only a handful of reporters cover religious or gay issues on a regular basis, and few are well versed on the intersection of the two. Confronted by two worlds that are alien to them, journalists too often turn to the conventional wisdom about their subjects, which is pat and superficial, instead of delving below the surface to see what actually motivates the activists. Alternately cowed by the fear of offending either group and ignorant of the complexities of the topic, journalists rarely raise tough questions about the intemperate political tactics of each. Within the evangelical and gay press, the situation is not much better. Too much of the reporting and writing by both sides is intended to celebrate the cause rather than cast a cold eye on the players or strategies involved. Caught up in a culture war, each side is loath to show vulnerability by admitting mistakes, much less adopt a conciliatory tone to facilitate negotiations.

Ultimately, the religious right's antigay crusade boils down to reasserting the right not to associate with homosexuals in diverse areas of American life, from the military to the workplace, a right they do not apply nor dare advocate with regard to any other minority group. Such reckless arguments, going far beyond recognizing the right of religious people to make up their minds on matters of morality, improperly establish discrimination as a theological imperative, thus rendering gay activists' suspicion of religious arguments in public policy all the more well-founded and driving the wedge between the groups still deeper. Similarly, antidiscrimination protections, which have also come under attack from gay conservatives, embody for the religious right the federal government's propensity to force homosexuality on an unwilling citizenry. But the logical extension of that argument is that gays and lesbians should be denied a roof over their heads and the ability to earn a living. That position is not only cruel but represents an abdication of the responsibility all Americans share to learn to live and work with one another. This responsibility, again, however, cuts both ways, as gays and lesbians also must learn to respect the sensibilities of their evangelical neighbors and coworkers, refusing to succumb to stereotypical Southern accents in lampooning antigay adherents just as those ignorant about gay people should not stoop to mimicking gays with a deliberate lisp.

Neither the religious right nor the gay movement has been fully able to acknowledge the challenge of those who question the standard left-right dichotomy of the debate or to recognize their constituencies' severely flagging interest in waging a culture war. As the conservative evangelical leader Tony Campolo has demonstrated, it is indeed possible to adhere to a strict interpretation of biblical dictates against sex outside of traditional, heterosexual marriage while granting that, as hardworking, tax-paying, God-fearing American citizens, gays and lesbians deserve an equal place in the military and in all aspects of American life. Campolo, who has nearly impeccable credentials among religious conservatives, believes that some religious-right activists find refuge for their reflexive prejudice in the Bible. "It is too easy for any of us out of intense emotion to use Scripture in inexact ways to affirm what we believe to be right or to condemn what we believe to be wrong," he wrote in 20 *Hot Potatoes Christians Are Afraid to Touch,* which was published in 1988. "The fact that homosexuality has become such an overriding concern for many contemporary preachers may be more a reflection of the homophobia of the church than the result of the emphasis of Scripture." Campolo's measured stance, however, satisfies neither evangelicals, who consider it heretical, nor gay activists, who are offended that he continues to insist that homosexuality is a sin. After publicly advocating that the military ban on gay and lesbian service members be lifted, Campolo was inundated with criticism from conservative evangelicals, who seemed more concerned that he was calling into question the nearly unanimous opposition to equal rights for homosexuals on the religious right than about the merits of his argument. Gay activists who say they're only seeking "tolerance" while refusing to settle for anything less than "approval" risk precluding the possibility of finding common ground with the religious right for the sake of an admirable, but unobtainable, principle.

If the religious right and the gay movement are ever to enjoy the mainstream political acceptance that they seek, they are going to have to put aside their more destructive urges and engage in the hard work of politics: educating the public about the merits of their positions. Otherwise we will only see more ugly skirmishes where the participants go at one another and forget everyone else. Even if one side should emerge victorious, its integrity will have been so besmirched by its behavior that its triumph will be hollow. There's no honor in winning a culture war but losing the hearts and minds of a nation.

22. KEITH BOYKIN

Keith Boykin, Executive Director
of the National Black Gay &
Lesbian Leadership Forum, is the
articulate voice of a rising
generation of African-American
gay men. In this excerpt from his
book *One More River to Cross,*
Boykin lays the groundwork for
closer cooperation between the
black and gay communities.

Are Blacks and Gays the Same?

ADVANCING DOWN PENNSYLVANIA AVENUE LIKE AN ARMY OF THE
unwanted, legions of lesbian and gay marchers repeated a mantra-like
chant: "Gay, straight, black, white: same struggle, same fight." The organizers of the event—the 1993 National March on Washington for Lesbian,
Gay, and Bi Equal Rights and Liberation—liberally invoked the name of
Dr. Martin Luther King, Jr., and freely conjured up memories of the historic March on Washington for Jobs and Freedom thirty years earlier. By
labeling their march "A Simple Matter of Justice" and positioning themselves as the natural successors to the civil rights movement's legacy of
protest, the 1993 marchers were challenging the black community and the
public-at-large to welcome them into the mainstream of the American civil

rights tradition for social justice. Although the lesbian and gay movement had won the support of high-profile black leaders such as Coretta Scott King, the Reverend Jesse Jackson, and NAACP executive director Benjamin Chavis, conservatives in the black religious community balked, and since the black church had led the three-hundred-year struggle against the nation's most pernicious inequity, black religious leaders spoke with unparalleled credibility when they rejected any comparisons between blacks and gays.

By marching on Washington, lesbians and gays launched a major volley in the battle to reclaim the civil rights mantle, but they did so with the same strategy employed by their opponents. All the various factions—including the conservative religious community, the conservative military, and a relatively progressive black community that jealously guards the memory of the black struggle—have fought to extort, exploit, and appropriate the good name of the civil rights movement and its most visible icons. Each side, quoting selectively from history and speeches, portrays itself as the direct descendant of Dr. Martin Luther King's dream. White religious conservatives, who have discovered a fund-raising jackpot by exploiting homosexuals, seek to divide blacks against gays by playing on the black community's worst fears, telling blacks that their "legitimate" civil rights are threatened by the "special rights" requests of lesbians and gays. The religious conservatives, many of whom had not favored civil rights for blacks in the 1960s, suddenly call out the name of Dr. King to *oppose* gay rights as freely as King's widow uses his name to *support* gay rights.

While many mainline black civil rights leaders have endorsed in words, if not in deeds, the principle of equal rights for lesbians and gays, not everyone in the black elite agrees. General Colin Powell, former chairman of the Joint Chiefs of Staff, has become the most visible African-American opponent of the comparison between blacks and gays. In rejecting what he called the "attempts to draw parallels" between the ban on gays in the military and the segregation of black soldiers, Powell positioned himself in the tradition of Dr. King's vision when he wrote in May 1992 to white liberal representative Patricia Schroeder: "I can assure you that I need no reminders concerning the history of African-Americans in the defense of their nation and the tribulations they faced. I am part of that history."

Powell dismissively rejected the comparison between blacks and gays with three simple sentences: "Skin color is a benign, non-behavioral characteristic. Sexual orientation is perhaps the most profound of human behavioral characteristics. Comparison of the two is a convenient but invalid argument." Although the general spoke with the clarity and brevity that usually convey authority, each of his three statements can be proved wrong. Race is not merely a matter of skin color, nor has it ever been considered benign or nonbehavioral. The whole history of America's troubled race relations contradicts such rose-colored historical revisionism. In addition, sexual orientation is not just about behavior. To assume that sexual orientation is merely behavioral suggests that individuals have no sexual orientation when they are not behaving sexually. While the act of having sex, whether heterosexual or homosexual, is certainly behavioral, the mere orientation toward one gender or another is not. Finally, the comparison of race with sexual orientation is not only a convenient argument but a valid one, not because the two characteristics are exactly the same but because most people have misunderstood them. In his letter, Powell himself misunderstood the two and failed to consider that race is not only about blacks and that sexual orientation is not only about gays. Nevertheless, even Powell recognized some similarities between the plight of the two groups when he told President Clinton privately that he would oppose the segregation of homosexual soldiers if the gay ban were lifted.

In many ways, Colin Powell's public opposition to gays in the military shut off the debate prematurely. Coming from the nation's highest-ranking black soldier, his analysis allowed white conservatives to hide behind his unquestionable credibility and discouraged white liberals from challenging him directly. The general's comments deprived the country of a much-needed discussion about race and sexual orientation and allowed us to retreat to the safety of our cocoons, where we did not need to think for ourselves because someone had already done our thinking for us.

Rather than educating or leading the public about gays and blacks in the military, Powell's analysis simply echoed the popularly perceived distinctions between race and sexual orientation. In fact, much of the division between blacks and homosexuals can be traced to fundamental misconceptions that each group holds about the other. Arguing from positions of raw emotion, blacks and homosexuals and others often ignore the complexity involved in comparing race with sexual orientation. We find ourselves hopelessly mired in simplistic sloganeering rather than seriously considering similarities and differences of identity, behavior, mutability, and oppression. Only when we examine carefully how race and sexual orientation are defined and (mis)understood in this country can we better determine what common ground, if any, exists between blacks and gays.

Comparing Oppression

The basic elements of oppression are the same for nearly every group, including blacks and gays. Virtually all oppressed groups suffer from three types of oppression: internal oppression as the individual struggles with his or her identity; group-based oppression from others in the same category; and external oppression from those who dislike the group. Of course, the specific manifestations of oppression differ from group to group, so racism differs from anti-Semitism, which differs from sexism, which differs from homophobia. One group is enslaved and segregated, another is "exterminated," a third is dominated, and the last is "bashed."

Despite the differences, the experience of dealing with prejudice is, perhaps, the defining attribute of both blackness and homosexuality. Racial prejudice, whether they choose to realize it or not, affects all African-Americans, including black lesbians and gays. Of course, not all blacks feel they have suffered discrimination, and some say they have not been *overtly* victimized by racism. Similarly, although some homosexuals say they have not experienced discrimination or prejudice, the overwhelming majority of lesbians and gays are affected by antigay bias. Consciously or not, they often make changes in their appearance or behavior to conceal their identity and prevent discrimination, and this self-policing becomes a form of discrimination when it prevents them from being themselves.

Black heterosexuals might better understand the oppression experienced by homosexuals if they tried to put themselves in the position of lesbians and gays. In fact, the whole comparison between blacks and gays is better understood by substituting the word "black" for "gay" whether we talk about oppression, behavior, mutability, visibility, or discrimination. When we hear someone complaining "Why do gays have to be so vocal and militant?" we might as well ask "Why do *blacks* have to be so vocal and militant?" When black straight people laugh at "fag" or "dyke" jokes, they should remember how they feel when white people laugh at "nigger" jokes. When blacks find themselves complaining that gays have taken over or ruined their neighborhoods, think how similar that rhetoric sounds to the oft-heard complaint that *blacks* are taking over or ruining white neighborhoods. One of the most enduring qualities of oppression is not only that it teaches the oppressed to hate themselves but also that it teaches them to hate one another, pitting minority against minority in a senseless contest to replicate the oppressor. Remarkably, the oppressed absorb and accept the values of the oppressor. The external oppression directed at minority groups from outsiders becomes internalized both in the culture of the minority and in the individual's self-esteem. Thus, blacks and homosexuals learn to hate themselves and each other, and to overcome this hatred requires conscious reprogramming of their self-images.

The internal oppression suffered by individual blacks and gays, even as we recognize obvious differences in specifics, suggests similarities in how they experience oppression. Both are taught to see themselves as second-class citizens, often undeserving of society's acceptance unless they live up to the highest standards and assimilate into the majority culture's stereotypical view of itself.

Internalized racism seeps deep into the psyche of black people and their understanding of themselves. Nowhere is this phenomenon more evident than in our obsession with the various hues in our skin color, which we mistakenly use as a measure of attractiveness, intelligence, sophistication, class, racial purity, and racial identity. As law professor and author Patricia Williams observes in her essay "Alchemical Notes: Reconstructing Ideals from Deconstructed Rights," "The simple matter of the color of one's skin so profoundly affects the way one is treated, so radically shapes what one is allowed to think and feel about this society, that the decision to generalize from that division is valid." What Williams seems to articulate is a black self-identity not independently chosen but rather thrust upon us by the treatment we receive from nonblacks.

As with African-Americans, many homosexuals carry a unique set of psychological baggage with them. For example, a gay military man described to me the terror he experienced when he had to be interviewed for a top-secret security clearance. He had joined the military at a young age and did not then recognize his sexual orientation. But by the time of the security clearance interview, he knew that he was gay. He walked into the interview petrified that he would be hooked up to a machine or some mysterious device that would somehow read his mind to discover his homosexual thoughts. Another closeted gay man told me he had declined to sign up for sleep studies conducted by a university because he feared the electrodes would somehow telegraph his homosexual desires to the researchers. In these examples, homosexuals internalize the oppression of the larger society and conform their behavior accordingly, even before they come in contact with outsiders.

For African-Americans, internalized racism encourages conformity of appearance, which leads some of us to lighten our skin color or straighten our hair so we can pass as white, just as internalized homophobia encourages many homosexuals to pass as heterosexual. Any group that respects itself and its uniqueness will not need to define its status based on its assumed similarity to another group. However, my own mother, with natural, unrelaxed hair, once confided in me her reluctance to join our family for the winter holidays because she knew the other women in the family would chide her about her hair. "Girl, when you gonna get rid of those naps?" they would ask; or they would tell her, "I know you're not going anywhere with me looking like that." These messages reinforce Eurocentric images of beauty and underscore the internalized racism still suffered even by proud black women and men.

The fact that blacks divide themselves along color lines suggests two things: first, that skin color is not benign; and second, that internalized racism stigmatizes not only individuals but whole groups as well. With group-based internalized prejudice, a whole group or its leaders attempt to define themselves by drawing lines that include what they are and exclude what they are not, often borrowing the definitions of their oppressors. On the slave plantations of the Old South, lighter-skinned blacks were often selected to perform the master's household duties, while darker-skinned blacks were left to work in the fields. Because white was the highest standard, the lighter slaves were considered more refined by blacks as well as whites. Though white slaveowners probably never held either light- or dark-skinned blacks anywhere close to the white level, in the hierarchy among slaves the lighter-skinned blacks could claim some pride and superiority over their darker-skinned brothers and sisters.

The antebellum slave mentality toward color has not disappeared entirely from American black thought. In a landmark legal case in 1989, a black woman in Georgia filed a lawsuit against her employer, alleging that her black supervisor had her fired because of her skin color. The lighter-skinned black employee, a clerk-typist for the Internal Revenue Service, claimed that her darker-skinned black supervisor constantly harassed her. "She told me I needed some sun . . . that I'd had life too easy and I was going to have to work for my position under her," the employee testified in court.

Black people constantly divide themselves based on skin color, creating exclusive social cliques such as "brown paper bag" clubs, which restrict membership to those blacks with skin color lighter than a standard grocery bag. We even allow our skin color to affect our perception of ourselves. In my family, for example, I was always thought of as light-skinned because I was a shade or two lighter than others in the family. It was not until years later that my own perception of my skin color changed, when a darker-skinned friend described me as having a skin color similar to his own. My first inclination was to protest my friend's label by objecting that I was not as dark as he, but I resisted the temptation when I realized it reflected my own bias about skin color. I eventually no longer thought of myself as light-skinned.

Lesbians and gays, like everyone else in society, are bombarded with images of gender conformity from their families, their employers, their friends, and, especially, the media. The images tell young people that men may be intimate only with women, not with other men. They teach little girls to play with dolls and little boys to play with toy soldiers. They instruct children that men are tough and don't cry, while women are emotional and do cry. Most disturbingly, the pursuit of these images ultimately punishes even young practitioners of gender nonconformity with epithets and labels such as "sissy," "tomboy," "punk," "faggot," and "dyke." By using these terms to challenge outward expressions of gender role difference, society regulates the perception of the pervasiveness of homosexuality. Society's compulsory heterosexuality, as well as the related risk for those who challenge the norm, ensures that fewer homosexually oriented persons than actually exist will choose to identify themselves as such.

Group-based oppression leads to the difficult question of who decides exactly who or what is an acceptable part of the group. For instance, at a Harlem press conference after New Alliance Party presidential candidate Lenora Fulani shouted down then Arkansas governor Bill Clinton, a man in the audience interrupted her remarks: "I came here to hear him," the New York Times reported. When she told the man that she was speaking up for black people, he shot back, "Don't tell me about black people. I've been black all my life."

To challenge another's blackness requires confidence in knowing just what that blackness consists of, yet can we agree on what it means to be black in America? What is uniquely black in thought, culture, and experience? Is it a blue-collar family in the projects of Chicago, or is it an upper-middle-class family in a brownstone in Brooklyn? Is it a family at all? Who represents black values? Is it the millions of Sunday worshippers praying to Jesus, or is it the millions of Muslims turning east to bow to Allah? Is it the couple working two jobs to support a family of four kids, or is it the stereotypical single mother watching soap operas and talk shows at home with her boyfriend? And who represents black political values? Do blacks agree more with former Supreme Court Justice Thurgood Marshall or with current Justice Clarence Thomas? What is the essence of blackness anyway? Is it the color of the skin, the shape of the nose, the curvature of the lips, the size of the butt, the kinkiness of the hair? Is it the soul food, the R&B music, or the mud cloth scarf that makes someone black?

We experience the same problems when we attempt to define homosexuality. What does it mean to be gay in America? What is uniquely gay in thought, culture, and experience? Is homosexuality ultimately reducible to a simple sexual act? If so, what is that act and how do we classify self-identified lesbians and gays who do not engage in it? How do we define people who engage in same-sex sexual behavior but do not consider themselves gay? Are those who live in stereotypical urban "gay ghettos" more gay than those who live outside these enclaves? Is gay marriage a betrayal of gay liberation or an affirmation of homosexual responsibility? Do lesbians and gays identify more with radical ACT UP protesters or with conservative Log Cabin Republican Club members? Who decides what is or is not gay, and to whom are they accountable?

The fact that we ask these questions of ourselves with any expectation of acceptable answers reflects an internalized prejudice that disrespects the diversity of our many different people. Often in an effort to put forward a "positive" image for our oppressors, we foolishly attempt to construct a single image of blackness or homosexuality to incorporate millions of different people. Rather than challenging the oppression that such values represent, our efforts to present "positive" images reinforce the dominance of cultural values with which minority communities may disagree. For blacks, this desire to project "positive" images sets up a tension between the need to include all black people in the struggle and the need to exclude certain blacks from the projected image. Therefore, we criticize those blacks who self-exclude from the community and simultaneously exclude and ostracize blacks who we believe do not fit our own stereotypes and biases about what it means to be black.

Of course, most blacks are fairly well settled with what it means to be black: It means our day-to-day experiences. But this does not stop us from—in fact, it may encourage—challenging the experiences of other blacks as being less authentic than our own. A poor black person living in the "hood" might label another black person living in a prosperous *black* suburb as an "Uncle Tom," but the black suburbanite might label still another black person as an "incog negro" because that person lives in an all-*white* suburb. By creating our subjective hierarchies of black authenticity, we arbitrarily divide ourselves into acceptable and unacceptable categories of racial identification. Although we may think we understand what it means to be black based on our own experience, this thinking often clouds, rather than clarifies, what it means for our race as a whole.

Lesbians and gays are not immune to the same divisions that plague black people. We, too, create hierarchies of authenticity and criticize those who self-exclude from the community as "closeted" or unable to deal with their homosexuality. For both blacks and gays, we start to see the ridiculous nature of our litmus tests when we realize that we end up excluding not only blacks who are not black enough and gays who are not gay enough but also those thought to be "too black" or "too gay." We blacks, for example, call ourselves "niggers," joke among ourselves about our stereotypical behavior, and even distance ourselves from those who "show their color." We homosexuals call ourselves "fags" and "dykes," sometimes in an effort to reclaim the language of our oppressor, but just as often to criticize one another. "I hate fags," one gay man said to me, as if to distance himself from his own identity.

At times, black people seem to shoulder the burden of the entire race whenever another black person makes a spectacle of himself in front of whites. When a stereotypical black homeless man strolls onto a city bus and begins to talk loudly to himself, some blacks admit that they internalize the expected perception of the white passengers on board. This is why we half-jokingly say that someone has "set back the entire race," as though any one individual could or should be allowed to cause such damage. Many black parents, therefore, have taught their children to act the way white people want them to behave or to dress in a way that makes whites feel comfortable and unthreatened. Not surprisingly, homosexuals shoulder similar burdens, distancing themselves from "flamboyant" gay men, "butch" lesbians, drag queens, or whoever does not fit the image we want to project about our identity.

Group-based censorship of "negative" images takes on heightened proportions among lesbians and gays because the community actually buys into many of the dominant culture's stereotypes about itself. The frequently raised question of whether to include bisexuals and transgendered people in the lesbian and gay community highlights this tension. Bisexuals are thought to portray the wrong image because their existence suggests that homosexuality might be a choice rather than an orientation. Transgendered people, including transvestites and transsexuals, project the image that lesbians and gays are actually just confused about their gender. The mainstream lesbian and gay community fears both of these groups because they confirm the larger society's stereotypes about homosexuality. As with the black community, the gay community seeks to present not an accurate image of who its members are but, instead, a questionably "positive" one that ignores the group's diversity.

Some African-Americans, like some lesbians and gays, would prefer to assimilate and do not feel oppressed by responding to societal pressure. Black writer Shelby Steele, for example, has discouraged the black search for difference from white society and encouraged a more color-blind, racialless attitude. Similarly, in the gay community, columnist Andrew Sullivan argues for gay marriage not only because it legitimates gay unions but because it facilitates the process of assimilation into the dominant culture.

I do not want to understate the potential value of creating a "positive" image in terms of shaping public opinion. If the goal of the gay rights movement is to pass laws that protect average-looking, mainstream lesbians and gays, then "positive" images will help. However, if the movement's goal is to liberate and challenge the larger culture to welcome and celebrate all types of difference, then the use of only "positive" imagery will backfire. Virtually all minority communities, including blacks and gays, wrestle with the conflict between assimilation and liberation as they struggle for their freedom. Few minority groups are sufficiently homogeneous to advance their entire community's goals with only one strategy. It makes sense to use "positive" images if they facilitate the passage of antidiscrimination legislation that protects the entire community, but it also increases the need for the movement to go beyond political transformation into social transformation so that the people not included in the legislative promotion campaign are not left behind.

How we choose to define ourselves is important because the descriptive informs the prescriptive: what we *prescribe* to heal our many wounds as a people depends on how we *describe* the injury or the wounded.

Comparing the famous 1963 March on Washington with its 1993 lesbian and gay counterpart reveals the strengths and weaknesses of the assimilation strategy. The 1993 march participants consciously borrowed from the rhetoric of the 1960s civil rights demonstrations, but they planned their event without the rigidity that characterized the 1963 march.

Bayard Rustin, the black gay man who coordinated the 1963 march, scripted every detail down to the second. He scheduled the buses, plotted the route, and threatened the speakers with embarrassing removal if they did not stick to their time limits and their approved remarks. Male participants wore shirts and ties, and female participants wore skirts or dresses. Black New York City police officers were designated to serve as marshals, lobby visits were supervised by march organizers, and the banners and placards were produced by the march staff. The theme of the march was carefully focused on "jobs and freedom," and the marchers' demands included passage of President Kennedy's civil rights bill, a $2 minimum wage, desegregation of schools, a federal public works program, and federal action to bar racial discrimination in employment practices. (All these demands were accomplished in a matter of years.) Rustin even accepted a lower title and less visible role because some civil rights leaders feared he projected the wrong image as a gay man. All these things were designed to send a message that black people should be given their civil rights because they are just like everyone else in America.

The 1993 March on Washington was quite different. It was arranged by a four-person, cogender, biracial cochair coordinating structure, under the guidance of a 250-person nationwide steering committee. The speakers' remarks were not scripted or reviewed in advance for approval, and even though the entire event was broadcast live on C-SPAN, a lesbian comedian told jokes that many Americans must have considered offensive, including one about "fucking" the First Lady. Another speaker, AIDS activist Larry Kramer, had been excluded from the speakers list but managed to speak anyway by orchestrating a temporary coup with the marshals, who physically blocked a march cochair from the stage. There was no dress code for the speakers, let alone for the participants, who came in T-shirts, tank tops, bare chests, and even bare breasts. The march organizers presented a list of seven demands and fifty-five related items, ranging from lifting the ban on gays in the military and passing a federal antidiscrimination bill to finding a cure for AIDS, ending sexist oppression, and implementing graduated age-of-consent laws. (None of these demands has been accomplished.)

Although the nonthreatening assimilation strategy employed by the black community paid off in legislative victories, the social revolution necessary to transform America's attitudes toward blacks never took place. The same negative stereotypes have persisted long after passage of civil rights legislation, and the socioeconomic changes that enabled the black middle class to develop did little to eliminate the prejudice against the black underclass. In other words, it became acceptable to be black and prosperous and well educated, but poor, undereducated blacks were still despised.

Similarly, we might expect that a homosexual assimilation strategy that puts forward only "positive" images of lesbians and gays will leave behind the parts of the community that suffer double and triple discrimination because of other differences based on race, class, gender, appearance, or education.

23. DAVID BERGMAN

Best known as a poet and as editor of the *Men on Men* gay fiction collections, David Bergman wrote this essay in response to what he considers a dangerous assimilationism exemplified by Bruce Bawer and other gay conservatives.

A Place for the Rest of Us: An Open Letter to Bruce Bawer

DEAR BRUCE,

I've read your book, *A Place at The Table : The Gay Individual in American Society* and some of the reviews of it. A few of the reviews I've read have been positive, but none of them, I think, have been just to you. They've failed to note the really heroic sincerity of your book, your painful effort to be evenhanded to those you oppose both on the left and the right. They've ignored the passion of the book and your deep love for your companion, Chris Davenport. In some way *A Place at the Table* is a long valentine to him, and I find that very moving. The reviews have ignored the deep moral examination of your own conduct. But most of all they have ignored your concern for young gay men and women growing up in this society. I am sorry that these virtues haven't been acknowledged by the critics, because without recognizing these qualities they will not be able to account for the profound influence your book will have. I don't want to hide that I think your book is very wrongheaded, but I am glad you have written it because it articulates what many people feel in ways that can lead to much better mutual understanding.

Like me, you show a great concern for young people; in fact, you see the worried, frightened, isolated teenager as your ideal reader. You open your book with an account of a young man, whom you assume from his "neat dress and good posture" and from the "wholesomeness and sensitivity" he radiates to be "the much-loved son of a decent family." You watch him at a magazine rack slowly gravitate to a copy of the *Native,* and you are "irked" because the journal contained "the narrow, sex-obsessed image of gay life" which "bore little resemblance to my life or to the lives of my gay friends—or, for the matter, to the lives of the vast majority of gay Americans." (I will spend a lot of time quoting you, because I don't want to put words in your mouth in the way that you put words in other people's mouths.) However, at the end of the anecdote, you do nothing to help the young man, and it's not clear from anything in the book that with the exception of writing *A Place at the Table* you have done anything for young people despite your expressed concerns for their welfare.

I'm sorry your contact with young gay people has been so limited. They need the help. Moreover, you might learn from them not to be so anxious about the harmful effects of the *Native* or other gay publications, and finally, if you spent some time with young people you might be less censorious of others—the teachers at the Harvey Milk School, professors in Gay Studies Programs—who have dedicated themselves to working with the young.

I know it's been a great privilege for me to serve for the last few years as the faculty advisor to the gay, lesbian, and bisexual student organization at Towson State University, a rather large state institution in Maryland. I've also taught such courses as Images of Masculinity, a look at both gay and straight male autobiography, and The Literature of AIDS—courses you may sneer at as being "subcultural-oriented courses." So I've done my share of working with just the types of young people you're concerned about.

What I learned is that teenage and college-age people don't have to read the *Native* to be "sex-obsessed," their hormones will do that quite nicely. Even your well-scrubbed, much-loved boy is no stranger to sexual obsession. Second, the students are quite good at deciding which fantasies are theirs and which are someone else's. Your young man had enough self-knowledge that he didn't want to look at *Penthouse,* and I feel confident that he won't start wearing nipple clamps just because he saw them advertised. Finally, if you want to help young people develop as individuals, you can't impose on them your standard of how they should express themselves as gay men or lesbians. That well-scrubbed boy may, in fact, want to wear leather or taffeta. One of the nicest, sweetest men in my student group—who has adoring parents and who works part-time in a bookstore—took an extra job as a go-go dancer at a local bar. It's not something I or his school friends encouraged him to do; they are as puzzled by this decision as I am. When I asked him why he took the job, he told me he liked dancing and the job brought in good money. I don't think those are the only reasons, but I'm not going to presume to know his motives. I would not be helping the young man if I said, "How awful! How disgusting! That's not what decent, middle-class males do." Nor would you be helping the young man at the magazine rack if you told him, "Believe me, most gay people don't do those disgusting things." He might feel even more alone than he already feels.

What is of the utmost importance in working with young people is not to impose what you like, what you feel comfortable with on them, or to presume that you know their hearts better than they do. As you point out, the range of human emotion, the rate of growth and maturity, the levels of comfort differ in every individual. Again as you point out, one needs to be more than tolerant, one needs to be accepting. It seems to me that you should take your own words to heart if you really mean to help people develop as happy individuals. Helping that young man is not at all as simple as you seem to think. Twenty years teaching have not always shown me what to do. I don't suppose you've gotten calls in the middle of the night from a gay student ready to commit suicide because his parents threaten to kick him out on the street, or from a bisexual mother whose two-year-old daughter has been diagnosed with leukemia, or from frightened teenagers of both sexes who learn their best friend has AIDS. Their lives are more complicated than ours ever were, and the picture of a drag queen or a man in leather doesn't faze them.

If you had worked with young people maybe you wouldn't be so critical of the teacher at the Harvey Milk School who excused the lateness of students by saying they were on "Gay People Time." You thought the teacher was reinforcing a stereotype, and "stereotypes are prisons." I understood his joke as an attempt to bring to students' attention their tardiness and their stereotypical behavior without turning the matter into a big deal. As you point out, the students at the school are "emotionally bruised young people" and coming down hard on them at this time in their lives may not be the best strategy for their overall development. I suppose the point I'm making is that for all your talk about wanting to foster individuality, you don't give people much room to find their own way to live their lives. You make your pronouncements about what's good and bad for people from a safe distance. I'm not so ready to second-guess the teacher at Harvey Milk as you are.

But it's not only the teacher at the Harvey Milk School you patronize, it is everyone involved with education. You tar with a very wide brush anyone involved in Gay and Lesbian Studies. First you claim that we're interested in "therapy" more than in "education." But since Socrates, the basis of Western education has been the injunction that "the unexamined life is not worth living" and that educational institutions were meant to fit young people to be fully productive members of society. I don't see how helping students understand themselves and function better (which is what I suspect you mean by "therapy") can ever be divided from the accumulation of facts and the development of cognitive skills (your limited idea of "education"). The two must go hand in hand.

You mock any attempt to teach students—gay, straight and in-between—about homosexuality. Here's what you say based on reading merely the titles of workshops and course descriptions (a typical strategy of the reactionary right):

> Gay Studies might have a valid purpose if it could help students better
> understand certain heretofore neglected aspects of Marlowe's plays, say, or
> Raphael's paintings, or Benjamin Britten's music. In reality, however, far from
> probing and questioning and attempting to understand, Gay Studies imposes
> reductive, politically correct ideas upon its subjects, mindlessly celebrating gay
> solidarity and the untying of lesbian tongues, for example, instead of seeking
> to understand major historical figures as individuals in whose lives and work
> sexuality functioned in very different ways.

Now I am highly critical of much of the work in Gay Studies, and have published my criticism in some detail, but your statement takes no notice of the very wide debates going on within Gay and Lesbian Studies about methodology and subject matter. In your words, no one is studying major figures, all gay studies celebrate "solidarity," no distinction is ever made between artists. How many of these classes have you attended? How many conferences have you gone to? I don't know what works in Gay Studies you have been reading, but a more careful examination will indicate that it is you who are reductive. May I suggest Claude Summer's *Gay Fiction,* Mark Lilly's *Gay Men's Literature in the Twentieth Century,* James Saslow's *Ganymede in the Renaissance,* Michael Moon's *Disseminating Whitman,* Jonathan Goldberg's *Sodometries,* or my own *Gaiety Transfigured*? These books take very different approaches, come to very different conclusions, have very different goals. Some of these books I thoroughly disagree with; in others I find larger areas of agreement, but nobody who has read these books carefully and without prejudice could come away believing they are cut from the same cloth. Did you think you were doing young people a service by tearing at everyone who tries to address Gay and Lesbian Studies?

Indeed, one of the largest contradictions in your book is between your rather moving attacks on the inadequacy of labels, the dangers of pigeon-holing people, the intellectual dishonesty of large groupings, and the way you like to pin labels on people, just as you've done in the passage above where you lump all people in classes on Gay Studies together. Here, for example, is what you say about labels:

> Labels, political and otherwise, have often seemed to me to create divisions where there need be none, to magnify minor divisions into greater ones, and to bind people to extreme positions that they might in other circumstances find anathema. . . .
>
> A friend of mine once complained that my views on various issues didn't add up neatly into any ideologically orthodox position. . . . She wanted to be able to label me, to put me on a shelf. This is what most people want, because focusing on labels makes life easier. Label yourself and you'll always know what to think, even without thinking; label others and you'll always know who are your enemies and who are your friends.

Bravo! These are fine words. And yet your analysis over and over divides gay people between two camps. "There is a broad cultural divide," you tell your reader. "We might call them, at the risk of drastic oversimplification, 'subculture-oriented gays' and 'mainstream gays' " (p.35). This oversimplification could admittedly be useful if you then went on to show the groups are far more complicated than that. But to the contrary, even though you know the dangers of labels and that your own labels are "drastic oversimplification," you stick to them. Is it because with these labels you can pretend to know who are your friends and who are your enemies?

I must admit that I never really understood this distinction between "subculture-oriented gays" and "mainstream gays." Whenever I thought I was getting a clear notion, you'd say something that thoroughly confused me. Here, for example, is how you describe the "subculture-oriented gay" living "near one extreme" of the gay lifestyles: he is a person "born into a more or less ordinary family in Wisconsin or Missouri or Georgia" who comes to live in a gay ghetto, works at a "marginal [or] at least vaguely artistic" job, patronizes gay business and cultural events, belongs to "at least one AIDS-related organization," and whose " 'lifestyle' would probably be considered aggressively nonconformist by most Americans" (pp.33–34). What first struck me about this description is that it doesn't seem to me extreme at all. I know a lot of people a lot more "deviant" than this man. In fact, your aggressive nonconformist in many ways appears to be a model citizen. After all, here's a guy who works for a living, pays his taxes, obeys the law, contributes to the local economy, remains politically informed and civically conscious, helping out people less fortunate than himself. If most people regard him as "aggressively nonconformist," where's the terrible sin? Isn't this a land of liberty and freedom where people are supposed to be allowed to live as they choose as long as they don't hurt anyone? What's the difference between being a "nonconformist" and "individualistic"?

In your disdain for the "aggressively nonconformist," I am reminded of John Stuart Mill, who wrote in *On Liberty:*

> In this age, the mere example of nonconformity, the mere refusal to bend the knee to custom, is itself a service. Precisely because the tyranny of opinion is such as to make eccentricity a reproach, it is desirable, in order to break through that tyranny, that people should be eccentric. . . . the amount of eccentricity in a society has generally been proportional to the amount of genius, mental vigor, and the moral courage which it contained. That so few now dare to be eccentric marks the chief danger of the time.

You might find that those nipple clamps and bike pants are not an enemy of democracy, but two of the foot soldiers in the war against "the tyranny of opinion."

Anyway, after reading the above description, I believed I did know what you meant by the "subculture-oriented gay," but then I came to your encomium to the characters in *Longtime Companion.* Unlike the hypothetical man described above, the couples in *Longtime Companion* were drawn from the "everyday life of middle-class gay male couples . . . like me and my lover; they walked the same streets we did, shared the same body of cultural references . . . held up a mirror to a version of 'gay life' that was familiar to me." In short they represented the "mainstream gay male." But how do the characters in *Longtime Companion* differ from the extreme "subculture-oriented gay"? In *Longtime Companion,* much of the action takes place in the Pines at Fire Island, which is as much of a gay ghetto as one is likely to find. Their friends seem to be exclusively gay, except for the one young woman, who is clearly (to use the vulgar expression) a "fag hag." When one pair goes out to celebrate, they patronize a gay restaurant. One is an actor on a daytime drama, another a writer for a daytime drama, a third a gym instructor—these seem to be the marginal or "vaguely artistic" jobs you criticize the poor extremist for holding. And like the extremist, the characters in *Longtime Companion* don't seem to be from New York—two are clearly Southern. By the end of the movie, four work for "AIDS-related organizations." So why are the people in *Longtime Companion* "mainstream gays," whereas your earlier figure was "subculture-oriented"?

The only answer seems to be that "subculture-oriented gays" are poor whereas these men are not, as you claim, "middle-class" but fairly wealthy. David, for example, is described as "filthy rich" and his lover is a writer for a network show—clearly they have big bucks. Fuzzy is a theatrical lawyer, and seems to be doing quite well for himself, while our soap-opera actor makes well over $100,000 a year. And they are all so pretty. When I showed *Longtime Companion* in my AIDS literature class, the students—most of whom were straight women—disliked it. They said it had the blandness of "an afternoon special," although they were disturbed by seeing men kiss in bed together. These suburban teenagers wanted to know where the black people were. (The only black is a practical nurse.) It didn't strike them as "real life" in the least.

I found my students' reactions especially interesting, because one of your greatest claims about "mainstream" gays is that they face reality. For example, one of the components that divide "subculture-oriented gays"— and as a usually graceful writer you should have recognized that there was something wrong in your analysis by the clumsiness of these classification titles—from "mainstream" gays is that subculture gays like to live in ghettos whereas "most adult homosexuals simply don't *want* such a life."

> They were raised in conventional middle-class neighborhoods, and they want
> to spend their lives in similar homes and neighborhoods, and they don't see
> why being gay should prevent them from doing so. Nor do they like the idea
> of inhabiting an exclusively, or even mostly, gay world: such a world feels

artificial to them, feels like an escape from reality. They want to live in the *real* world" (p.35).

Like you, I grew up in Queens, and I know those Queens neighborhoods. They are almost always racially divided; they are usually ethnically and religiously divided. They tend to be economically homogeneous. Queens, for example, is the borough of Archie Bunker. I grew up in Laurelton, an all-Jewish, all-middle-class ghetto. I'm not sure what is the *real* world, but I do know that Laurelton is no more "real" than Chelsea or the West Village. In fact, I can't think of anyone but you who would call the Lower East Side, where many gays and lesbians live, an escape. I now live in Baltimore, which has lively neighborhoods, almost all of them fairly divided along racial, ethnic, and economic lines. The area I live in around John Hopkins University is a place many gays and lesbians live, but it also one of the most ethnically, racially, and socially varied parts of the city. Do you really want us to believe that the suburbs are the *real* world, and the urban centers are an escape? Really, Bruce, that is too, too easy.

But I will agree with you that gays and lesbians should be able to live wherever they want, which is why those subcultural types—that supposed cadre of alien escapists—worked so hard to try to pass housing and employment antidiscrimination laws and why in Baltimore when a gay couple was being harassed by their neighbors because they didn't want gays living in *their* neighborhood, subcultural types rallied to the couple's support and made sure they got the police protection they needed. If there is an element of escapism, it is in the person who wants to shut himself off in the neighborhood he has always known, unwilling to explore what it would be like to live elsewhere among less familiar surroundings. If you want to live in Queens, all the more power to you. But don't defend your choice by claiming that others want to escape reality.

Another oversimplified distinction you make is that "to be a subculture-oriented gay, then, is to center one's identity on one's homosexuality" (p.36). Toward the end of the book you write: "Homosexuality is not (or should not be) a fixed, defining identity; for each gay person it should be a *part* of a distinctive individual identity" (p.217, italics yours). Yet you also write: "As with Jewishness or blackness, a gay person's homosexuality is almost invariably a key component of his identity" and "for the average gay person, sexual orientation is at least as important an element of individual identity as race, ethnicity or gender" (p.86). Later you write, "Sexual orientation is an essential element of a person's identity" (p.141). And you write that "homosexuality is so essential and deeply rooted a part of . . . identity as to be unchangeable" (p.111).

Now as I quoted above, you've written that labels can be used to exaggerate differences that are really only small semantic distinctions. I suppose there is a shift between the subculture-oriented gays who would *center* their identity on the sexuality, and your claim that it is an *essential* and *key* component. But, honestly, are these positions so far apart? Don't you both believe that sexuality touches all areas of a person's life?

In fact, it seems to me that both you and queer theorists hold similar notions of identity and are hostile to identity politics for similar reasons. You both regard identities as rigid formulae that inhibit behavior and require highly regimented behavior. Identities, you claim, give people a false sense of themselves and stop the processes of development and growth.

Of course, identity *can* and *does* force people to conform to certain standards. But it does other things that both you and the postmodern theorists you dislike conveniently forget. If one regards identity not as a normative formula but as a name for relationships held together as Wittgenstein argues by "a family relationship," then much of what you resent and resist will be less threatening. Take, for example, your identity as a son. It has not remained something unitary but has changed—I hope—as both you and your parents have changed. Moreover, it has altered in relation to other sorts of identities—as a lover, as a writer, as a Christian. Rather than something rigid and well defined, identities tend to be very vague, baggy, and interlocked with other identities. It seems to me that being gay is just as much an evolving identity as being a son, and it means something very different when you first identify yourself as gay than when you have lived as a gay man for many years. The mistake that so many people make is assume that everyone who shares an identity has to be *identical*. But one of the reasons people join groups is so they do not have to duplicate behaviors; groups allow people to focus on what they prefer to do, while leaving others to perform their own preferred tasks. Look at a family: The shared familial identity allows each member of the family to cultivate his or her own individuality. If they lived as strangers, there would be much more duplication.

Both you and your much-despised subcultural gays ignore the benefits of identities. First, they allow people to feel less alone, and for young gay people this is a particularly important benefit. Few things can be as frightening and alienating as believing you're the only homosexual in the world. This need to belong is probably the reason that young people when first coming out seem to drift to the most easily identifiable, most stylized and stereotypical behaviors. But I have noticed that people, once they have achieved a sense of security, begin to see that under the rubric lies a wide area of behavior, and they begin to define themselves in less stereotypical terms.

More important, identities can provide a sense of purpose. Because identities arise in part out of relationships to others or to certain causes, they can give people a sense of acting for something larger than themselves. As a son, as a Bawer, you act with other people in mind, and it's not surprising that the postmodern attack on identity comes from a generation that arose in the "age of narcissism." The AIDS programs that developed rapidly across the country could not have existed had there not been a shared identity that gave some people a sense that they should act beyond their own immediate self-interest.

Your narrow sense that all people who share an identity must be nearly identical affects not only how you regard gay people but your sense of being an American. Thus you attack multiculturalism, because "instead of recognizing the many things that unite people with one another across lines of race ethnicity, class, gender and sexual orientation, . . . these scholars are preoccupied with the differences that divide group from group" (p.210). I think you've got it all wrong. By emphasizing the diversity of class, gender, race, and sexual orientation, multiculturalism is celebrating the way all groups are tied together in society, united together, sometimes by tensions and conflicts, but also by the interlocking mesh of identities. But as scholars describe the push and pull between groups, the complex interactions among and within identities, you feel threatened, not confirmed. You want all the rough edges filed away, the mirror made smooth, so that it can reflect your own glowering stare. It is you who can't take any joy in the polyphony of voices within American culture or within gay people; it is you who want to impose a monody—that most primitive of musical forms. You don't like the raucous, sometimes vulgar, many times cacophonous sounds of the Gay Pride March or the March on Washington.

And with this emotional and imaginative failure to appreciate the invigorating complexity of society, you also seem unable to recognize the inconsistencies in your own argument. For example when discussing the speeches at the March on Washington—admittedly not my favorite part of the event—you describe such "eloquent speakers" as Ian McKellan alternating with "vulgar comediennes," Eartha Kitt leading a "rousing" rendition of "God Bless America" followed by someone who argued that

"America was irredeemably corrupt," "fire-breathing radicals" and "a brave, intelligent speech by the first openly gay member of the Canadian parliament." As you described it, the March on Washington seemed a livelier event than I remembered it. But despite this variety, you draw the conclusion that the speeches "confirm[ed] every last stereotype about homosexuals" (p.220). How could an event so diverse confirm stereotypes? What stereotype could you make out of RuPaul, Jesse Jackson, Martina Navratilova, Kate Clinton, and Ian McKellan? True, a bigot could find in this highly diverse crowd the stereotype it wanted to see, but the bigot can find what it wants to see wherever it looks, even if the only speakers were you and Marvin Liebman. The open mind, I hope, would come away realizing that all gay people are not alike, that there is no single gay lifestyle, that some gay people are silly and vulgar, while others are wise and polished. In short, they would get a better idea of the range of lesbian and gay experience than they would have gotten from one eloquent speech in the manner of Martin Luther King.

The problem is not merely intellectual—it's deeper, on the gut level. You don't seem to connect with people who are clearly different. Uptight, prim, stiff, you can't enjoy the great spectacle of human difference and variety even as you proclaim the utmost respect for individuality. And this limitation goes along with your seeming lack of humor. Frankly, Bruce, your book lacks any sign that you can laugh at yourself or the world. You exude an earnestness, which although at first somewhat charming like the deadly seriousness of my best students, soon grows tedious with its air of self-importance. I agree that you're not a self-hating homosexual—that is far too facile a diagnosis. If anything, you are far too pleased with yourself. Even at the end when you discuss the snobbery of others, you seem complaisantly delighted with your own modesty.

Because you are so pleased with yourself, you can't believe that others might hate you for being gay. You want to blame those others, those subcultural types—those really weird gay people—who are messing things up for people like you. The heart of your political position is wonderfully simple and utterly naive: "Prejudice . . . can be most dramatically challenged by personal exposure to the object of prejudice" (p.88). "Our aim," you write, "should be not to use 'power' to change laws but to use our humanity to change hearts and minds. If the heterosexual majority ever comes to accept homosexuality, it will do so because it has seen homosexuals in suits and ties, not nipple clamps and bike pants; it will do so because it has seen homosexuals showing respect for civilization, not attempting to subvert it" (p.51).

If only a three-piece suit would win us love, then, Bruce, we would all gladly don them! But as your own experience reported in your book over and over again shows, the hearts and minds of heterosexuals don't want to change even when showed the most respectable, civilized behavior.

Let us go back in history. My father was one of the first American soldiers at Bergen-Belsen. He rarely speaks of it, but he knows that German Jews were the most assimilated minority in Weimar Germany. They wore suits and ties. They showed respect for civilization and did not want to subvert it. They believed that this alone would protect them, and they were exterminated. As a Jew I was brought up never to forget, and as a gay man I am constantly reminded that assimilation is no guarantor of acceptance. The tactic you are advocating is exactly the tactic used by the Mattachine Society. In their demonstrations, lesbians and gays had to act like little ladies and gentlemen. The effect—zero.

But if that is not enough, look at your own experience at the *American Spectator,* which published vitriolic attacks on homosexuality, knowing perfectly well that they were untrue. You even admit: "The truth is that conservative publications and foundations that oppose gay equal rights nonetheless publish and employ numerous individual homosexuals, many of whom they know perfectly well to be gay" (p.110). Did you fail to wear the right clothes to work? Were you insufficiently civilized? Why hasn't your friendship changed their minds? And how could you, Bruce, be a part of this hate-mongering journal for six years?

You discuss a letter of Robert B. Reilly in *Newsweek,* who believes that homosexual practices are being shoved in his face. Your conclusion was that people like Mr. Reilly don't "even want to be reminded that homosexuality exists" (p.121). If people don't want to hear that "homosexuality exists," how then can you make them understand it, win their hearts and minds if you're not willing to make them uncomfortable?

Yet the saddest story—the most revealing tale—comes at the end of your book. Two friends whom you and your lover introduced, who asked you to be the best man at their wedding and Chris to be in the wedding party, these people who knew your lives and saw how deeply committed you were to one another, how civilized and respectful you were of mainstream values and Christian beliefs, and had even seen you in suits with matching ties—these very people wrote into their wedding vows that the "marriage between a man and a woman . . . was 'the only valid foundation for an enduring home' " (p.261). How did you explain this "traumatic" experience, which you rightly felt was "patronizing"? Your explanation is "that some straight people consider a close friendship with a gay person to be a part of their wild and colorful youth.... Then they reach a certain age and decide to settle down; they find responsible jobs, get married—and kick the gay friend in the teeth" (pp.262–3).

What does this incident do to your theory that "prejudice ... can be most dramatically challenged by a personal exposure to the object of prejudice"? That all we have to do is make America understand us as suit-wearing, civilized human beings, and it will gladly extend to us the equal rights which are our proper share? You are "disheartened" because "many 'enlightened' opponents of gay rights ... don't rethink their opposition" even "if an argument they have advanced fails to stand up to scrutiny" (p.112). But do you rethink your position, when your own painful experiences show it to be—if not wrong—inadequate, for I do believe that education and understanding and, yes, personal exposure are necessary steps in winning equal rights even if not sufficient engines of change. Come on, Bruce, if people were so generous, so rational, so empathetic, would there be the kind of hate we now face?

Let's be clear about it—I'm *not* saying that all Americans are yahoos and bigots, but I'm also rejecting your fantasy that they are just bewitched, bothered, and bewildered. There are a great number of people out there who don't want to think about homosexuality. There is an even greater number who don't have the intellectual or emotional flexibility to understand that difference is not a threat. They believe that only one way can be right, and they have come to live the way they do, not because they have selected it from among different options but because they have been told it is the only right way to conduct themselves. Gay rights threatens their fundamental belief systems. And there is a final group who can feel good about themselves only if they can feel superior to others. For these groups—and I don't know how many of them there are, but from votes in Cincinnati, Colorado, and Oregon we can assume they form a large number—just being nice won't do the trick. Organization, political pressure, raising money, using the media—all of the tricks of political power you rather balk at as being too rough and uncivilized—are necessary to win our fair share of equal rights. And it's not going to be clean, polite, or civil. There's no hostess from Miss Porter's serving at the table, but a lot of hungry, demanding lodgers who believe that we are another mouth to feed—which means less grub for them. I wish it wasn't so because, like you, I'd rather have pleasant dinner conversation than the pandemonium that usually happens when the family of man sits down together, but there it is.

Nor does it have to be as particularly grim as I've painted it. In fact, the kind of carnivalesque atmosphere of many gay events—a raucousness you so sniffily turn away from—is exactly the antidote to the serious work that needs to be performed. I know you didn't find it made much sense for the March on Washington to be both "serious and festive": "At a party there was room for frivolousness and self-indulgence; a serious protest required restraint and self-discipline" (p.222). But many occasions are both serious and festive—weddings, Christmas, political conventions. The March on Washington was an event more important for showing numbers and re-energizing activists than for changing the minds of the Joint Chiefs or Jane Doe. Do you really think those "enlightened" conservatives would have changed their mind if the march had been grimly sober?

What I want to say, Bruce, is that there is a place at my table for you—with starched linen napkins, and my grandfather's silverware, and pleasant dinner conversation, all the things you like. The guests may be a little wild, and the cuisine a little rich and spicy, but it's good home cooking. Yet I don't think you will set a place for me at your home, because you keep telling me I'm not your sort. I'm a bit too different; I might speak too loudly and embarrass you, and I do have the habit of spilling the wine, as well as my beads. Nevertheless, you're welcome at our place anytime you want—you and Chris—just pull up a chair and dig in. We don't rest on ceremony.

Best wishes,

Daniel Mendelsohn's gimlet-eyed assessment of gay culture was the talk of the town when it ran as the cover story in *New York* magazine in September 1996. The Princeton-educated critic writes frequently for *The New York Times Book Review* and other national publications.

Decline and Fall: How Gay Culture Lost Its Edge

I can catch a ball. I genuinely like both my parents.
I hate opera. I don't know why I bother being gay.

ARTHUR, in Terence McNally's *Love! Valour! Compassion!*

WHAT BETTER SYMBOL OF THE DECLINE OF GAY CULTURE OVER THE past decade than the fall of Rome? Not, obviously, the city or even the empire, but rather the opulently appointed gay bar that opened late last year at the corner of Eight Avenue and Twenty-fifth Street, at the northern outskirts of Chelsea, New York's newest, most bustling gay neighborhood.

When it opened just a year ago, Rome promised to be the most dazzling and high-concept gay nightspot since the eighties. Upstairs, gym-bunny bartenders outfitted in skimpy leather centurion kilts and surrounded by enough pediments to give the Vatican a run for its *lire* fixed your drinks; downstairs, you could check your coat or heed the call of *Natura* amidst grottos adorned with *faux*-Pompeiian frescos of naked boys. Colored marble rumored to have cost upwards of a million dollars provided an appropriately Versace-esque backdrop for a clientele that seems to divide its time between lifting weights and hoisting little black Barney's bags. Compared to the relentlessly (if rather optimistically) *sportif* décor of Champs, on Nineteenth Street, or the almost touchingly retro murk of The Break, the old neighborhood stand-by on Eighth at Twenty-second, Rome's imperial aspirations seemed to presage the return of grand high style to gay nightlife.

Yet despite its promise of Neronian excess, going to Rome proved to be a depressingly Gibbon-esque experience of decline and fall: A year after its opening, those who venture beyond the wrought-iron gates on an average night are likely to find paying customers vastly outnumbered by centurions. To find where the Chelsea boys are *really* going, you have to go three blocks south, to the Big Cup coffee house. Here, the prevailing aesthetic is less Cecil B. DeMille than Dick Van Dyke: Slouchy mismatched couches and funky sixties dinette sets are crammed with guppies pretending to use their laptops; behind the cash register, the girls and boys have that new, exoskeletal cKOne look. It's not just that Big Cup is about caffeine rather than alcohol. Things don't look noticeably less PG-13 half a block away at Barracuda, the neighborhood's newest bona fide gay bar, which looks like the Big Cup in a brownout. And like Big Cup, it's almost always packed.

"This is 1996," one club promoter told me. "It's just not about style any more."

Not too long ago, that assessment would have been unthinkable. Whether verbal, sartorial, or social, style has been inextricably linked with urban gay culture pretty much since the moment when the word *homosexual* was first coined—not coincidentally, the very moment that Oscar Wilde began offering the world his glitteringly arch critiques of bourgeois Victorian convention, a hundred years ago. Ever since, gay culture has in one way or another played Wilde to the world's West End, making style rather than substance the point—or, better, making style a pin with which to prick the overinflated certainties and assumptions of the "normal" world. You see that *outré* sensibility at work from Wilde and Noël Coward to Larry Kramer and Tony Kushner. (The character in Wilde's *The Importance of Being Earnest* who declares, "In matters of grave importance, style, not sincerity, is the vital thing," is the literary ancestress of Kushner's ghostly Ethel Rosenberg, saying Kaddish at Roy Cohn's deathbed: The outrageousness of each gesture forces audiences to rethink concepts like "seriousness" or "justice.") And you see it even in everyday gay life, where the emphasis on stylization metamorphosed the most banal routines of everyday life—breakfast, say—into tableaux worthy of Vincente Minelli. "In America," Camille Paglia wrote in her 1994 book *Vamps and Tramps,* "gay men brunch—where interesting conversation is a *sine qua non.*"

Almost exactly ten years ago, the distinctive gay cultural and creative energy that Paglia was talking about seemed to be breaking through from the margins to the center. (By "gay culture" I'm referring, of course, to gay *male* culture. For various historical reasons, lesbian culture has had neither the visibility nor impact on the larger mainstream that gay male culture has—it hasn't had time to rise, let alone fall.) Former *New York Times* theater critic Frank Rich famously discussed this phenomenon in a 1987 *Esquire* essay called "The Gay Decades," which traced the increasing assimilation of gay style and sensibility into the American mainstream: from social life (the mid-eighties advent of clubs with exclusive door policies à la Studio 54) to pop culture (the infiltration of high camp à la Bette Midler, the enormous popularity of the shoulder-padded glitzfest *Dynasty*) to fashion (the apotheosis of Calvin Klein's narcissistically self-absorbed ephebes as . . . well, the *sine qua non* of male self-image). All this, Rich concluded, pointed to "the most dramatic cultural assimilation of our time": what he called the "homosexualization of straight culture."

Yet as the fall of Rome suggests, times have clearly changed; Joan Collins wouldn't be caught dead at Big Cup. Pretty much everyone you talk to feels that the edge has disappeared from urban gay culture; as the gay community "matures," both its substance and its style are increasingly hard to tell from those of the straight mainstream. Today, the biggest issue in gay politics isn't the moral justification for outing uncooperative closeted politicians or stratagems for disrupting Easter services at St. Patrick's Cathedral, but the "rights" to marry or serve in the military. ACT UP's politics-as-theater is, if not dead, then beside the point, supplanted by what one AIDS writer calls "a more reality-based disease activism" of outfits like the Treatment Action Group (TAG), which works closely with the institutions ACT UP once protested. The happeningest gay magazine isn't the abrasive *OutWeek* but the glossy "lifestyle" publication *Out.* Gay books and plays are less likely to treat the triumphant initiation into a world of avid sexuality, or the tragedy attendant on political hypocrisy about the AIDS epidemic, than they are to emphasize the importance of family values. Even Paglia's axiom about gay men at brunch seems, on second thought, to be fueled more by nostalgia for a vanished world of handkerchief-brandishing exquisites than by the hyperbolically muscled reality of gay life today. You're unlikely to find any incipient Ronald Firbanks among the workbooted regulars at Food Bar, Chelsea's most popular gay restaurant.

Gay culture, in other words, has gone from *épater*-ing *les bourgeois* to merely aping them. In the brief space of a decade, the phenomenon that Rich was talking about has been inverted: The most dramatic cultural assimilation of *our* time has been the heterosexualization of gay culture. As homosexuality has moved, however slowly, from the margins to the center of American cultural consciousness, there's been less and less for gay culture to do what it's best at, which is to stand on the margins and throw shade. No one, of course, would dispute that the political and social progress made by the gay movement has substantively benefitted the lives of gay people as individuals; and surely no gay person would want to reverse that progress. But the blunting of gay sensibility suggests that those gains come at a certain—and high—cultural cost. In purely aesthetic terms, at least, oppression may have been the best thing that ever happened to us. Without it, we're nothing.

The best way to understand how gay sensibility has paradoxically become the victim of political progress by the gay community is to look at what happened to political activism. It's no accident that so many of the gay people you talk to mention the late eighties—the time when Frank Rich was writing, as it happens—as the high-water mark for gay culture. It was the last time the gay community could easily place itself at the political edge, the last time it had a single, easily-identifiable, clear-cut political agenda: the fight against AIDS. That particular outside oppressor provoked the last great explosion of trenchant, outrageous, critical gay style, which was ACT UP. The nature of and reasons for ACT UP's demise tell you a lot about why style is being leached from the rest of gay culture as well.

As a way to focus attention on the AIDS crisis, ACT UP brilliantly put *outré* gay style-consciousness in the service of a substantive political goal— a new, distinctively gay kind of activism that Andrew Sullivan rightly (if disapprovingly) characterizes as "the politics of style." "The moment of ACT UP was really 1987 and 1988," says Mark Schoofs, a *Village Voice* AIDS reporter. "You can be very precise here. That was the *floruit* of the movement. You had this really wonderful string of attention-grabbing demonstrations: stopping traffic on Wall Street, shutting down the FDA— amazing stuff." Schoofs's description of this period dovetails nicely with Sullivan's evaluation of ACT UP as—fittingly enough for a movement founded by a playwright—an essentially artistic production, with demonstrations that were often conceived of in theatrical terms, as "performances" for (admittedly often hostile) "audiences," complete with fake blood and ghoulish props. It seems only appropriate that when describing ACT UP in its heyday, Spencer Cox, a twenty-eight-year-old former ACT UPper and currently the director of the anti-viral project at TAG, resorts to the buzzword of gay sensibility. "It was all about this *fabulous* vibrant AIDS movement, and all this creative energy that was going into it and that was really producing results," Cox says, not without irony. Not surprisingly, ACT UP generated its own sartorial style as well: "Look at the fashion that gay men wore in the mid-to-late eighties," Schoofs says. "The military leather jackets, the big Doc Martens—there was a whole paramilitary thing going on. It was because we were, in fact, *fighting.*"

If ACT UP's explosive mixture of style and politics was a typically gay way of commenting on a crisis precipitated by the mainstream, it's interesting to ask why the group, and not the crisis, has disappeared so thoroughly from public consciousness—rarely taken into account, and occasionally not even taken seriously. "In Vancouver, they were a bit of an embarrassment," Schoofs says, referring to ACT UP San Francisco's demonstration at the 1996 International AIDS Conference. "No one would even stop walking when ACT UP San Francisco appeared. It might as well have been a car alarm on a New York street."

When trying to account for the disappearance of ACT UP as a real player on the political scene, many people formerly associated with the group, and a lot of gay people in general, talk about the emotional devastation wrought by the disease. Sally Morrison, the vice president of external affairs for AmFAR, sums up the problem. "Many, many people who worked in AIDS are just exhausted—exhausted by grief, *not* work. It's overwhelming." But the disappearance of ACT UP-type activism isn't merely a matter of emotional exhaustion; after all, a whole new gay generation has come of age since the mid-eighties, but they're all sitting in Big Cup reading *Details* rather than dumping their friends' bodies on the White House Lawn. In a strange way, the present-day superfluousness of ACT UP and its style-as-politics is the result of success, not failure.

For once ACT UP had achieved its goals, it had nowhere to go but down. "A lot of what ACT UP was pushing for has been met," Michelangelo Signorile, the *Out* columnist, legendary outing renegade, and former ACT UPper, says. "We are *on* panels; we did change the FDA and NIH. We've pushed research and gotten our people *inside*." Jay Blotcher is the director of media relations at AmFAR; it's interesting that, in describing the trajectory of his own career in fighting AIDS, he echoes Signorile's crucial spatial metaphor. "I started out in the city working at the St. Mark's baths and then worked at ACT UP, and now am nestled in the bosom of an institution. Once we were pariahs at the gate, and now we're inside. There was once a time to fling epithets and homilies, but that's changed."

These repeated allusions to the inside/outside split reminds you that even in the political arena, the epithet-wielding sensibility that defined the gay cultural ethos only made sense when gays were "chained to the gates," as Morrison puts it when recalling the group's mentality. "The bitchiness, the irony, all of the brilliance came of repression," Schoofs declares, and most theorists of gay culture would agree. So do many former ACT UPpers. The artist Vincent Gagliostro belonged to the artists' collective Gran Fury, which designed the famous "Silence = Death" logo with its brazen appropriation of the Nazi-era pink triangle. "Ten years ago," he recalls, "my thought process as I worked on something was never 'Will this offend someone?' If it was a political piece, it was *supposed* to offend."

But offensiveness became less productive as the difference between the institutional "inside" and the gay "outside" increasingly eroded; it's harder to subvert, to use your ironic sensibility to fight the power, when you *are* the power—when you're nestled in the bosom of the institution, as Blotcher put it. ACT UP *had* to come apart as the progress to which Signorile referred became apparent; the group's successes resulted in the disappearance of the conditions—call it the special outsider's perspective—that had made its ironic style both possible *and* meaningful. With less and less to critique, to be edgy *about,* the group's tactics could only look more and more irrelevant—and foolish. "It's one thing to demonstrate because people can't get effective antibiotics that will prolong their lives," Cox says. "But it's another thing entirely to get all worked up because Sharon Stone in *Basic Instinct* carried an ice pick."

ACT UP's increasingly shrill irrelevancy stands in overwrought contrast to the operative mode of its successor, Cox's Treatment Action Group—the group Mark Schoofs pointedly uses to exemplify the "mature" phase of AIDS activism. (The striking frequency with which people refer to TAG as "mature" suggests that if ACT UP was the AIDS activist movement's narcissistic adolescence, TAG is its responsible adulthood.) Founded in 1991, the not-for-profit agency provides in-depth analysis and policy recommendations not only to the HIV/AIDS community but to the mainstream institutions against which ACT UP once raged: government, academia, and the pharmaceutical industry. "Today," Sally Morrison remarks, "the cutting edge of AIDS activism is TAG. What's interesting about TAG though, is that its m.o. is so different from ACT UP—that whole way of channeling anger in a public way. It's very different, and much more effective for the times we're living in. It's certainly about maturation—a different way of doing things."

ACT UP's demise and the subdued TAG's almost ironic transformation into the "cutting edge" suggests how much gay edge depends on a straight center. Without the latter, in fact, gay sensibility can only curdle into kitsch. The symbolism of the pink triangle once seemed a shocking gesture; today, you can buy darling little pink triangle flags for sale at Chelsea's one-stop gay-shopping store, Rainbows and Triangles—an example of what Gagliostro bitterly calls the "Hallmarkization" of gay sensibility. And if you take away both the edge *and* the kitsch, there's nothing left. What remains doesn't look all that different from anything you find in straight culture. "Let's face it," Jay Blotcher told me, "when you're a story line on 'Friends,' it's hard to keep thinking you're radical."

The eclipse of ACT UP serves as a useful paradigm for the rest of gay culture. As Blotcher's reference to the popular TV show suggests, one of the best places to gauge that assimilation process is in the popular culture itself. You see it best of all in gay literary culture, and in gay literary culture you see it best in popular gay magazines.

In magazine publishing, the most egregious example of this phenomenon is in the evolution of gay magazines from the raucous *OutWeek* of the ACT UP period to today's best-selling gay magazine, *Out*. (Full disclosure: the author is a contributing writer at *Out*.) The *OutWeek* sensibility was exemplified by the style and tactics of its most famous columnist, Michelangelo Signorile, whose caps-locked "outings" of closeted celebrities constituted a literary version of ACT UP's flamboyantly public "actions"—an editorial manifestation of what Helen Eisenbach, the author of *Lesbianism Made Easy* and the former executive editor of another, short-lived *OutWeek* epigone, *QW,* calls "the notorious bitchy gay edge." (She thinks *Out* doesn't have it.) "For all its flaws," says one gay publishing insider, echoing Eisenbach's choice of words, "*OutWeek* was funny, passionate, and had an edge. Now where's the edge? Gone. You want to know what happened to gay culture? Michelangelo is writing for *Out* today. Period. End of discussion."

The whole point of *Out,* of course, was to distance itself from *OutWeek.* Five years ago, when *Out* was still a twinkle in the eye of its founder and former editor-in-chief Michael Goff, the word among publishing people was that it was going to be a "gay *Vanity Fair."* Expectations ran predictably high. After all, it was pretty well known that the Condé Nast glitzfest owed its success to its just-under-the-surface gay ethos—the result of the notoriously high percentage of gays on its masthead. (A *Spy* piece about the publishing giant was called "Vanity Fairies.") So it seemed inevitable that *Out,* a magazine by, of, and for gay people, would be the cuttingest of the cutting edge.

But while there's no question that *Out*—which carefully balances its celebrity cover stories on Keanu Reeves and straight Calvin Klein model *du jour* Antonio Sabato, Jr., and its fitness, health, and travel columns with more sober and substantive news and politics features—is infinitely more polished than *OutWeek,* it's not clear to some that it's as sexy or fabulous as *Vanity Fair,* either. To Eisenbach and the publishing maven, it looks pretty much like any other magazine—surprisingly predictable, its libido kept carefully under control. (*OutWeek,* you remember, relied on phone-sex lines for its advertising, but somehow it seemed a good fit; libido and rage were what the magazine, and the zeitgeist, were all about. The closest thing you get to libido among *Out*'s advertisers, on the other hand, is WASPy boys cuddling in the Abercrombie & Fitch advertisements.) Their disappointment in *Out* makes you wonder whether *Vanity Fair*'s famous edge was due precisely to the fact that it wasn't—at least patently—a gay magazine. When the gay stuff becomes patent and becomes the whole point, the sensibility evaporates, and you're bound to end up with something that's neither as sexy nor ultimately as *gay* as *OutWeek*—or, for that matter, as *Vanity Fair.*

But *Out*'s thirty-year-old editor-in-chief, Sarah Pettit, an *OutWeek* alumna, dismisses accusations of editorial slickness with an impatient expletive, and is especially resentful of the in-flight magazine crack. "First of all," she says, "that was my fucking joke"—about another gay magazine). "Second, I find that kind of glib analysis as being sort of *faux*-activist. Let's remember that people were nostalgic for *OutWeek* even before it folded. It's impossible to argue that [*Out*] is not a magazine of a different era. You can't freeze time—*OutWeek* would never work in 1996." She concludes by making an analogy inspired by *le goût* ACT UP. "Today, I wouldn't be wearing black boots and tank tops. We've worn that outfit already. Maybe there are other costumes we can don without changing the political body underneath. It's just a different way of presenting yourself to the world."

As it turns out, that way startlingly resembles the mainstream way. Pettit's sartorial metaphor is picked up by Signorile himself, who, Pettit argues, is an "infinitely more mature and resourceful" reporter for *Out* than he was for *OutWeek*. "You have to keep wrapping your ideas in a different cloak," Signorile says of his current style. But although he claims that his idea has always been the same—a post-Stonewall version of "to thine own self be true"—he doesn't dispute that his *Out* columns are considerably more domestic, quieter, more couch-potato-ey than the "shrill screeds" (as one editor calls them) that he used to produce for *OutWeek*. Recent columns include "thirtysomething" meditations about the paradoxes of monogamy ("Sex and the Not-So-Single Guy") and the difficulties of reconciling a gay lifestyle with traditional family life ("Homo for the Holidays")—stuff that isn't all that different, come to think of it, from what you find in *GQ* or, for that matter, what you found in the 1987 *Esquire* issue that featured Frank Rich's piece. Signorile goes on to make a remark that nicely sums up the difference between Then and Now in gay culture. "It's very much about interacting with the larger culture," says the writer. "I can write today about the most contentious political issues, but the most responses I get are invariably to the really personal subjects—in particular, things dealing with family and boyfriends."

Signorile's larger projects reflect a similar shift. His last book, *Outing Yourself*—a sort of how-to for being a well-adjusted gay person—was a downsized, domestic version of his earlier book, *Queer in America,* which was about . . . well, outing everyone else. A grandiose and sweeping exposé of the "closets of power," *Queer in America* marked the apogee of the *OutWeek* phase of the author's career. The more recent book plays ideological Big Cup, so to speak, to his previous work's Rome.

Out is not the only gay periodical to symbolize a shift in both focus and style. A few years ago, copies of the broadsheet *Diseased Pariah News* exemplified the bite and irreverence of the ACT UP moment in gay culture: One famous cover drawing depicted George Bush getting a manicure, à la Palmolive detergent commercials of old. "The Blood of 86,000 Americans

Who Have Died of AIDS, Mr. President," the title caption went, "You're *Soaking* in It!" Today, it's hard to find copies of *DPN* at New York's biggest gay bookstore, A Different Light; the popular magazine of today's HIV culture is *POZ,* as glossily produced and self-consciously "professional" as *Out.* But oddly enough, there's nothing really *gay* about *POZ.* With its careful mix of solid information and easily digestible poppy features ("Rating the Rappers" in the recent "Music Issue")—all wrapped up in a soberly designed package—*POZ* today is about as edgy as *The Economist:* a respectable TAG, so to speak, to *DPN's* outrageous ACT UP.

The same shift is evident in other areas of gay literature as well. Fifteen and twenty years ago, the self-consciously exquisite style of books like Edmund White's *Nocturnes for the King of Naples* mirrored the rarefied sexual and cultural milieus of their gay narrators (to say nothing of their readers' equally stratospheric cultural aspirations). Five years later, it seemed as though every gay book you picked up was yet another thinly disguised autobiographical tale of exuberantly discovered gay sexuality. (Well, nearly every book. The fiction of David Leavitt, with its blandly infantile characters forever fixated on children's books, remained chastely aloof from the proceedings—to the point where he actually recycled almost verbatim one of his rare moments of erotic *frisson* from one published work to another.)

What's interesting about today's gay book scene is that Leavitt has become the rule rather than the exception. The sober lessons of the AIDS epidemic have made themselves felt in both the style and subject of contemporary gay novels. The invitingly reclining youth on the cover of John Fox's spirited 1984 coming-of-age novel *The Boys on the Rock* is an apt enough symbol for what lies within; now it seems like—well, *is*—an artifact from another culture. Or at least you can't help thinking as much when you compare it to the empty Adirondack chairs that adorn the preciously miniaturized Farrar, Straus and Giroux packaging of *The Weekend,* Peter Cameron's slender and almost painfully restrained 1995 novella of a middle-aged art critic's struggle to resume life after his lover's death. It's not that the newer books are somehow worse, or less interesting; it's just that they aren't all that different from the other fiction you're likely to find right now at Barnes & Noble. A crop of recent gay epics—Felice Picano's *Like People in History,* Ethan Mordden's *How Long Has This Been Going On?,* and Michael Cunningham's *Flesh and Blood*—better as usual by far than the others—

suggests the extent to which the focus in current gay fiction is less on out-law sexuality than on that which connects gay experience to larger social and familial currents. "Not just gay-specific themes," as gay literary agent Jed Mattes says, "but things that *merge* with gay issues."

There's little doubt that the literary shift of which Mattes speaks is a sign of a "maturing" in gay letters as striking as the one you see in gay politics. Still, when you take away the libidinous edge from gay drama—which, since Wilde, is perhaps the preeminent vehicle for the expression of gay sensibility—what you're left with isn't much more than upscale dinner theater. The furniture on the cover of Cameron's book may make you think of Terence McNally's huge hit *Love! Valour! Compassion!*—an exercise in self-consciously Chekhovian wistful bourgeois angst ("Desire is a terrible thing," one character moons at the opening) whose slender accomplishment stands in almost parodic contrast to the ambitious Socialist-Realist sloganeering of its title. McNally's hit play dovetails perfectly with the cultural moment: It's certainly a far cry from what Frank Rich admiringly referred to as the "big juicy incantatory political speeches" in Tony Kushner's *Angels in America,* which appeared on the cultural stage just a few years earlier. Clearly the product of a different era, *Angels* can best be seen as the final expression of the late-eighties ACT UP phase of gay culture. The only stylistic—or indeed ideological—risk McNally takes is the spelling of *valour.*

Recent and wildly popular revivals of gay theatrical classics like *Valley of the Dolls* and, especially, Mart Crowley's *The Boys in the Band* provide a useful then-now comparison for seeing not just what has changed in gay culture but *why.* The revival of *Boys* is particularly rich in cultural ironies. For Frank Rich, the 1968 drama epitomized the acidic gay ethos of an earlier, closeted age; it is a play so annihilatingly bleak in its assessment of the emotional prospects of gay men that Michael Cunningham, writing in the *New York Times,* recalled being almost "scared straight" when he saw the film version as a teenager. Now, as you watch the hunky, empowered, aromatherapized Chelsea boys stream out of the Lucille Lortel Theater on Christopher Street, where *Boys* has been playing to packed houses, you realize how much the ethos Rich described is increasingly seen *within* gay culture as a relic of a different age—a part of cultural history in need of preservation. And if the late-sixties milieu of *Boys* has received the full Masterpiece Theatre treatment, lovingly recreated in every detail, it's because the bitchy exchanges you get in Crowley's play—and indeed the taste for the kind of *outré* bitchiness that springs from profound emotional dissatisfaction—no longer make sense in today's gay culture, with its psychologically pumped-up "I Am What I Am" ethos; they're now as passé as the Nehru jackets and ankh worn by the play's central character.

But if the scathingly amusing *Boys in the Band* was the child of the unholy union between oppression and its neurotic mate, self-loathing, it certainly makes for good theater. From a strictly cultural point of view, at least, you can't help wondering what happens when one of its characters' wishes comes true: "If we . . . if we could just not hate ourselves so much." One answer is *Party,* an enormously popular play that's made the round of several major cities to great acclaim. *Party* shamelessly rips off *Boys*—its cast is also a mixed bag of gay nuts gathered for a soirée, and its plot, such as it is, is generated by an obvious contrivance, a truth-or-dare-like party game—but the hydrochloric verbal élan you got in *Boys* has degenerated here into gooey generic gags. ("Why are fart jokes so funny?" one character in the later play asks, rather hopefully.) Comparing the stylistically and thematically toothless *Party* to its fanged pre-Stonewall model reminds you that gay sensibility, for better or for worse, only makes artistic sense if it has something to *critique.* In art as in politics, when that sensibility is forced to accommodate a "positive," value-laden agenda ("gay people can have 'families,' too!"), it fades into irrelevance or disintegrates into kitsch—or both. You think of William Finn's tirelessly gloopy *Falsettos,* with its bar-mitzvah-at-the-AIDS-deathbed climax and Williwear-wearing gay angel. Finn's play looked like it was going to explore the possibility of a new gay family but merely ends by killing off Dad's boyfriend and reuniting the original biological family—a confirmation, rather than a questioning, of the norm.

The comfortable upper-middle-class setting of McNally's drama and the saccharine neo-conventionality of Finn's *Weltanschauung* suggest the extent to which some recent gay theater makes rather than questions the very kind of bourgeois assumptions that gay sensibility once so trenchantly poked at. It's interesting that the one really ironic, culturally aware character in *Party*—the host of the eponymous event—is an anomaly even at his own gay gathering, his wit and self-deprecating quips as angular and arresting as he is himself in comparison to the other guests, who look (and sound) like models for phone-sex ads. You get the same kind of thing in the amateurish film version of Paul Rudnick's *Jeffrey,* where the focus of the new gay audience's identification is clearly meant to be either of its blandly good-looking and witless romantic protagonists instead of the movie's only vivid—and classically "gay"—figure, the shopping-bag-wielding decorator played by *Star Trek*'s Patrick Stewart.

What's really interesting about some of the new, gay-themed movies—

not only the independent film *Jeffrey,* but, even more, major studio releases like *To Wong Foo* and *The Birdcage,* the Mike Nichols remake of *La cage aux folles*—is that they're considered even inside the gay community to be triumphant incursions by gay sensibility into a once-prohibitive mainstream. But what they really seem to represent is the taming of a once-vivifying gay shrew.

In artistic terms, drag can be used to subvert and call into question what you thought you knew about gender and identity—how completely clothes make the man (and woman) in our culture. But for all the long fingernails they flash, the drag queens presented in some of the recent popular drag films can't really tear our cultural preconceptions to shreds, because the only reason they're there, oddly enough, is to reinforce smiley-face "messages" about the importance of essentially mainstream values: family, say, or "community." *Birdcage* is no more a critique of sexual norms than was *Guess Who's Coming to Dinner?;* ditto for *To Wong Foo,* which is really a buddy movie in skirts, a parable of togetherness and learning about who your family really is. In neither film is the drag really *about* anything. In *To Wong Foo,* a nice straight boy unwittingly falls for one of the drag queens, but the film never does what a Wilde or an Orton would have done with the crisis precipitated by its inversion of gender conventions. The boy is never forced to confront the possibility that he loved the person beneath the dress; instead, the movie Band-Aids over all this, hustling the drag queens away, sparing both the straight boy and moviegoers the effort of serious thinking about the "issues" it pretends to raise.

If gay culture has become either indistinguishable from the mainstream or pasteurized into total consumer-culture irrelevance—RuPaul selling cosmetics for MAC—the reason became very clear at last year's real-life New York drag fest, the annual Labor Day bash called Wigstock.

Drag has traditionally represented the margin of the margin: the most flamboyant example of gay culture's special penchant for style-as-critique. So nothing could have been a more shocking illustration of the homogenization (and, therefore, heterosexualization) of gay sensibility than the comment one drag queen shouted from the bandstand during the 1995 festivities—the last, as it turned out. (The interesting thing about the cancellation of this year's event wasn't the much-lamented failure to attract corporate funding, but the fact that organizers assumed they would get corporate funding in the first place.) The drag queen's words summed up all the cultural and social shifts over the past ten years, the transition from being fabulous to being nice, from flamboyant exterior style to inner "health," from the exoticized gay margin to the normalized straight center. "Look around, people" this queen cried, surveying the wigged and sequinned throng below. The genial crowd may have come with the idea that they were going to be part of something carnivalesque, something that explored the boundaries of "otherness." But as the queen's invocation of the diction of armchair-psychiatry suggests, the joke was on them. Beaming, she threw back her head. "It's all about *self-esteem*!"

The drag queen's exclamation was to be echoed by the forty-three-year-old party promoter and *Homo Xtra* publisher Marc Berkley, who notes that comfy, grungy hangouts may be the wave of the future. "I think we're getting back to trying to feel good," he says.

It would be foolish, to say nothing of just plain wrong, to suggest that gay nightlife today isn't booming, or that you can't go out to a number of big gay clubs and dance and do as many drugs as you want with a dizzying number of cute and eager men. But what's interesting is the emergence of places like the Big Cup as a new and popular alternative to the mobbed clubs or to the clinical cyberefficiency of AOL hookups—places that manage to make stylelessness hip, that emphasize "self-esteem," perhaps, over fabulous (and at least instantaneous) self-gratification.

"Most places you can dance and connect sexually," says Joe Fontecchio, the phenomenally well-muscled co-owner of Food Bar, "but I think there's a need right now for dialogue. Big Cup is a perfect example—a more sedate situation, where even strangers can connect and talk without it necessarily leading to sex. Right now, talking may be the sexiest thing there is." ("When you're at Twilo," Big Cup co-owner Cliff Bradshaw asks, referring to one of the three big gay dance clubs in New York, "what kind of interaction can you actually have?") Like a lot of gay men in their thirties and forties, Fontecchio declares himself "a little bit more sober" in his social life than he was ten years ago; he's over the "sex-only posturing" you get at the big gay clubs. "You'd go to clubs and see these go-go boys gyrating," he says, rolling his eyes, "and it got to be like watching the Nature Channel."

So it's a nice coincidence that Fontecchio and his partners are opening a new club this fall in Chelsea—"a place for grown-ups," the restaurateur says, only half joking. Called, simply, "g," lower case, the new lounge—its restrained blond-wood and brushed aluminum interior coolly antithetical to the Augustan pretensions of Rome—is clearly meant to appeal to a quieter social energy, and to respond to the needs not only of upscale gay singles and even couples, but of gay women, too. For Fontecchio, the real marker of the new maturity in gay social life is in fact an increased desire to mix the sexes in stylish atmosphere—something, he remarks, that he's always seen in stylish local straight bars like Merc Bar and Temple Bar, but rarely in gay bars.

g may well be the ultimate expression of the new gay social life. But it's interesting to try to imagine what the lounge will look like on a typical weeknight. Well-dressed young men and women slouched comfortably on stylish divans, freshly arrived from their jobs, briefcases tucked beneath their seats, drinks in hand—it's a pretty picture, to be sure. And, when you think about it, not all that different from a hundred other places in town—anybody's places, normal places, straight places. Which brings you to the final irony of the new "maturity" in gay culture. AmFAR's Jay Blotcher recalls his standard retort to those who questioned the meaning of gay pride parades and ACT UP demonstrations. "Why are we making such a fuss?" he'd say, parroting the question. "We're making a big deal about it so that one day it won't be a big deal."

But then what? Once you give up what both Blotcher and Schoofs called "the security blanket of oppression"—the outside hostility that, while admittedly making gays easily identifiable as targets, at least made gays identifiable at all—it may not be so clear that you're all that different from everyone else. Indeed, something Jay Blotcher says reminds me that, for all its claims to artistic and cultural exceptionalism, gay culture as a whole is suffering today, ironically enough, from a classic and well-documented assimilationist dilemma: You can't take away what's difficult about being a subculture without taking away what makes the subculture interesting and distinctive to begin with. Blotcher's choice of words inevitably brings to mind the comparable dilemma of American Jewry. "We are the chosen people—there'll always be this amazing dynamic to the gay psyche," he says, a bit defensively; and yet a moment later he wonders whether the "fast-talking, bon mot slinging" gay persona was anything more than a "protective coating"—a response, in other words, to an outside oppression whose elimination we paradoxically crave.

The high and occasionally disorienting price of assimilation was on my mind as I wound up my long telephone conversation with Blotcher. He recalled a favorite line of the film critic and author Vito Russo, who died of AIDS. "Vito always used to say to me, 'You know, someday we will be accepted and the world will understand and accept us, and when that day comes we're going to miss that secret world.' " Blotcher paused, and I could almost hear him shrugging. "I guess that's progress," he said. "Sort of. Kind of."

25. JOHN WEIR

A brilliant novelist (*The Irreversible Decline of Eddie Socket*), John Weir has also made his mark as an inventively cantankerous commentator for *Details, The Advocate,* and other magazines. In this essay from the anthology *Anti-Gay,* he pointedly renounces identity politics.

Going In

THIS WILL KILL MY PARENTS AND RUIN MY CAREER, BUT LISTEN, I take it back: I'm not gay. I don't mean I don't still fall in love with guys, or that I wouldn't be willing to go to a gay rights demonstration if I thought it would enhance someone's civil liberties. I never said I was straight. However, for most of my adult life I've insisted on being thought of as a gay man, and I just want to say right now that I'm over it. Big deal, I'm homosexual. According to identity politics, however, my sexuality is all important. It sets me apart from the mainstream. Well, duh, I never felt like part of the mainstream anyway. Not when it seemed to be filled exclusively with scary straight men, and not now, either, when it's making room for scary gay ones.

It used to be an insult to accuse a guy of acting gay. Lately, it's discreet praise. It means he's sensitive, really well-dressed and probably friends with someone who knows Barbra Streisand. Accepting an Oscar for his role as a dying fag in *Philadelphia,* Tom Hanks even managed to make homosexuality sound patriotic. "God bless America," he said, weeping for dead gay men like they were Veterans of Foreign Wars. Recently, the most unlikely people have been cashing in on queer visibility, from Robert Altman, who is planning a screen version of playwright Tony Kushner's homo-anthem *Angels in America,* to Stephen Spielberg, who produced the drag extravaganza *To Wong Foo, Thanks for Everything, Julie Newmar* as if it were an all-American family entertainment.

Homosexuality is being repackaged and resold to Americans as a traditional family value. And homosexuals are emerging as the yuppies of the 1990s. They're the new class of urban professionals with money to spend and aggressively marketed products to choose from. Absolut Vodka, Ikea, Benetton, Dewar's, Calvin Klein, Levi's 501s, Brad Pitt and Nine Inch Nails are just a few of the commodities secretly or openly aimed at upwardly mobile, straight-acting, white-appearing gay guys and the handful of lesbians with comparable economic power. It's not enough to say that these people are patsies to a culture that takes their money without granting them their rights. The sad fact is that homosexuals are desperate to be exploited.

If you read any of the new or newly mainstream advertising-laden gay magazines, *Out* or *The Advocate* or *Genre,* or if you saw the thousands of identically clad homosexuals who flooded New York City during the June 1994 Stonewall 25 celebration, you know where the gay community is headed. It's not moving towards legal rights. It's not focused on mourning its dead, or insisting self-preservingly on safer sex, or on finding a cure for breast cancer or AIDS. The collective impulse of the chic lesbians and the brave young gay Republicans who captivate the media today and titillate each other is shopping.

That's what the gay magazines are for, to target and create a consumer demographic. Their interest isn't politics of sexuality. Indeed, they're so worried about offending their few loyal corporate advertisers with copy that is too sexy or political that the only thing homosexual about them is their shame. They tell the world that the characteristic homosexual act is compulsive spending. Otherwise, they're merely a cheerleading squad for anything gay or remotely gay-friendly, no matter how banal. If Melissa Etheridge burps, she gets covered in the gay press. Then there are the "gay leaders" who show up on the covers of gay magazines: Roseanne. Bill Clinton. Barbra Streisand. Marky Mark. During New York's 1995 Gay Pride week, *The Advocate* put New York Republican Mayor Rudolph Giuliani on its cover, which is like putting Joseph Mengele on the front page of *Hadassah* magazine on Yom Kippur.

Streisand of course is ubiquitous. Does everyone who has ever had a homosexual impulse owe her a personal thank-you? For what? For directing George Carlin to play a sissygirl faggot in *The Prince of Tides?* For leaving out of the film the lesbianism that was central to the book? Homosexuals are suffering from a collective case of Stockholm syndrome—falling in love with our tormentors. How else to explain what makes Marky Mark a gay icon, except that he looks like the guy from high-school gym class who spent half his time exciting your ashamed desire, and the other half shutting your head in his locker? Self-identified gay men lament that they have no national leaders, that the community can't "support" its leadership, that the gay rights movement is too diverse and mistrusting, too "hurt" to walk behind a representative figure. But I don't know a fag who wouldn't follow Marky Mark into a firing squad if he so much as winked.

Gay magazines still arrive in your mailbox in discreet wrapping, if you request it. But it would be far more startling for your neighbors and mail carriers to learn that you subscribe to truly politically radical and sex-obsessed journals, like bulletins from the religious right. Actually, there are a lot of similarities between the gay rights movement and Christian fundamentalism. Like homosexuals, Christians are increasingly open about their practices. Like some fervent queer activists, many Christians are shrill, dogmatic, paranoiac, combative, and separatist. The difference is that while Christians rally around God, homosexuals only have sex. You don't have to look your best to win God's love, but if you're searching for a gay man, you'd better have tits. Gay men are such a straining, susceptible horde of self-loathing, hump-happy pleasure seekers that anyone with a decent set of biceps and a smidgen of media savvy could lead them where no fascist, or televangelist, has ever gone before.

The entire gay male community seems at times to be colluding against the possibility of independent thinking. The gay rights movement, too often, is focused on theatrics rather than on discourse: We want to be entertained and flattered, not criticized. As a group, self-identified gay men are especially resistant to thinking about issues of class and race, and they steadfastly deny their sexism. The irony of gay liberation is that it has made room in the mainstream only for those white men who are already privileged, and disinclined to share their wealth. This is the charge that many Christian fundamentalists make against us: that we are a bunch of affluent men who think our homosexuality shouldn't interfere with our God-given right to rule the world. Fundamentalists aren't exactly strangers to feeling both martyred and entitled, of course. Maybe that's why, in vilifying us, they're partly right.

There was a time in my early twenties when being gay meant everything to me. I felt like my sexuality explained my entire life. It was the missing puzzle piece which, clicked into place, finally brought the whole picture into focus. The ten years after I came out, at age twenty-three, were a very heady time. I marched in Gay Pride celebrations throughout the 1980s. I got arrested for protesting because homosexuals weren't allowed to join New York City's St. Patrick's Day parade. I went to ACT UP meetings and networked with all the smartest, cutest, most energetic dykes and fags in Manhattan, and thus, I thought naively, in the world. I hooked up with Queer Nation and raided straight bars. I remember one night precisely: We went to a skinhead dive in the East Village and kissed each other every fifteen minutes. There were no skinheads in the bar that night—the bar, in fact, was nearly empty—but it was a thrilling thing to do. It felt redemptive. It felt like I was facing down everyone who had ever called me "faggot" in high school and saying, "Yeah so?"

That part of my life was important to my self-respect. I won't disavow the years when I wore "Queer Nation" T-shirts or pinned pink triangles to my lapel. Lately, however, I want to trade all my gay paraphernalia for a button that says "NOT ME." I'm postgay, a counterqueer, the ungrateful beneficiary of the gains of gay liberation. It's not just that I'm frustrated with the mindlessness of the gay male community, and the elitism of its leadership. I've decided to reject the whole category of "gay." Lately, I've been agreeing with Gore Vidal. In his introduction to the 1963 edition of his infamous 1948 homo novel *The City and the Pillar,* he says, "There is of course no such thing as a homosexual. Despite current usage, the word is an adjective describing a sexual action, not a noun describing a recognizable type."

Theoretically, Vidal is right. Effectively, however, there is currently no more recognizable type than the self-identified, politically active, sexually predatory gay American man, the kind of guy who wants not equality for everyone but entitlement for himself. And big pecs. If gay men ruled America, there would be tax credits for joining a gym. This was abundantly clear to me at the New York Stonewall 25 celebration, the twenty-fifth anniversary of the uprising that inspired the gay rights movement. It was a weeklong festival of pod people twirling their multi-colored freedom rings.

There were so many hairless young men in nipple-hugging white T-shirts wandering the streets that I began to wish that it was 1969 again and paddy wagons would come and take them all away.

I spent the week with my best friend, the writer David B. Feinberg, who was dying of AIDS. He was having a hard time eating. Parasites were wearing away the undulant walls of his intestines, and he couldn't keep anything down. Wherever we went, our main concern was finding the john. As it happened, when I wasn't with David, I was reporting a magazine article about aspiring gay male porn stars. I went from club to club with members of my community, bare-chested men in cut-off blue jeans and black combat boots. Gay liberation has made it possible for every male homosexual in America to look the same and act too beautiful to talk to. If David had come along, he would have looked around the dance floor and said, "Cute boy, cute boy, cute boy." But David was home shitting his beauty into the toilet, and the cute boys he might have wanted were busy trying to look like storm troopers.

In our fervor to be part of the mainstream, we are creating stereotypes about ourselves that are just as clichéd as anything the religious right might dream up. This is evident in openly gay playwright Terence McNally's *Love! Valour! Compassion!,* a recent Tony Award–winning Broadway hit. The play concerns some upwardly mobile, well-dressed gay white men— artists and performers and urban professionals—who spend summer weekends together at a lovely country house in upstate New York. They swim, play tennis, make meals, serenade each other on the piano with Chopin waltzes, sunbathe nude, lament about AIDS and finally, triumphantly, dress up in tutus and dance to *Swan Lake.*

The play is full of sentimental notions of gay male solidarity: All gay men, except for the ones who know about musical comedy, have beautiful bodies; they are all epicures; they love to sit outside in the sun; if they're bitchy it's only because they're wounded; if they die it's somebody else's fault. Their pain is cured by women's clothing. Their desire is aroused, most fervently, by Puerto Ricans. Of course, there is an equally sentimental and misleading version of the 1990s male homosexual as an angry young queer. Picture a line of brave protesters confronting police officers in riot gear. The activists' faces are contorted in rage. "We're here, we're queer, get used to it," they chant, their voices raised as one in agonized lament.

I have been such a radical queer, and I have spent cozy weekends at some rich man's country house, eating gourmet food and talking politics and art. It's easy for me to spend time in both camps, because they are essentially the same. Nevertheless, critics from both sides support a false distinction between them. In *A Place at the Table,* self-identified "conservative" gay writer Bruce Bawer contrasts "subculture" gays with conservative ones, "elegantly turned out" gay men who go to church on Sunday. Radical queers say Bawer is self-loathing and anti-sex. But the two groups are haggling over style, not ideology. Both Bawer and Queer Nation belong to the privileged upper tenth of the gay community, the class of urban artists and professionals who dictate gay politics to the rest of the country. There are no statistics to prove it, of course, but if mainstream means "majority," I bet the mainstream of homosexuality in America today is in the Marines.

And in the Navy. And living on public assistance in Idaho. And leaving Latin American enclaves in Los Angeles to cruise for wealthy gringos wearing beautiful sweaters in gay bars lining Santa Monica Boulevard. The mainstream of homosexuality in America today is living at home with Mom and Dad in a two-family house in Whitestone, Queens, acting "straight" all day with friends held over from high school, but getting on homosexual phone-sex lines at night and saying things like, "Anybody out there like a lot of body contact?" Mainstream homosexuals are straight guys who go to gay bars once a week on Fridays and warn their girlfriends not to ask them what they're doing on their one night out. They are lesbians whose order of preference for sexual partners is: (1) straight women, (2) bisexual men, (3) other lesbians.

Yet the gay community represented in Ikea ads, the comfy image of a couple of middle-class white guys out shopping for furniture, is the one that has been identified as the mainstream. It's a lie. It is a lie for which radical dykes and fags are just as culpable as assimilationist lesbians and gays. The true division in the gay community is between the entrenched, privileged, politically active urban and suburban trend-setters and policy makers, and the mass of people with homosexual urges who feel represented more by *Reader's Digest* and *Soldier of Fortune* magazine than by *The Advocate* or *Genre* or *10 Percent* or *Frontiers* or *Deneuve* or *On Our Backs* or *Out.* If indeed they have even heard of them.

Nothing reveals the self-absorption of the gay ruling class more patently and damningly than its response to the problems of being homosexual in the military. Radical gays, hiding behind a veneer of pacifism, are especially guilty of classism and elitism in this instance. During the 1993 debate about President Clinton's proposal to lift the ban on gays in the military, radical queers very nearly colluded with anti-gay politicos, like Georgia Senator Sam Nunn, who organized the Congressional hearings on tolerating homosexuals in the armed forces. "If they're in the military, they get what they deserve," homo radicals told me, over and over, throughout the hearings.

Knee-jerk anti-military feeling dictated the radicals' official response. And a widespread and often petty mistrust of journalist Randy Shilts prevented the radical homo community from taking into account Shilts's devastating 1993 study of gay life in the military, *Conduct Unbecoming*. Shilts recounts severe and repeated civil rights violations, inflicted by military brass on gays or suspected gays, most of them women and/or African-American. The practice of homo witch-hunting actually intensified during the 1980s, roughly paralleling the AIDS crisis and ruining thousands of lives. But the activist gay community largely ignored the evidence in Shilts's book, because many gay men were still sulking over Shilts's role in closing gay bath houses in San Francisco in the early 1980s.

It's more important to get blown by a grunt in public than it is to defend his civil rights. Fags like to fetishize Marines, in part because of their mostly working-class appeal. But if somebody in the armed forces complains about how the military treats him, a lot of gay men tune out. "Abolish the military altogether," radical fags say, overlooking the fact that enlisting in the armed forces is often the most viable economic alternative for working-class young men. If you're seventeen years old and you don't like musical comedy, and you don't want to move to New York or Chicago or Los Angeles, and you don't have enough money for college; and if you know that you like sweaty, male environments; and if you want to get the hell out of your small town, why not the Marines? Not every gay man in America is a chorus boy or a sensitive poet or a Harvard MBA.

Of course, there were plenty of gay lawyers and Washington lobbyists who did try to help gays in the military. But they were defeated by a false sense of security. They assumed that because they were middle-class white guys they would naturally get what they wanted. The gay rights movement, from radicals to conservatives, is crippled by a sense of entitlement. Sometimes I think the difference between the two factions is just a question of contrasting fashion statements. In either case, I'm no longer dressing for either party. I'm sick of gay men. The next time I see a bunch of dudes from Jersey beating on a faggot from Greenwich Village, I'm going to cheer them on. Being gay used to feel like an expression of difference, but I lost my otherness, and now I want it back. I'm not gay anymore. I'm not even queer. I'd almost rather be mistaken for a registered Republican. After all, there's no distinction anymore between conservative Republicans and self-identified homosexuals. A conservative is someone who wants to keep what he has. So is a gay man. The gay rights movement is largely helmed by white men who crave what they were promised as children but denied as adults because of their sexuality; they want their guaranteed access to power. And they're not necessarily interested in extending that power to you, just because you happen to like having sex, sometimes, with guys.

26. JAMES EARL HARDY

James Earl Hardy's trilogy of novels, beginning with the best-selling *B-Boy Blues,* boldly explored a previously undertapped gay, African-American aesthetic. This *Advocate* column expresses his anger at the continuing bigotry evident in the language white people use when discussing racial matters.

The River of De-Nile

I WAS ON A PANEL ABOUT THE TOKENIZATION OF AFRICAN-AMERICAN homosexuals in the media when another participant, a white gay publisher, was asked why his staff is lily-white. His answer? Because he hasn't been able to find any "credible" African-Americans.

Credible?

I explained that this word (like *merit* and *qualified*) is often used by affirmative action foes to imply that African-Americans don't have what it takes to compete. After all, when's the last time you heard that someone couldn't find a "credible" white applicant?

The incident highlighted a problem many whites fail to grasp—even those who think they don't have a racist bone in their bodies. Fact is, it isn't their bones they should be worried about but their language. There is a special dialect white America has adopted to endorse the racial construct on which white supremacy has been built—and I'm not just talking about the word *nigger.* Being a member of a sexual "minority," even having a Negro as a lover or friend, doesn't mean you are more enlightened in this regard than your heterosexual cohorts. How many of the following "epithets" have you used?

Divisive and *separatist:* The conventional white wisdom about the Million Man March was that it would increase "racial tension." (Translation: How *dare* those Negroes do something without our permission or participation?) But for whites and African-Americans to be "divided," we have to first be "united," and we're not. We already live in "separate" worlds. So the only way the march (or the O. J. Simpson verdict) can divide or separate us (more than we are already) is if whites want it to—and the irrational reactions some had to both events say they do.

Transcend race: This means the Negro is "acceptable" because she or he has proved her or his worth as a human being (whites don't have to "transcend race," because they just *are*). Colin Powell is the flavor of the moment, and the empty praise expressed by some whites has been "I see him as an American hero, not a black man." (Guess he can't be both, huh?)

Race card: With this expression, race is reduced to a game—and I guess we would be the spades. Whites accuse African-Americans of "playing" the race card whenever whites want to deny that race matters. But if America was conceived on race and thrives on it, how can it ever *not* matter?

Politically correct: This ridiculous label is pulled out when people not white or male demand that they be called what they wish and treated with respect. With the charge of "PC," the slave-master syndrome kicks in: "I have the divine right to define and devalue you."

Reverse discrimination: There certainly have been and will be white victims of discrimination. But even though discrimination is discrimination, the *reverse* tag makes it clear that *real* discrimination isn't supposed to happen to whites ("It's OK for us to dish it out, not to receive it").

Black racism: Black people can certainly be bigots. But to be racist, you need the *power* to inflict your prejudiced views on others. Racism is institutional; it manifests in subtle ways. Take the Gay and Lesbian Alliance Against Defamation (GLAAD): Instead of reporting on how gay men of African descent were overlooked in media coverage of the Million Man March, they compare the event to the 1993 gay rights march, employing the tired "black versus gay" tactic arrogantly championed by white homosexuals (*"My* struggle is like *yours"*—when it ain't). In the end, members of the "community" GLAAD claims to represent were ignored and, like the Million Man March itself, marginalized.

Color-blind: "I don't see color," some whites argue. Yeah, right. You will admire a blue sky, a burnt-orange sun, and a red rose but refuse to even *see* my brown skin? People who say they are color-blind are just blind. Acknowledge and appreciate all I am—just don't hold it against me.

And then there are pejorative identifiers like *black-on-black crime* (doesn't "white-on-white crime" exist?) that allow whites to view African-Americans as a group whose attitudes and conduct are indicative of an "inferior" race.

Every time whites (and people of color who should know better) use these terms, the much-ballyhooed "dream" for us all to "just get along" is betrayed. It is hypocritical to expect people of color to work toward racial harmony or fight for gay rights while whites hide behind code words that uphold the status quo. Whites want "healing" yet refuse to treat the illness; they want "understanding" while dismissing the experiences of others. So while the nation has been embroiled in an overdue race debate for months, much of the debate has been misguided—because you can't have an honest dialogue if *dis*honest language clouds the discussion.

And as the year 2000 looms, we are still talking about race in riddles instead of reality. Maybe if the valueless vocabulary were dropped, gay America (where the river of De-Nile runs deep) and the rest of society would *really* be able to have good "race relations."

Whatever that means.

27. ANDREW HOLLERAN

Almost two decades after the publication of his novel *Dancer from the Dance,* a hallmark text for the urban fast-lane gay generation, Andrew Holleran now writes about aging and becoming estranged from the culture he helped define. In his novel *The Beauty of Men,* and here, in this *Christopher Street* column, he chronicles the trials of what he's called "gay geezerhood."

Survivors

MY FIRST NIGHT IN NEW YORK, WE DO A STUPID THING: WE GO OUT to dinner at a small Italian restaurant on Second Avenue that has a *prix fixe* pasta dinner after nine o'clock. The place is jammed. They seat my friend and me at a small table near the entrance. Around us are much larger groups of eight and nine, at larger tables, laughing, talking, eating. The din is tremendous. It's Friday night. I've been away so long I've forgotten the first rule of living in New York: Wait for the Weekend to Pass. The weekend is the invasion of the body-snatchers—when St. Mark's Place turns into a zoo; lines for movies, waits for tables, all become intolerable. Wait for Sunday night, when the whole frenzy vanishes, like Christmas, at a single stroke.

It's not just the irritation of the noise, the crowd, the long wait, the feeling that we have walked right into a moving airplane propeller, this time, however; it's not just that I'm tired from my trip, or that one has to make an effort to fight sleep, and make small talk against the restaurant roar; it's that this time I feel self-conscious about looking old. We're two gentlemen with silver hair, my friend and I, seated at our little table, while around us people much younger blare and bellow; I feel like one of the two spinsters who have ventured out from Grey Gardens. This feeling only increases the next day. In the darkness of the Metropolitan Museum, in the timelessness, the serenity of Art, the feeling momentarily vanishes; moving through the shadowy rooms, looking at glass cases filled—in dark chambers—with gold jewelry from Sumeria and ancient India, spotlighted on their pedestals, one forgets altogether that one is old. Then we find ourselves resting, on the stone perimeter of the Temple of Dendur, watching six young men play football on the green grass outside the huge glass wall; grabbing their crotches, lifting their shirts, pinching their butts at an angle as they pause between plays—all young, either indifferent to the audience within the Temple of Dendur, or quite conscious of the fact—displaying their youth and grace in a moving frieze.

Inside the museum, of course, when we resume our tour, are many other people, who vary conspicuously in age and condition; some of the gods are plaster, and some are walking around. When a man our age, standing at a glass case containing ceramics in the Tiffany wing, turns to us and starts talking about the Mad Potter of Biloxi, I realize how similar we are—three gay men of a certain age in a museum—and, watching my friend and the stranger speak, how the old reflect each other when they are together; which is why straight men dump their wives for younger women, I guess. No one wants that reflection staring back at them.

That evening, a friend brings to a (much quieter) Indian restaurant on Sixth Street, where we meet, a photo album given to him by the hosts of his thirty-fifth birthday party. I am astonished looking at the pictures, not by the obvious fact—how many of the guests are dead—but by how handsome my friend was then. Tall, well-built, in custom-made black leather pants and shirt, his pictures offer a striking contrast to the man across the table from me now; his face puffy, his stomach, beneath the double-breasted coat, that of a pregnant woman. He's not had sex in years and has eaten himself into what he calls "gay social withdrawal." What else is one to do? I wonder at this point. If one feels guilty for being old—if one feels one has disappointed one's friends by looking one's age—if one feels a certain pain in merely walking up the steps of a museum, or down a street, shouldn't one just stay in? Pascal asked why people ever leave their rooms. They leave their rooms, I think, to copulate; to look at other people and to be looked at. Social life is about mating—after you mate, you return to your burrow and reproduce. That's why the young—even the gay young—go out, presumably. When your mating time has passed, you feel odd going out, so you stay home; like the Parisian who drew her drapes the day she saw her first crow's foot and never went out again; or Marlene Dietrich making friends on the telephone in her apartment in Paris, never once allowing anyone to meet her. People who were once admired for their looks don't want to show their loss.

My friend's photo album of his birthday party reminds me oddly of the pictures a friend of mine in San Francisco used to see when he went to parties for people with AIDS: gaunt men showing snapshots of themselves when they were bartenders, men everyone drooled over. The next morning I stand in the foyer of my apartment building on St. Mark's Place behind a glass door and watch the people passing on the sidewalk. I'm used to seeing people now in a rural context, where one dresses basically for comfort; here comfort gives way to packaging—the city as a vast exercise in retail. We're told it's what's inside, not outside, that counts, but on the street the outside is the medium of exchange. I go back upstairs to my apartment— gay social withdrawal—open my copy of Reinaldo Arenas's *Before Night Falls,* and read, in the second paragraph of the introduction describing his feelings of mortality when he had AIDS: "Besides, some months ago when I entered a public rest room I became painfully aware that my presence failed to arouse the old expectant feeling of complicity. Nobody paid any attention to me, and the erotic games going on proceeded undisturbed. I no longer existed. I was not young any more. Right then and there I thought that the best thing for me was to die."

An extreme reaction, perhaps, like most that follow in this marvelous memoir—intense, passionate—but still true. But this is absurd, I think: One can't withdraw, stop living, because one is no longer young. This feeling disgusts me, it is so craven, so masochistic. Yet the fact that it is real only recalls the incredible assumption that lies beneath Youth—that when it walks into a room, it is doing the room a favor. (A gay man, whose identity is dependent on cruising, assumes that more than most, I suspect.) Now I go out with the attitude that I don't expect to be cruised; I'm happy if no one asks me to leave. (Leave what? The sidewalk? The restaurant?) At lunch, in a coffee shop in SoHo, I'm reminded that the reason people go to gyms is to have a body to show off in the innumerable places New York offers for exposure. "You can't be too big," a friend, just turned forty, tells me, when I remark that his chest is larger than it was the last time we met. "The Big Boys only want other Big Boys." Some of them, including a doctor he knows, are taking steroids; the steroids have caused the man's testicles to shrink. "But why would you exchange muscles for testicles?" I ask. "The muscles are there to attract people *to* the testicles."

It doesn't matter, he says, everybody on the Circuit wants to be bigger. He's got a new trainer himself, who's going to help him with his arms and shoulders, which is why he can't come to A Different Light that evening, to hear two writers read.

In the room downstairs at the bookstore, filled to overflowing, are men of all ages, men with white hair, and lined faces, clean-shaven young men with beautiful eyes, and men in the middle with wonderful beards, men at all stages of life from the twenties to the sixties. Mark Merlis reads from his novel *American Studies* a passage in which an older man reminisces about his diminishing ability to cruise, including a phrase about being so old that people avert their eyes from you "as if from an accident." (The accident, of course, is age; the truth of this is borne out in any walk down a street in this city, where looks are given and exchanged and parcelled out as carefully as money.) It's odd listening to this passage, which elicits laughter in several places; odd because it is so accurate, and because as he reads I watch the faces of the silver-haired men around me and wonder what they are thinking. Does having these truths expressed publicly in a novel alleviate the humiliations of age, or only accentuate them? I used to think that talking about age was like talking about hemmorhoids: Don't. But tonight I'm glad to hear this brought out into the open: the way we think, feel about age in this subculture of homosexual men—because if we are going to pay such elaborate attention to coming out, we must also face its denouement: what is going to happen after you come out, how you will evolve years later.

The standard fear—voiced most often by the family when a young man comes out—is that their sons and brothers will end up alone, or at least lonely in their old age. And in fact I have several friends right now who are wondering—like one in California whose lover just died in a house by the Russian River—just how it is that they have ended up by themselves. This experiment called gay life—this new arrangement, as Arenas points out in his book, of segregating oneself as a homosexual from the rest of society, to be with other homosexuals—has yet to address that question. Why *do* gay men end up alone after a certain age, why do they feel exiled from the bars, baths, restaurants, and meeting places men in their twenties and thirties flock to?

The answer, I suppose, is at the café my friend and I visit after the reading on Seventh Avenue. Seventh and Eighth Avenues have lately become clone corridors. This stretch of sidewalk on Seventh has always seemed to me to be one of the ugliest in New York: The gas station on the east side is the only cheerful note in this drab, characterless segment of Manhattan that could just as well be Hoboken, or Detroit. The sidewalk is like the runway at a fashion show, however, as the buffed boys with their perfect haircuts pass the window—it is the very ugliness of New York, the gritty, greenless grime of stretches like this one on Seventh Avenue, that makes the beauty of the face, the human figure, on the concrete and asphalt, all the more enticing. Everyone who walks down a street in New York— like these men with pompadours passing the café—is on display, and, as in the modeling business, the competition is fierce, and it is best to be young; even if tonight's parade is won not by any of the gay men walking by in parkas and jeans, but by a policeman who looks like Fabian patrolling his beat—an absolute knockout.

When I glance away from the show outside, however, to address my companion (I sit facing the wall, he the room behind us), I notice a peculiar expression passing over his features and say: "What's wrong? You look as if you'd just seen a worm." "The waiter is serving another couple," he says, "who came in after we did." "Are they straight?" I ask. "No," he says, "they're gay. But younger. It's ageism," he says, raising his hand. "I'm going to call him on it." I am torn between admiration for his courage, and embarrassment over what I hope will not be a scene.

There is no scene; the waiter, when my friend gets his attention and points out the unfairness, protests that he is sorry, he hadn't noticed the order of our arrivals. "Of course he did," says my friend after the waiter leaves, "even if unconsciously. They are young and cute, so he went over to them." So it's not just me, I think; we're all feeling this absurd, self-conscious paranoia. "I'll be protesting the White House in a wheelchair when I'm ninety-five," my friend laughs.

"By the way," I ask, "how many men from our generation in New York do you think are still alive?"

He looks at me and says flatly: "Two percent." I suspect the figure is quite low but say nothing; he's made his point. In his circle, it's probably true. "I am the *only one* alive," he says now, "from the party Clovis and Vito gave me in 1983. The only one."

It's a double whammy, Survivor's Syndrome: the ordinary humiliations of growing old that attend all people, straight and gay, blended with accumulated grief and the fact that there are far fewer peers to share this with. (The only comfort for this new feeling of embarrassment; that, and a sense of humor.) Middle age and the losses of AIDS play upon one another, increase synergistically the fact and feeling of isolation. When we say good-night to each other on the street, we go our separate ways—back into gay social withdrawal.

28. RAFAEL CAMPO

At the age of thirty-one, Rafael Campo has already published two critically hailed volumes of poetry and a book of essays, *The Poetry of Healing*—all the while caring for his patients as a doctor in Boston. This concluding essay from his collection speaks to the difficulties—and possibilities—of belonging to many different communities.

Giving It Back

THE THEN DEAN OF STUDENT AFFAIRS AT HARVARD MEDICAL SCHOOL was musing over my future career options as a physician the first time I heard the phrase "giving back to the community." Puzzled by what she might mean, I wondered what it was that I could have unwittingly stolen. (Having grown up in white America, I suppose I must have been taught that the dark one in the room must always be guilty of *something;* in my case especially, this was usually in fact true.) It seemed virtually impossible to me that I owed anybody anything, given the history of numbing loss which was all that I had inherited from my Cuban relatives. Indeed, it seemed to me that someday reparations would have to be made to *me,* for the lost sugar plantation and the one thousand slaughtered head of cattle, for the nameless stream that ran with our blood and the salt and sand quarries in which our murdered bodies were dumped—all that was my birthright as proved by the yellowing deed I imagined my grandfather clenching in his fist as he tearfully told and retold his stories of the revolution.

So what could I now give back, one who had so very little, one who was still so busy trying to make his selections? Yes, the Americans had turned their backs on us at a crucial moment, but in the end they had given us a new home in a glaring white supermarket of opportunities, bargains, and possibilities. The point of my American journey seemed to be what else I could acquire for *myself;* the state-of-the-art home entertainment center or the swank beachfront vacation home in Florida each more clearly imaginable to me than my grandfather's out-of-tune guitar or the modest house that faced toward the sea from which he and his family once made their dramatic escape. As I listened impatiently to the Dean wax eloquent on the needs of poor Latinos who lived in neighborhoods through which I would avoid driving if at all possible, people who might try to pay me for my services with chickens or tortillas, people whose teenage sons might mug me on my way home from a night shift in the Emergency Room, I grew more and more concerned about paying back the sixty-thousand dollars in student loans I had amassed during my academic career. I was contemplating a lucrative career in Diagnostic Radiology—whatever youthful idealism I had brought with me to medicine had long since evaporated. I had started to like the fluid look of my reflection in the shiny Volvos and BMWs parked around the hospital in the spaces reserved for the radiologists as I walked in each day; I liked having my boundaries blurred. What could be wrong with the soft, pink, perfectly made body of success? I wanted to wear America like an expensive suit, the best that money could buy. I deserved it.

Of course, I conceded on some level that there were others like me who had been dispossessed as well, perhaps just as unfairly, those same Spanish-speaking people from so many cultures, races, and nations who were fast becoming my patients as I embarked on my first ward rotations. I saw, too, how what they had lost oftentimes was recorded physically upon their bodies: the missing limb amputated after inadvertently stepping on a land mine, the empty eye socket where the globe had been ruptured after a gun-butt's brutal blow to the face, the lost uterus removed during a government-enforced sterilization program. Sometimes their illnesses were less obviously caused by the conditions in which they were now forced to live, or the jobs hunger urged them to take: the green-eyed woman from Mexico who burned her arm in the hungry maw of a laundry press, the gray-haired Salvadoran man with scarred lungs and a nerve disorder who probably had inhaled pesticides sprayed while he was picking fruit, the cinnamon-black man from Cuba whose infant daughter was bitten by a hungry rat in the housing projects where they lived. I felt sorry for them, to be sure, but if there was one thing I had by then learned during medical school it was how to protect (if not exactly to take care of) myself.

Moreover, my own once-downtrodden family of immigrants had not only survived, but prospered. Despite their own personal litany of hardships—the omnipresent language barrier, the matter-of-fact but subtle discrimination and the especially savored moments of blatant persecution—their durability, much more than their industrious achievements, had been always a source of great pride to them. So I expected no less of these people for whom I was beginning to care, whose bodies were my laboratories and my classrooms. If they were vaguely "my people," it was more in the sense of "property" or "baggage" as opposed to "spirit." The myth of the uniqueness of fingerprints was making a dangerous kind of sense to me; human beings were so inalterably different, even when they shared a dietary staple or a mother tongue or an unsurprising susceptibility to bullets, I believed it was impossible for an embrace or a prayer or a handshake or a poem to bring them together.

Then there was the larger problem of what was meant by "community" in the first place. Was this well-intentioned Dean referring, when she pronounced this polysyllabic word, only to the Cuban expatriate community, whose rabid patriotism and reactionary anti-communist/anti-Castro right-wing politics repulsed me, but to whom I nonetheless belonged in the most obvious ways? Or did she mean the more broadly defined Latino community, which in Boston at the time was comprised not only of Cubans but also of much larger contingents of Dominicans and Salvadorans, as well as a significant number of Puerto Ricans (some born on the U.S. mainland, some back on the island itself) and a growing number of Mexican-Americans? Or, perhaps worst of all, did she simply relegate me to the most broadly defined category available, that clamoring undifferentiated heap of the darker-skinned oppressed, those pitiably disadvantaged and generically "poor" people in America? Or were there other groups of people—ones I was afraid to acknowledge in her genteel presence, or even others at the moment unknown to both of us—with whom I shared yet another different homeland?

I had felt many times, or had been made to feel, that I had been admitted to Harvard Medical School for a very specific reason. I was not really expected to think independently or to have original ideas but to satisfy a quota, to represent someone's stereotype of the Latino student—who, by definition, could not aspire to a career in research or in some high-powered superspecialty, but instead, after his brief elevation into the world of privilege, would dutifully go back out into his underserved "community" to practice medicine. Less intellectually demanding jobs existed for me in the ghettos, there were always plenty of openings for relatively low-paid Primary Care providers. Disenfranchised as I was often presumed to be, I was forced to play that most thankless of roles, that of the one who desperately needs that life-changing hand-up. Presumably, otherwise I might have made nothing of myself. This particular recasting of my identity was especially painful to bear, because it was authored by the acts and attitudes of the kindly liberal people whom I knew were allies, people who wanted to do something, anything to help—whether out of a sense of what was morally just, or out of religious or personal guilt, or fear of eventual retribution—as long as they did not have to reach out into those needy communities themselves with their own clean, well-manicured hands.

They were preferable, at least, to their most visible alternatives, the outright bigots who angrily bemoaned my presence among them. To them, I was the reason their sons did not get into Harvard. Perhaps they imagined I was another tenth baby born out of wedlock who would someday have ten illegitimate children myself and thus take over the world by outbreeding white people. Or I was the beneficiary of Head Start, food stamps, and other expensive government-sponsored entitlement programs that siphoned off their tax dollars from more worthy uses such as Star Wars or the B-1 bomber. I was responsible for the resurgence of tuberculosis in the United States, the illegal immigrant who smuggled the organism into the country hidden in my lungs like contraband. I was not fully human to them, so I myself could not suffer; I was simply a vector. I was all the potentially lethal vermin and the terrible scourges they carried, the fierce African killer bee, the ravenous Medfly, the repulsive cockroach, the blood-sucking mosquito, the typhus-infected rat. I was the pathetic monkey trying to imitate them, to steal their precious American know-how and cutting-edge technology and take it back to my own country. I was dragging their gloriously free society down the tubes by taking insatiable advantage of and twisting that same freedom to serve my own selfish purposes. Sadly—and this seemed to be the extent of their emotional response to the remotely uncomfortable problem of my assumed-to-be-impoverished existence—I could never be as smart, or as productive, or as innovative as they were. Only my inherent genetic deficiencies were to blame. Pseudo-Darwinian theories of survival and genetic advantagedness explained everything, and at the same time were conveniently thought to be unchangeable natural laws—while I knew that some of the audacious researchers among these most dangerous of my enemies paradoxically attempted to manipulate human genes to cure cancer. I worried that perhaps someday I myself might become an unwilling subject in one of their diabolical experiments, my dissected rat-brain floating in a great glass vat of saline, an anti-Frankenstein of sorts by whose gruesome disembodiment they hoped to salvage my least-impaired working parts and so re-engineer me into something more useful before discarding the rest. In my overactive imagination, I envisioned them as high-powered "mad scientists" who secretly hoped that they could purge by their ultrasophisticated genetic techniques the human race of all its debilitating differences.

Then there were the few other Latinos in medicine whom I encountered, mostly older, disgruntled men who worked in chronically underfunded, technology-poor Primary Care settings. Their own bitter intolerance for points of view discordant with their own sometimes shocked me. I recall vividly the harrowing experience of an interview with the Director of Minority Recruitment and Retention at one West Coast medical school, who demanded to know why I had not checked any of the boxes next to the various categories that allowed the school to identify disadvantaged minority candidates. He implied that I was either ashamed of my heritage, or that I was a sellout too eager for the promised assimilation that would never come. When I tried to defend myself, on the basis that I was not sure I qualified for this special consideration since I was ambivalent about whether in fact I had been in any way truly disadvantaged—indeed, on some of my applications where the question was worded differently I *had* checked the box in question—he attacked me again, saying it was not special consideration but redress of past inequities that the admissions process was attempting to effect in its application review process. He then accused me of possibly the worst of all crimes, namely the abandonment of my own community. That word again, "community." And so I was banished from the comforting embrace of my own people before I had ever found the strength in their warm arms in the first place.

These three disparate but oddly complementary views of the community of origin to which I might belong only partially accounted for my resistance to this strangely altruistic notion of "giving back." That Latino cultures are stereotypically seen as welcoming, colorful, and musical made its rejection of me when I came out all the more painful. The quietly closed doors and withheld invitations of the Anglo world literally paled in comparison to all those melodramatic and exaggerated tears, the near-violent disowning of my lover by his father, and the various sanctimonious sermons from Catholic priests that I endured when I was surrounded by Latinos, by my own family. Spanish words, because of their melodious gentleness which allowed me to carry them closer to my heart, were much more capable of inflicting mortal wounds when turned against me. The Latino "community" fostered a surprisingly greater innate hostility to homosexuality, yet it was also the one place where I expected to be unconditionally loved. I reacted to its renunciation of me with a particularly potent mixture of anger and alienation. I began to think of myself as the most desperate of desperados: I was doubly illegal and doubly an ingrate, at once the unwanted and detestable immigrant who would disappoint the great nation that had reluctantly taken me in, and the repugnant and sinful castaway who would give all of us in the boat a bad name, who would shame the culture that had given me life. After all, we as a people were too poor for such an extravagance of love, an excessive love that was more like a sickness and so must have penetrated me during my adventures in the decadent white world.

Ironically, it was this unspeakable love that ultimately led me to the place where I am now, to a career not in Diagnostic Radiology but in General Internal Medicine, which allows me to provide primary care mostly to Latino patients in Boston. It was the love of another man, Latino himself, who taught me to love my culture, who led me to my place at the banquet table. It was his nurturing that sustained me through the cold winters of my New England college, and later through the chilling anatomy labs of medical school. It did not matter to him whether on occasion I listened to old Broadway show tunes or to Led Zeppelin instead of salsa; we could still communicate in Spanish, we could still cook paella, or *plátanos* and rice and beans, and then discuss politics late into the night while chain-smoking cigarettes. I was forgiven for my awkward mispronunciations, in both English and in Spanish, because bilingualism for us came to mean that my tongue was sometimes wrapped around his. We created our own country of origin, crossed oceans to our own undiscovered continent, wrote anthems for our own America the Fabulous. We planned to create a new life together in blissful harmony in Cuba someday—the choice of that most impossible and unimaginable of all locations was not exactly accidental—reclaiming my grandfather's lost plantation as our own, liberating it from the centuries of both capitalist and communist oppression. We would invent our own utopian political system, we would make idealistic lyrics like Martí's the law of the land. We who belonged neither to Spain nor to the United States but to one another.

Under the tutelage of his love, I began to understand democracy and human rights in a revolutionary way. I saw particularly that in illness, as in desire, all people were indeed created equal. Suffering did not respect national boundaries or speak in only one approved language. The color of blood in every flag was monotonously the same unfathomable red. Need paid no attention to what part of whose body was placed where. Death visited every neighborhood, riding in on the subway or in a stretch limousine at any hour of the day or night. Though wealth might have the power to promote health, and maybe even to prolong life, in the end all my patients needed me to hold their hands, or to smile and to touch their faces. Everyone needed a witness, all of them wanted someone to whom they could tell their final stories. Afterwards, the agonal last breaths always followed the same basic pattern, and the flat green line on the monitor always failed to be rekindled with the electrical waveform of a beating heart.

Oppression, too, became even more physically embodied, all the more obvious in the quotidian lives of my patients, to whose suffering I was finally awakened. The infected rat bite, the debilitating toxic exposure, the relentless spread of AIDS were no longer simply the documentation of losses that I had learned, from the history of my own family, to compile passively, losses about which nothing could be done; rather, each became a form of active violence perpetrated by the powerful against the weak, calling for an immediate, drastic, and equally purposeful response. I began to understand how one atrocity led to another: from the genocide of this land's indigenous peoples (a fact I had once haughtily questioned), where European diseases were literally employed as weapons against native people, to the murder and starvation of *mejicanos* and *californios* who remained in their homes after Mexico ceded its northern territories to the United States, to the ongoing American embargo of Cuba, where because of the lack of vaccines and antibiotics children continue to die each day.

I learned from reading the newspapers many things that were never mentioned in my medical textbooks. I witnessed that the health-care policy of the moment was being shaped by the same aggressive impulses to control and to subjugate other people that had led to the wars and the destruction of the not-so-distant past. The contentious debates over funding to combat AIDS raged in ever-more hostile terms during my four years of medical school. It was for all intents and purposes a war, one which had led desperate and misguided ACT UP members to interrupt a Catholic mass and to desecrate St. Patrick's Cathedral in New York by laying bloody handprints on its cold stone walls, and one where the rhetoric of hate and bigotry has had its most venomous expression from Jesse Helms, the senior Republican Senator from North Carolina, who spoke the following words of enlightenment on the Senate floor:

> What originally began as a measured response to a public-health emergency has become a weapon, frankly, for the deterioration of America's Judeo-Christian value system. There's not a chance this bill will be stopped because there's a powerful lobby out there in the media and in the homosexual community, and senators are scrambling to put their names on anything that has to do with AIDS.

Weapon, community, homosexual, America, values, Judeo-Christian, AIDS. Was my community after all "the homosexual community" that Jesse Helms seemed so adept at identifying and annihilating while I, one of its own members, had struggled so long to find it? Did my assent to this question therefore mean that I was not American? Or not Christian? Or not Latino? These questions about labels began to swirl in my head as I made my rounds in the hospital each morning, and though their answers might seem obvious, my education and my pride in my accomplishments rose to a painful hard knot in my throat as I stared into the eyes of those who were actually dying, those gaunt men and women who were neither senators nor physicians, those people who asked me quietly in Spanish for a glass of water before I left, those who were not necessarily gay or Latino or heterosexual or African-American or female or white; their most conspicuous defining characteristic was that they were suffering. How convenient, I thought, that the same terrible disease could be used to decimate minority cultures and simultaneously to destroy the values of the much stronger Helms-inspired mainstream one.

I have come to appreciate how little one's own sense of identity ultimately seems to matter in the definition of communities, in the drawing of national or sexual or linguistic boundaries, when such tremendously powerful adversarial forces are at work. Out there somewhere in the larger culture, whether in an institutionalized form of human nature that insists on separating us into digestible groups, or as an aggregate of individual human choices to know only one version of any story, there must exist a principle by which all are probed and assigned a place. Because my training is both in medicine and in poetry, because my languages are both English and Spanish, because my love is at once conventional and queer, and because I was born in only one place and at one moment in time, once I had this fantasy: the invention of a single blood test whose undeniable result could be related and understood by anyone in a few spoken words and then sealed with a kiss, a test that proved beyond all doubt that we were all fundamentally the same creatures. I have seen our naked bodies, so often the instruments or the objects of our divisions; I know I am just as human as Tom Cruise, whose beautiful image is worth millions of dollars, just as human as my IV drug-using AIDS patient in the ER whose name I forgot probably within minutes of her death in my arms. I freely admit I am still naive, believing at times that a touch can heal even in an ICU, or that a prayer can be heard well outside the confines of a church.

It has been suggested to me that my problem, however it is defined, has resulted from an exaggerated capacity on my part for sensing the innumerable wrongs done to me. I have been told that I must always remember how to forget. The organs of my voice have become hypertrophied from saying the same things over and over again to a world that refuses to listen; no matter how hard I try, I will never recreate the Aztec canon or the Mayan system of arithmetic. And enough with the queer thing, they say, warning me that I am beginning to sound like the frustrated *mariachi* who wants to wear his pink ruffled shirt to sing in a restaurant that only serves tacos. Too serious, too sensitive, too insistent, my parents say. My poems have an unfortunate tendency to wallow in the misery of their own creation, besides being obsessed with my patriarchal past. Perhaps I have driven my community, whoever they might be, away from me with my unending questions and saturnine social skills. Perhaps I have told one too many a story about a patient whose life or death changed my own. If these criticisms are accurate, then I accept them; but since even before my awkward conversation with the Dean, really since the moment I realized I shared the world with other people, sometimes in spite of myself and some-times with the fullest of hearts, I have felt compelled to search for some way to give.

Once I felt that the most insurmountable of all the obstacles facing me in the care of my patients was my own selfishness. I was too busy to listen to the pathetic story of another person's suffering, too hungry to stay a few minutes later to comfort another person in need, too important to be bur-dened with another person's trivial concern. The next great hurdle I en-countered also had to do with the imperilment of empathy: Will the heart of the seventy-five-year-old grandmother of eight from Guatemala with congestive heart failure finally burst when she learns that I am gay? (She cried the same tears as my own grandmother once did, and revealed to me one of her own grandchildren was a lesbian.) I have tried to internalize what I have learned from my patients themselves. I remember how they have endured, and how they have taught me what I once thought was im-possible, something I thought I might never learn: the limitless ways that I can give back to many communities.

I wonder who you would see if I were to come to you for help. What would you give me? I am not tall, I have an olive complexion, I have dark straight hair, I have green eyes. I am a bit overweight, I have a job, I have enough money for shelter, for food. I look like the hybrid that I am. Like most hybrids, I will never reproduce. I am toxic to my own aspirations and dreams; in my veins run both the promise of a better life and its incessant denial. My physical appearance marks me now, though it remains un-marred, unlike the bodies of so many others of my kind. I walk down the street in San Francisco, and I am mistaken for a Mexican. I could be ille-gal. Once, an elderly American lady driving a white Cadillac asked me whether I was Jewish. I thought she recognized me. I am the Jew of the Caribbean—isn't that what they call Cubans? My mother was born in Dover, New Jersey. Her parents' relatives still live in Italy, that's what they always said. My father is a U.S. citizen, but I never asked him where he keeps his documentation. I should know that. We memorized an Ameri-can version of his own history. Maybe I can give that back. Maybe I can teach you to love something new, like salsa or black beans and white rice or Gloria Estefan or Andy Garcia or Celia Cruz or Albita. I want you to know something about me, about us, after you finish reading this. I am writing a new poem later today. I want you to read it, too. I want to be mistaken for your brother, or your son; I want to remind you of your daughter, your mother, your sister. I want to give you something, not a disease, but perhaps a cure. I want you to look into the liquid mirror of my eyes, and see someone you recognize. Someone you have always known, someone you might even love.

Yourself.

Contributors

BRUCE BAWER's book *Stealing Jesus: How Fundamentalism Betrays Christianity* will appear from Crown Publishers in the fall of 1997.

DAVID BERGMAN is the author or editor of a dozen books, including *Cracking the Code,* which won the George Elliston Poetry Prize, and *Gaiety Transfigured: Gay Self-Representation in American Literature.* He is the editor of *Men on Men,* the biennial collection of the best of recent gay short fiction. His work has appeared in such magazines as *The Harvard Gay and Lesbian Review, The Kenyon Review, Men's Style, The New Republic,* and *The Paris Review.* He lives in Baltimore and teaches at Towson State University.

KEITH BOYKIN is the author of *One More River to Cross: Black & Gay in America.* A 1992 graduate of Harvard Law School, he worked for two years as Special Assistant and Director of Specialty Press for President Clinton, serving as the principal liaison and spokesperson between the White House and minority—including African-American and gay—media. Currently, he serves as Executive Director of the National Black Gay & Lesbian Leadership Forum.

MICHAEL BRONSKI is the author of *Culture Clash: The Making of Gay Sensibility* and *The Pleasure Principle: Culture, Backlash and the Struggle for Gay Freedom,* and editor of *Taking Liberties* and *Flashpoint.* His writing has appeared in *The Los Angeles Times, The Village Voice, Z Magazine, Out,* and *Gay Community News,* as well as in the anthologies *Gay Spirit, Friends and Lovers, Personal Dispatches, Acting on AIDS,* and volumes 2, 3, and 4 of the *Flesh and the Word* series. He has been involved in the Gay Liberation Movement for more than twenty-nine years.

FRANK BROWNING is the author of four books, including *A Queer Geography* and *The Culture of Desire.* He is currently completing *Apples: History, Mythology, Delights,* for Farrar, Straus & Giroux. Formerly an award-winning correspondent for National Public Radio in Los Angeles and Washington, his writing has appeared in periodicals such as *The New York Times, The Washington Post, Mother Jones, Playboy, Penthouse,* and *The Saturday Review.* He divides his time between Brooklyn, New York, and Wallingford, Kentucky, where he is co-owner of Browning Orchard.

CHRIS BULL is the co-author of *Perfect Enemies: The Religious Right, the Gay Movement, and the Politics of the 1990s.* A journalist living in Washington, D.C., he was for three years the national reporter for *Gay Community News,* and after that the Washington correspondent for *The Advocate.* He received the National Lesbian and Gay Journalists Association's 1994 honors for his coverage of gay youth suicide.

RAFAEL CAMPO teaches and practices internal medicine at Harvard Medical School's Beth Israel Deaconess Medical Center. W. W. Norton recently published a collection of his prose entitled *The Poetry of Healing: A Doctor's Education in Empathy, Identity, and Desire.* His books of poetry are *The Other Man Was Me* and *What the Body Told.* He is the recipient of a Guggenheim Foundation Fellowship for 1997.

BERNARD COOPER'S most recent book is *Truth Serum,* from Houghton Mifflin. His work has appeared in *Best American Gay Fiction 1996, The 1995 O. Henry Prize Collection,* and *The Best American Essays of 1995.*

MARK DOTY is the author of the memoir *Heaven's Coast* and four collections of poems: *Turtle, Swan; Bethlehem in Broad Daylight; Atlantis;* and *My Alexandria,* winner of the National Books Critics Circle Award, the *Los Angeles Times* Book Award, the National Poetry Series, and a finalist for the National Book Award. He has been the recipient of a Whiting Writer's Award and grants from the National Endowment for the Arts, the Guggenheim Foundation, the Ingram Merrill Foundation, the Massachusetts Arts Foundation, and the Vermont Council on the Arts. He lives in Provincetown, Massachusetts.

JOHN GALLAGHER is the co-author of *Perfect Enemies: The Religious Right, the Gay Movement, and the Politics of the 1990s.* He has been a national correspondent for *The Advocate* for the past five years, where his reporting on regional and national politics has received numerous awards. Previously, he was a reporter at *Time* magazine for seven years. He lives in New York City.

JESSE GREEN is an award-winning journalist whose articles have appeared in such publications as *The New York Times Magazine, New York, Premiere, GQ, Philadelphia, Mirabella,* and *Out.* His first novel, *O Beautiful,* was published by Ballantine in 1992, and is now in its third printing. His short stories have appeared in many magazines; "Mirandas" was anthologized in the collection *Waves,* published by Vintage in 1994. Green lives in New York City, where he is now at work on a second novel and on *The Velveteen Father,* a nonfiction memoir to be published by Hyperion in 1998.

JAMES EARL HARDY is the author of the national bestseller *B-Boy Blues,* praised as the first Africentric, gay hip-hop love story. It has spawned a sequel, *2nd Time Around,* and a third title, *If Only for One Nite.* He is featured in collections including *Shade: An Anthology of Fiction by Gay Men of African Descent.* An honors graduate of the Columbia School of Journalism, he is also an award-winning entertainment feature writer and music critic who has penned biographies of Spike Lee and Boyz II Men. He lives in New York City.

HARRY HAY founded the Mattachine Society, the first gay liberation group in the United States. He remains an outspoken activist in the gay liberation and New Age spirituality movements. He lives in Los Angeles.

ALEC HOLLAND is the pseudonym of a writer who lives in San Francisco.

ANDREW HOLLERAN is the author of three novels, *The Beauty of Men, Nights in Aruba,* and *Dancer from the Dance;* and also a collection of essays, *Ground Zero.* He lives in Florida.

FENTON JOHNSON is the author of two novels, *Crossing the River* and *Scissors, Paper, Rock,* and a memoir, *Geography of the Heart,* which received the American Library Association Award for best gay/lesbian nonfiction of 1996. He is the recipient of National Endowment for the Arts literature fellowships in both fiction and creative nonfiction, as well as a Wallace Stegner Fellowship from Stanford University and a James Michener Fellowship from the University of Iowa Writers Workshop. He currently teaches in the Writing Program at Columbia University.

TONY KUSHNER is the author of *Angels in America, Part One: Millennium Approaches,* and *Part Two: Perestroika,* for which he received two Tony awards for best play on Broadway and the Pulitzer Prize for Drama. His other plays include an adaptation of Corneille's *The Illusion, A Bright Room Called Day,* and *Slavs!* His essays have appeared in many publications including *Esquire, The Nation, The New York Times, The Los Angeles Times, The Washington Post,* and *Newsweek.* He lives in New York City.

MICHAEL LASSELL is the author of *Poems for Lost and Un-lost Boys, Decade Dance* (winner of a Lambda Literary Award), and *The Hard Way.* He is the editor of *The Name of Love, Eros in Boystown,* and, with Lawrence Schimel of *Two Hearts Desire.* His work has appeared in scores of journals and newspapers in this country and abroad, and in such anthologies as *Gay & Lesbian Poetry in Our Time, Men on Men 3, Hometowns, Flesh and the Word, Friends and Lovers, Wanderlust, Best Gay Erotica 1996, Queer View Mirror 2,* and such college textbooks as W. W. Norton's *New Worlds of Literature.*

RABBI YAAKOV LEVADO (a pseudonym) received his B.A. in philosophy from Yeshiva University and his rabbinic ordination from the Rabbi Isaac Elchanan Theological Seminary. He is presently working on a book to be titled *Wrestling with Men and God: Torah, Tradition, and Illicit Love.*

CRAIG LUCAS is the author of numerous plays and movies, including *Prelude to a Kiss, Longtime Companion, Reckless, Blue Windows, Missing Persons, God's Heart,* and *The Dying Gaul.* He has received the Obie Award, Sundance Film Festival Audience Award, L.A. Drama Critics Award, Outer Circle Award, and Guggenheim and Rockefeller fellowships. He lives in New York City.

MARK MATOUSEK is the author of the memoir *Sex Death Enlightenment.* A former editor at *Interview* magazine, and columnist for *Details* and *Harper's Bazaar,* he has contributed essays to many periodicals and anthologies, as well as being nominated for a National Magazine Award in 1992. He lives in New York City and is currently at work on a second memoir for Riverhead Books.

DANIEL MENDELSOHN is a New York-based critic and translator. His writing has appeared in publications including *The New Yorker, The New York Times Magazine* and *Book Review, The Nation, Lingua Franca,* and *Out* magazine, where he is a contributing writer; and has been anthologized in various collections, from *Beyond Queer* to *The Best American Humor.* He is currently working on two books for Knopf: an essay about gay culture, to be published next year, and a new English translation of the complete works of C. P. Cavafy. He was educated at the University of Virginia, and holds a doctorate in Classics from Princeton.

SCOTT O'HARA is a retired porn star, rentable from your local video store in at least twenty-six videos. He was the editor of *Steam* magazine—"The Literate Queer's Guide to Sex and Controversy"—for three years. His first collection of short stories, *Do-It-Yourself Piston Polishing (For Non-Mechanics)*, was published by Badboy in 1996. *Autopornography*, his memoir of life in the porn world, has recently been released from Haworth.

GABRIEL ROTELLO was the founding editor of *OutWeek* magazine, and was the first gay man to write a weekly column on gay and lesbian issues for a major American newspaper, *New York Newsday*. He writes frequently on gay and AIDS subjects for many publications, including *The Nation, The Advocate,* and *Out*. His book *Sexual Ecology: AIDS and the Destiny of Gay Men* was published in 1997 by Dutton. Rotello won the Gay and Lesbian Alliance Against Defamation Outstanding Journalist of the Year Award for 1995. He lives in New York City.

D. TRAVERS SCOTT is a writer/performer and author of the novel *Execution, Texas: 1987*. His work has appeared in publications including *Best American Gay Fiction 1997, Harper's, Best Gay Erotica 1996 and 1997, Holy Titclamps!, Reclaiming the Heartland,* and *Forbidden: Defiant Lesbian Writing*. He lives in Seattle with David Eckard, a great sculptor who's also very tolerant about having details of his personal life published.

MICHELANGELO SIGNORILE is the author of three books, including *Life Outside: The Signorile Report on Gay Men: Sex, Drugs, Muscles and the Passages of Life,* published in 1997. He writes a monthly column, "Signorile in America," for *Out* magazine, and has written for *The New York Times, The Village Voice, USA Today,* and *The Advocate*. He lives in New York City.

ANDREW SULLIVAN is the author of *Virtually Normal: An Argument About Homosexuality*. He is the former editor of *The New Republic*.

MARK THOMPSON worked for the national gay newsmagazine *The Advocate*—as a feature writer, photographer, and eventually senior editor—from 1975 to 1994. He is the editor of four books: *Long Road to Freedom: The Advocate History of the Gay and Lesbian Movement, Gay Spirit: Myth and Meaning, Leatherfolk: Radical Sex, People, Politics and Practice,* and *Gay Soul: Finding the Heart of Gay Spirit and Nature*—the latter two of which were nominated for the Lambda Literary Award. St. Martin's Press recently published his latest book, *Gay Body: One Man's Journey Through Shadow to Self.*

JOHN WEIR is the author of *The Irreversible Decline of Eddie Socket,* which won a Lambda Literary Award for Best Gay Debut in 1990. He has written for *Details, The Advocate, The Village Voice,* and many other publications. He lives in New York City.

Permissions

"Making Sex Public" by Michael Lassell. Redacted and updated from a talk delivered at "Flesh and the Word: A Celebration of the Work and Life of John Preston," Brown University, October 7, 1995. Published in different form in *Taking Liberties,* edited by Michael Bronski (New York: Masquerade, 1996). Copyright © 1995, 1997 by Michael Lassell. Reprinted by permission of the author.

"Why Gay Men Can't Really Talk About Sex" by Michael Bronski. First published in *Flesh and the Word 3,* edited by John Preston with Michael Lowenthal (New York: Plume, 1995). Copyright © 1995 by Michael Bronski. Reprinted by permission of the author.

"Flirting with Suicide" by Jesse Green. First published in slightly abridged form in *The New York Times Magazine,* September 15, 1996. Copyright © 1996 by Jesse Green. Reprinted by permission of the author.

"To Protect and Serve" by Gabriel Rotello. First published in *The Advocate,* June 13, 1995. Copyright © 1995 by Gabriel Rotello. Reprinted by permission of *The Advocate.*

"Talking with My Mouth Full" by Scott O'Hara from *Policing Public Sex,* edited by Dangerous Bedfellows (Boston: South End Press, 1996). Copyright © 1996 by Scott O'Hara. Reprinted by permission of the author.

"Flexible Fidelity" by D. Travers Scott. First published in different form as "At Home with the He-Whores" in *Steam,* vol. 2 issue 4, Winter 1994. Copyright © 1994, 1997 by D. Travers Scott. Reprinted by permission of the author.

"Sex and the Not-So-Single Guy" by Michelangelo Signorile. First published in *Out,* July 1996. Copyright © 1996 by Michelangelo Signorile. Reprinted by permission of the author.

"If and When" from *Truth Serum* by Bernard Cooper. Copyright © 1996 by Bernard Cooper. Reprinted by permission of Houghton Mifflin Company. All rights reserved.

"American Religion, Gay Identity" from *A Queer Geography* by Frank Browning. Copyright © 1996 by Frank Browning. Reprinted by permission of Crown Publishers, Inc.

"The Fundamentals of Faith" by Bruce Bawer. First published in *The Advocate,* March 19, 1996. Copyright © 1996 by Bruce Bawer. Reprinted by permission of the author.

"Alone Again, Naturally" by Andrew Sullivan. First published in *The New Republic,* November 28, 1994. Copyright © 1994 by The New Republic, Inc. Reprinted by permission of *The New Republic.*

About the Editor

MICHAEL LOWENTHAL studied writing at Dartmouth College, from which he graduated in 1990 as class valedictorian. Formerly an editor at University Press of New England, he has worked full-time as a writer and free-lance editor since 1993. His short stories and essays have appeared in literary journals such as *The Kenyon Review, Other Voices, The Crescent Review,* and *Columbia,* and have been anthologized in more than fifteen books, including *Best American Gay Fiction* 1996, *Men on Men* 5, *Wrestling with the Angel,* and *Friends and Lovers,* which he edited with the late John Preston. He is also the editor of Preston's final book, *Winter's Light,* and of the best-selling *Flesh and the Word* series. His journalism and reviews have appeared in *The New York Times Magazine, The Boston Globe, The Boston Phoenix, Out, The Advocate* and many other periodicals. Lowenthal is recipient of a 1995–96 New Hampshire State Council on the Arts Fellowship for fiction writing, and his first novel, *In the Shadow of His Wings*, will be published by Dutton in 1998. He lives in Boston.